Matthew Arnold, Thomas Brower Peacock, Thomas Danly Suplée

**Poems of the plains and songs of the solitudes**

Third Edition

Matthew Arnold, Thomas Brower Peacock, Thomas Danly Suplée

**Poems of the plains and songs of the solitudes**
*Third Edition*

ISBN/EAN: 9783337185541

Printed in Europe, USA, Canada, Australia, Japan

Cover: Foto ©Thomas Meinert / pixelio.de

More available books at **www.hansebooks.com**

# Poems of the Plains

AND

# Songs of the Solitudes

TOGETHER WITH

## "THE RHYME OF THE BORDER WAR"

BY

## THOMAS BROWER PEACOCK

AUTHOR OF "THE RHYME OF THE BORDER WAR," "THE VENDETTA, AND
OTHER POEMS," ETC., ETC.

*THIRD EDITION. REVISED*

WITH BIOGRAPHICAL SKETCH OF THE AUTHOR AND CRITICAL REMARKS ON
HIS POEMS BY
PROF. THOMAS DANLEIGH SUPLÉE, A.M., Ph.D.

NEW YORK AND LONDON

G. P. PUTNAM'S SONS

The Knickerbocker Press

1889

# TO THE POETS.

O minstrel of the golden tongue,
O minstrel of the mystic heart,
This gift accept—these songs I 've sung—
To you their soul I would impart.
From Homer to the lowliest son
Who ever dared his voice to raise,
I dedicate to each fond one
These Western border minstrel lays.

————

Away, my poems of the plains,
   Go, mingle with the busy throng ;
Whatever be your fate, remains
   This truth : my passion is for song.
I sing of solitudes unending—
   The solitudes that ever blight
Earth-life—that mystery extending
   'Round knowledge, with its walls of night.

# CONTENTS.

v

# *Contents.*

viii *Contents.*

# PREFACE.

BY THOMAS DANLEIGH SUPLÉE, A.M., PH.D.

THE statement will pass without challenge, I think, that the West has not produced many great poets. Excepting a few whose names might easily be counted upon the fingers of a single hand, the poets have hailed from the States described as " Original." The reason of this, I take it, is pretty nearly the same as that which is given for the scarcity of almost all kinds of literature in the earlier periods of American history. Just as the Puritans and their contemporaries were occupied with problems unfavorable to the successful cultivation of what we term the literary habit, so the pioneers of the unconquered West, and their immediate descendants, have found but little leisure for writing or even reading poetry. The Sierras have their solitary bard in Joaquin Miller, and the adjacent wilds may only claim Bret Harte. The great middle West is still more barren. Though many birds have made its wonderful prairie stretches vocal with strains of sweetest melody, but few dreaming poets have been there to echo their notes. Themes modest and lofty have not been wanting. Nature is simple and winning, grand and thrilling, picturesque and

ix

inspiring, but men have either not been impressed with these qualities in their surroundings, or they have lacked the power to properly interpret them.

What the world expects of the Western poet is rather vaguely understood, and the world will probably never be persuaded that the true prophet has arisen until it discovers in him some of the qualities of its somewhat sensational ideal. It expects this ideal poet to be the peculiar product of the region whose apostle he is to be. His poetry is to contain bold and dashing strokes, which shall be impressive, without exacting too much suspicion of fire without heat, or thunder without lightning. It awaits a master in the art of stimulating, who is something more than a journeyman artist at delineating. In short, the pictured ideal must be worthy of a big country, and some wonderful geographical details, equal to the task of doing full justice to the enterprise, generosity and " bigness " which are invariably associated with the West.

That there is a strong flavor of unreasonableness in much of this expectation, needs not be insisted upon. Let us rather expect a man strongly imbued with Western sympathies, to the manor born, and unquestionably able to picture or interpret the manor,—a man who needs not to be seated upon high mountains in order to be inspired to utter big thoughts, but who having lived under the brows of the eternal hills is so overwhelmed with their immense suggestions, that his thoughts are equally grand in inspiring mental pictures, lifting you, as do the mountains, into a higher atmosphere of serenity and purity.

" Great mountains lift the lowlands on their sides."

Such a man will lend a voice to the hills, catch the music of the streams, paint the sweet flowers of the prairies, and the radiant clouds in the skies above them, measure nature's strength, and praise her bounty, and men will crown him poet.

Let us see what there is in the life, the songs, and estimates of the critics of our author to warrant the belief that he is entitled to the distinction of being, what his critics claim him to be, the poet laureate of the West.

Mr. Peacock accomplishes what few of the world's living poets are capable of doing, and that is this, he frequently rises to the sublime.

In his later poems, particularly, virility is a noticeable merit—that fire and vigor rare in the poetry of every age.

Thomas Brower Peacock was born on the 16th day of April, 185 ., at Cambridge, Guernsey County, Ohio. He was the third son and the fourth child in a family of seven children, of whom four were sons and three were daughters. His father's name was Thomas William Peacock, a man highly esteemed in Ohio, as an able editor of several papers, and the president of a railroad. Mr. Peacock enjoys the proud distinction of being able to trace his ancestry back to King William of Holland, and is one of the thousand heirs to the Trinity Church property in New York City, commonly known as the Anneke Jans estate. His father's father was a native of Edinburgh, Scotland, and among his relatives in that connection, he numbers a Lord and Lady Peacock. The name " Peacock " originated long ago from the " Pea Mountains " in Scotland, where peacocks were formerly found in large numbers. Mr. Peacock is also related, though distantly, to Thomas Love Peacock, the intimate friend of the unfortunate Shelley.

His mother's maiden name was Naomi Carson, and her parents were among the earliest settlers of Guernsey Co., Ohio.

Mr. Peacock's boyhood was comparatively uneventful. In his seventh year the family moved to a farm about a mile east of Cambridge, where they resided two years, his father, in the meantime, editing the Cambridge *Jeffersonian,* a paper still in existence. After disposing of this paper, his father removed to Zanesville, Muskingum Co., Ohio, where he purchased the leading Democratic paper of that city, the Zanesville *Aurora.* He edited this paper for four years, his son Thomas, then a boy in his teens, carrying the papers to subscribers through the city.

When his father sold the farm near Cambridge the boy cried bitterly, not only because he was greatly attached to the place, but also by reason of a very remarkable attachment which he had formed for three purely imaginary friends, whom he had

named " Adixon," " Frawdixon," and " Sandborn."
His uncle, F. M. Carson, wrote a little book con-
cerning these fancied friends, who were quite as
real to the boy as any of his friends of flesh and
blood. This uncle was a superior man, some time
editor of the Wheeling *Intelligencer*. He died at
the age of twenty-seven.

Mr. Peacock's education was mainly obtained at
Zanesville, Ohio. From this place the family removed to Dresden, Ohio, where the father and the
son together edited the *Monitor*. To this paper
the boy contributed three romances in prose, and a
number of small poems.

In the year 1870, the young man caught the
Texas fever, from reading the glowing accounts of
it written in the shape of advertising pamphlets,
and also from letters received from persons living
there, and emigrated to the southwestern wilds.
During the two years that Mr. Peacock remained
in Texas, he taught school for one year, and kept a
hotel during the other year, entertaining, among
other characters, " Cole Younger," " Wild Bill,"
and " Jesse James,"—men whose patronage was
not solicited by the host, and rarely covered more
than a single night.

While in Texas, Mr. Peacock met with a number
of adventures. In an encounter between some
Union soldiers and a force of the so-called " Ku-
Klux," he was wounded, and laid up for six weeks.
He refers to this incident in his " Rhyme of the
Border War," when he says :

" I sympathize with those who fall
Down stricken by the deadly ball,
For I have felt the cruel thing
Tear through my flesh with angry sting."

He moved to Kansas, his adopted State, in 1872, making the trip overland, a distance of eight hundred miles, by wagon team. He first settled at Independence, and two years afterwards removed to the city of Topeka, where he has resided for the last thirteen years. For eight years he was associate editor of the Kansas *Democrat.*

Mr. Peacock's "Star of the East" was written in Zanesville, Ohio, at the age of sixteen. His "Vendetta" and some minor poems were written in Texas. "The Rhyme of the Border War," "The Doomed Ship Atlantic," and his later poems have been written in Kansas.

Mr. Peacock was married June 17, 1880, to Miss Ida E. Eckert, the second daughter of Daniel S. Eckert, a retired farmer. His wife is a woman of fine literary taste.

The first volume of poems published by Mr. Peacock was a very modest little book of verses issued in 1872. It was so liberally criticised and favorably noticed by the press that the author was encouraged to publish a larger volume in 1876, containing many of the old poems revised, together with many new verses. This second edition was also favorably received and very extensively noticed. "The Rhyme of the Border War" was published by G. W. Carleton & Co., New York City, in 1880.

The new volume, " Poems of the Plains and
Songs of the Solitudes," includes the former publications revised, and a large number of new ones for
the first time published.

In form, Mr. Peacock's poetry in not conven-
tional. One of the first and strongest impressions
which one gets from its perusal, is a certain freedom from restraint of regulation poetry which is
everywhere apparent. There is relaxation from
those cast-iron rules pertaining to metre and now
and then to rhyme which grace the concluding pages
of text-books of grammar and composition. The
stream of his diction glides at its own sweet will,
and is quiet or tempestuous, according to its burden of thought—but always free from the trammels
of canonical expression.

In the matter of his verse Mr. Peacock is a
poet in one peculiar sense that is too much over-
looked in the qualifications of the poet in these later
days. He is preëminently imaginative—a seer of
visions, a dreamer of dreams, a creator of pictures,
and whether it be vision, or dream, or picture, he
sees, and dreams, and creates in a way that is singularly imaginative. The world has been straying far
from the path of genuine poetry of late. We are
not ashamed to say that we never were converted
to these heretical ways of thinking, and greatly pre-
fer the poetry written for our reading shall not be a
homily, a system of philosophy, or subtle analysis
of human character,—but rather the story of what
one has seen who has soared far into the regions of

the fanciful. Something startling and unusual, even a little bit unreal if you please, but new, fresh, strange, imaginative, and picturesque. Walter Scott, or some one with gifts allied to his, will be enjoyed again when literary taste is corrected, and men dare to fling off the chains of mock admiration by which they are bound. The Platos will then stick to prose. A truce to them now. Let us, when we want poetry, get out of the regions of too fine discussions, of keen analysis, and tiresome definition, and enter the broad, open fields, and clear skies, to rest our jaded and tortured minds, renew our exhausted patience, and once more unaffectedly enjoy the pleasures of the imagination.

Mr. Peacock is essentially romantic, and is never more thoroughly inspired than when singing the praises of true woman. Here, for instance, is a lyric of love, sung by one of his characters, which Owen Meredith might be proud to claim :

" Give Heaven the good, and Hell the bad,
 Yield me the lovely and the fair,
For though my heart be sick and sad,
 A girl's sweet face dispels my care.
Drink, drink, the rosy, sparkling wine,
 To woman, lovely and divine.

" O what 's the poet's proudest wreaths,
 To sweeter wreaths of woman's arms
Encircling you when beauty breathes
 Her true love, gemm'd by all her charms !

Then drink the rosy, sparkling wine,
To woman, lovely and divine.

" Then drain the foaming, sparkling glass,
   To her who brings such peace and bliss,
Whose tender eyes we cannot pass,
   Without we long to woo and kiss.
Drink, drink, the rosy, sparkling wine,
To woman, lovely and divine."

There is no lack of love-making in "The Rhyme
of the Border War," but the passion is tender, notwithstanding it beats and throbs in the breasts of
rough men in rough times.

To afford a taste of Mr. Peacock's quality by
quotation would require space which the pre-
scribed limits of a preface do not afford. Frequently there is a peculiar beauty in single lines
and stanzas. Here is one rosary of thoughts :

" God is not far from him who prays."

" Great minds honor worth and brain."

" Who never doubted never thought."

" Great men are numbered by no year."

" Two souls are in the poet's breast."

" The stars are tears that God once wept."

" Christ's life 's a poem more sublime
   Than any given unto rhyme."

" A thousand poems unexpressed
  May be within the poet's breast,
  Which angels read that wander by,
  Sweet pilgrims from beyond the sky."

" Greater than kings, with kingdoms strong,
  Are the mighty kings of song."

" Greater than conqueror or king,
  The Thinker on his throne of Thought
A sceptre wields,—puissant thing—
  By which mutations great are wrought."

" The dew-drop on yon fragrant flower
  May be the tear of some sweet star,
That weeps for joy that God's great power
  Shields all creation near and far."

" Battle stamps his bloody feet ! "

" Though now and then a moment seen,
  The strange wild Indian of the plain,
His star is setting low between
  The Rocky Mountains and the main.
His fate and the buffalo's are one—
  They gather to the setting sun."

" The East with great omnipotent power
  Burns with the breath of God this hour."

" And like those sweet immortal flowers,
  True woman's love grows on sublime—
Like them it soars o'er mortal hours—
  It lives beyond the bounds of time ! "

" God secretes in places lone and still
  The rarest products of His will ;
For contact with the world disarms
  His fairest flowers of half their charms."

Mr. Peacock has won golden opinions from the most eminent critics, such as Matthew Arnold, Victor Hugo, the London *Saturday Review*, Hugh Hastings, the New York *Nation*, Bayard Taylor, George Ripley, Louise Chandler Moulton, Ray Palmer, Dr. R. Shelton Mackenzie, Oscar Wilde, Boston *Literary World*, Utica (N. Y.) *Herald*, New York *Christian Union*, New York *Commercial Advertiser*, Philadelphia *Press*, Philadelphia *Times*, etc., etc. They have not looked at him, sniffed lightly, uttered a few words of faint praise or angry contempt, and passed on. They have looked, listened, and praised. The following criticism, written in 1877, is Enrique Parmer's estimate of the Kansas poet :

" This man, whose lips have touched the rim of nature's poesy, who has drifted without bluster into the wind-swept forests of song, is young in years, and his genius is now stretching its wings for its first flight. Thomas Brower Peacock is gifted with poetic genius. The author of ' Vendetta ' develops in that effort alone evidences of all the elements of the poet, while in the minor poems many gems of purest ray flash out, which foreshadow the dawn of brighter imagery for the grand thoughts that lie here and there on the pages of the book.

"His poetry is thoroughly human—a poetry which reproduces, as we read it, all the feelings of our wayward nature—which shows how man was made to mourn, to be merry, to doubt. The descriptive and the picturesque have a large place in his writings. A picture with him is more than the mere drapery of a passion. The chivalric past has as yet received but little of his veneration. The conflicts of the ancient rival factions have somewhat greater enchantment than the gorgeous falsehoods of departed ages, to warm his fancy or to rule his pen. He has little to do with rank or reverence, except when he enters the pale of the supernatural.

"His imagery is true; it is also original. He meditated by himself and he studied the outward phenomena of nature with strange enthusiasm; hence it is not surprising that this youthful poet should have enriched his mind with truth, freshness, and originality, and that these should appear in imagery and description.

"The reader will find many beauties, many curious fancies, many strange pictures wrought out with marvellous power. He will find wild romances painted with a master pen, long rolling verse, almost as good as that of 'Childe Harold,' occasional bursts of inspiration vivid as that of Poe or Shelley, description as dignified and orthodox as that of Wordsworth, while many stanzas are as musical and enrapturing as Tennyson's 'Locksley Hall.'"

Mr. Peacock has received no less generous treatment at the hands of critics abroad. There is probably no safer guide in the matter of literary criticism than Matthew Arnold, and this is what he says of our poet : " He takes a subject which interests him and he treats it with liveliness and vigor."

The London *Saturday Review,* another great authority, says :

" What America needs is a poet of the soil, as the people say. The American bard should be a child of nature, ' self-taught,' like the minstrel of Odysseus, a warrior, a lover, a soaring human being. He should be inspired by the noble history of his own race in the New World. He should not look to the past for subjects, but ' live in the living present.' All these qualities meet, we think, in Thomas Brower Peacock.

" The poet, in a passage of grandeur, compares Quantrell to Satan. Both were on the losing side, both knew better in their hearts.

" Rich in imagination, Mr. Peacock is also inspired by experience ; like Æneas, he tells of broils *quorum pars magna fuit,* in his ' Rhyme,' as he modestly calls his truly remarkable contemporary epic. The hand that fired the field-piece strikes the lyre. War is his theme, and he leads us

" ' Where Battle stamps his bloody feet.'

" ' So that the poem hath expressed
The music of the poet's breast,"

everything else is unessential. In an age when form is everything, and substance is sadly to seek,

we welcome the virile daring of the Kansas singer.
Mr. Peacock not only charms us, but instructs us
too.   We have never read any American poetry so
exuberantly American."

Thomas Brower Peacock's poems have thus generally received favorable comments from a bright
galaxy of famous stars in the literary firmament.

# AUTHOR'S PREFACE.

ON the appearance of this volume, in its first edition, it had the fortune to be extensively criticised.

While most of these criticisms were favorable, others were tolerable, and some execrable. I do not wish to inflict upon my readers a rehearsal of my grievances, for indeed I am not inclined to consider them as such ; for it is seldom that an author does not derive benefit from even the most scathing abuse put forth by his antagonist. One of my critics has said : "' Battle stamps his bloody feet' is a superb metaphor. But when he gets hold of a striking phrase he is apt to overwork it."

If he means that I have used the same expression twice, he is in error. That line occurs but once in my productions. If he intends to say that I have expressed the same idea in other language than the line quoted, then he finds fault with usages of the greatest poets, and among them Lord Byron, who is much admired for his ability in giving a thought in varied language.

In "The Rhyme of the Border War" I have endeavored to deal truly and faithfully with that life denominated "Wild West," and to picture as accurately as possible those stirring scenes in the troublous days of the early settlement of Kansas and the West, before and during the great war of the Rebellion ; depicting battles on horseback with revolver and rifle, guerrilla warfare, pioneer experiences, border broils, and to keep intact historical data. This poem has been widely criticised, and is possibly my best.

It was " The Rhyme of the Border War," as it first appeared in 1880, with manuscript corrections, which called forth the words of commendation from Matthew Arnold and other eminent critics. And it was such expressions as Mr. Arnold's, in true appreciation of worth, however obscure, that led me to the revision and reprinting of all former publications in this book.

The New York *Nation*, in commenting upon "The Rhyme of the Border War," declares : "Matthew Arnold found in it, apparently, those qualities of distinction and interest which he declined to recognize in Emerson and others."

Assuming that the word "apparently" might to some imply a doubt as to the authenticity of the language quoted from Mr. Arnold, and with gratitude to the press and the literary world for the courtesy and kindness shown me, I herewith take pleasure in submitting to the public the following autograph letters :

Dear Sir

I have received your letter
and volume. A volume is
read at a disadvantage when
it is filled with manuscript
corrections; but I can see that
you have a subject which
interests you, and that you
treat it with liveliness and
vigour

Dear Sir

I have no objection to your printing the words of mine you quote.

I hope to visit America once more, and to reach Kansas and the West, but for the rest year or two I am bound at home.

Truly yours

Matthew Arnold

Mr. Peacock

Dear Sir

You seem to have now quite
adopted literature as a profession.
I am inclined to advise you
to read the English authors
of the last century rather
than your contemporaries

I will review your volume when

# MISCELLANEOUS POEMS.

# KIT CARSON.

A FRAGMENT.

H E comes! his steed with mighty bound
Flies swiftly o'er the echoing ground—
He seems a wanderer astray,
Whose past had been a better day;
A being which to earth was hurled,
Whose home is in another world—
Who rides mysterious o'er the earth,
Surprised and dazed with his new birth!
A river runs before his course,
Which he must cross, and soon, perforce.
The channel's bank is reached, the wave
His courser's sides doth hem and lave.
The shore is won, and once again
He thunders o'er the endless plain!
The rider's stern and flashing eye
Speaks courage, wrath, and vengeance nigh.
And well, I ween, his foes may fear
His anger in his mad career—
Ah! who is he that finds no rest?
'T is brave Kit Carson of the west!
And some dear friend he now doth aid,
Who stands on peril's brink, afraid.

3

## SPIRIT WHISPERINGS.

ONCE, disconsolate and lonely,
    When my fancies saddened only,
And my spirit longed to leap
To that realm beyond death's sleep ;
When I hungered for some token
Of that future life unbroken
By a breath or melody,
Or a tone of minstrelsy,
In the darkness all engloomed,
Was my soul, in night entombed—
When I felt the Alpine weight
Of life's burdens, pressed by fate ;
Then this boon of beauty only,
Came to me in secret lonely :
Though all men revile and chide me,
Yet the angels are beside me,
And they kiss the poet's brow,
As they kiss me even now.
When I sought some mystic rune
Which would charm my soul in tune
With harmony unheard by ear
Of wanderer through earth's valley here—
But no gonfalon of glory
Came to gladden with its story.
Then I sought the weird entrancement
Of Poe's poems for enhancement ;
Whose sweet haunting melody

Bore me toward Infinity—
Far beyond the outmost star,
To the golden gates ajar.
As I sat, I thought how sadly
Waned his life-star, and how madly
Drained he from the chalice, liquor,
But to feel its mad'ning ichor—
When black ravens came and stayed—
Spectral ravens perched and preyed
On his heart of melancholy,
And he felt the curse of folly.
Magician thou of poesy all,
Pray, my spirit disinthrall !
My heart 's shipwrecked evermore
On a goblin-haunted shore,
And I hear the fiends' wild laughter,
And the dreaded silence after !
From the spirit-shore of being
Wilt thou prove to me, in seeing,
That buds of promise never die,
But bloom in radiance o'er the sky !
From the golden gates of glory,
Come and tell a happier story
Than you told on earth before—
Come, O come to earth once more !
Oh, I feel that thou art near it—
Near earth and me, and mankind all,
As when thy chained and fettered spirit
Leaped from out its prison wall ;
Give me, Poet, I implore !
Hope or symbol glorious,

Which shall lift me evermore
Over earth victorious !
Are thy thoughts still steeped in gloom ?
Or do they through all heaven bloom ?
Like song-birds forever flown
To that hidden world unknown,
Like soft music heard in dreams,
Like sweet voice of sylvan streams,
Like harps played by angel power,
We hear in beauty some pure hour—
Startled from my doubts and dreaming,
With rich grace and beauty beaming,
Descending through the starlit space,
Where God's hills and heaven embrace,
As though to strengthen indecision,
There arose before my vision,
In his intellectual pride,
With his child-wife by his side,
The Author of " The Raven," smiling,
With this song my soul beguiling :
" The ocean of Eternity,
    Breaking on Time's troubled shore,
Returns with cries of agony
    To God forevermore !
And we pity and we sorrow
    O'er man's life, a tragedy—
And we hope a bright to-morrow,
    When the earth redeemed will be.
With the dawning golden morning,
    With the morn that is divine,

I 'd contrast the dismal warning,
    Of that past which once was mine.
I would read the runic story
    Of my life that 's wed to time ;
O I read it sad and hoary
    With a vice that seems a crime !
O I see the tempter sparkling,
    Glowing in the goblet bright !
And I see the shadows darkling
    Till I stand on brink of night.
Within a city maddening,
    With a dagger at my heart,
I saw the record saddening,
    Of my life the mortal part.
Lo ! there came from out the midnight,
    Into which my spirit peered,
A phantom toward the firelight,
    Which my craven heart had feared.
And from out his bosom, glowing
    With a beauty not of earth,
Drew a wondrous mirror, showing
    Images of lovely worth.
Angels therein flitted, saintly,
    Glided by, and me entranced—
And my being shadowed faintly,
    I beheld, that on me glanced.
By the aid of firelight's flicker,
    There, above, I 'm pictured dim—
And I quaff a fiery liquor,
    Ruby to a tankard's rim.

Then I knew my thirst so maddening,
  Had enslaved my soul full fast—
Since I 've left earth's moorings, gladdening,
  I have risen o'er the past.
Love is here, an endless sea,
  God and His eternal noon—
Here truth wakes into melody,
  Like echoes 'neath the moon.

---

## THE KANSAS INDIAN'S LAMENT.

### I.

OUR tribe is less'ning year by year,
    The pale-face drives us back—
With us, the bison, bear, and deer
    Before his onward track—
In battle with his armèd power,
The Red Man fears but dares now cower.

### II.

The footprints of our moc'sins fade,
    They once left paths for miles, .
And the Great Spirit hides in shade,
    No more we see his smiles :
Few wampum belts our tribe needs yet,
For soon the warrior's star will set.

### III.

These broad prairies once were ours ;
　We fished the many rivers ;
On yonder Kaw, embanked with flowers,
　With arrows in our quivers,
With dusky maids, wigwams behind,
We sailed before the singing wind.

### IV.

The sunflower waved its yellow head,
　Across the grassy plains—
And, like our chieftain, now are dead
　The spirit-herbs for pains :
Pale-face, our mild clime 's not for thee,
It moves, with us, toward sundown sea.

### V.

Our moons are few, our race is run,
　Some dark fate drags us down ;
Less bright the once all-glorious sun,
　The golden stars are brown—
The tall mounds black and dismal loom,
Each day speaks of our coming doom.

### VI.

Our wasted race—my father brave,
　My squaw and pappoose too,

All here lie buried in the grave,
   Here rots my swift canoe—
The things I loved have passed away,
Ah ! soon will I be gone as they !

## VII.

Methinks the pale race might have spared
   Some spot where we 'd abide,—
Spared us, who once owned all, and shared
   With them from tide to tide :
'T is strange, 't is passing strange to me,
Why they would drive us in the sea.

## VIII.

Our small tribe 's scattered like the leaves
   And wasted to a few—
Each warrior for the bright past grieves,
   Which vanished from our view !
They wait till Manitou's voice sounds,
Calling to Happy Hunting Grounds.

## IX.

We go ! the White Race takes our place ;
   Great Spirit, what am I !
Once thousands strong, where 's now my race—
   On plains beyond the sky ?
O take me too, I would not stay,
When all I loved have passed away !

### X.

Perchance, when many moons have fled
  And the Great Spirit's wrath,
Our many loved ones, from the dead,
  Will come back to earth's path,
To hunt again the buffalo,
And no pale race to bring us woe.

### XI.

But soft ! methinks I hear a voice ?
  Great Manitou's ! speaks He !
It makes my craven heart rejoice—
  O what wouldst Thou with me ?
"Be brave ! God's Happy Hunting Grounds,
Are great and good, and have no bounds !"

---

### SHAKESPEARE AND BYRON.

THE drama hath its Avon Bard, sublime,
  The one great eagle of the upper air,
To reach whose heights the mightiest e'en despair ;
In this, the one protagonist of time—
In spontaneity, the source and strength of rhyme,
Is Byron gifted less than he, Shakespeare ?
Who draws the line, and who can make it clear ?
Up Mount Parnassus, far ascents they climb,
Each one with voice and grandeur of the ocean.

'Neath fame's bright light men both must e'er ad-
    mire.
With heart and mind, with lover's true devotion—
In noble rage, each flames volcanic fire :
Puissant Powers ! names ne'er to be downtrod,
Immortal as the deathless stars of God !

    Sept. 24, 1887.

## BEYOND.

O HEAVENLY Muse ! with thy soft dulcet
    shell,    ·
Breathe unto me thy many fancies wild !—
Give me thy mighty magic undefil'd—
Boundless imagination's charming spell—
Heaven's highest inspiration yield as well ;
That I with these—though momentary power—
Behold beyond this lowly realm of Hour—
Beyond, where knowledge, power, and wisdom
    dwell
'Midst beauty's wealth sublime—where all we name
Eternity—and change as time is styled,
By which the life of mortal is beguiled.
Where Past, Present, and Future are one, th' same,
Where God's intelligence hath ever smil'd—
To world beyond ; where dwell Love, Hope, and
    Fame.

## THE DOOMED SHIP "ATLANTIC."

[The steamship "Atlantic," of the White Star line, of
England, Captain Williams commanding, was lost off Hali-
fax, Nova Scotia, April 1, 1873. Out of 1,000 souls of both
sexes and all ages, but between 300 and 400 escaped, and of
that number, with few exceptions, all were unmarried men.
Not a female survived.]

THE good swift ship "Atlantic," free,
   Rides at her moorings, trim and sound—
Ready for her voyage o'er the sea,
   With freight of souls, far distant bound.
A bride of peerless grace she seems,
   A sweet young bride whom Heaven doth bless
With th' beauty of which th' poet dreams—
   A queen of wondrous loveliness—
A queen whose kingdom is the sea,
Her sceptre floating wide and free.
A thousand hearts prophetic beat
On board—where Life and Love now meet.
The Future's veil is closely drawn,
Save where Hope points a lovely dawn.
The ship is loos'd—the farewells said—
They part, the living—how soon dead
Will many be, that, parting, hear
Their last love breathed in willing ear !
Now numbers to high Heaven pray,
   While down the Mersey's limpid stream
They 're floating on their joyful way,
   The emblem of a blissful dream.

The noble ship speeds on—away—
  On mighty ocean, broad and deep—
Rolls in her wake the foaming spray,
  Where oft the storms in anger sweep ;
The gentle, rolling, restless waves
Speak not of danger nor of graves,
But dancing blithesome o'er the sea,
List t' voices mingling merrily.
No cloud now frets the sapphire sky,
But all is bright—beneath—on high—
While swiftly wings their rapid flight,
Where wave and heaven blend on the sight—
And floating o'er the ocean swell
Go joyous murmurings—all is well.
Hope walks the wave—Despair, unseen,
Is sleeping down below; where green
The dank weed grows—where Ruin moves,
Preying on corses of lost loves.
Like mighty phantom of the past,
Wand'ring through space sublime and vast,
The ship glides on her lonely way,
And round the living breezes play.
Cloud-fleets appear far in the sky,
And through the upper deep float by.
As dying Day sinks on his bier,
And Twilight sheds the mourning tear,
From out the deep, as murderer can,
One steals on board, unseen by man,
And grins and chuckles at the thought :
" I soon will gloat o'er misery wrought ! "
'T is he, grim Death, dark, fierce, and bold—

He comes for victims young and old ;
But, ah ! too soon to triumph here.
    Hark ! hark ! a voice : "Away, ingrate ! "
He heeds ! slinks off in darkness drear—
    Death well obeys ! 't is the voice of Fate !
Descending, Night, with visage dark,
Drops her black mantle o'er the bark
And o'er time's pathway journeys on—
Many to dream's charm'd realm have gone.
Astray from port [1] where Hope abides,
    Through gloom, where Danger rides the blast,
The bark toward eternity glides—
    That mighty deep she 's nearing fast.
Upon the hazardous shore afar,
    There glows a false, weird beacon [2] light—
It seems some bright though fallen star,
    Torn from the curtained dome of night ;
Its phosphorous glare unveils the gloom ;
    Each shadow seems a sad, still ghost ;
Death holds the light that lures to doom,
    High over Prospect's headland coast !
O fearful woe !   What means that crash,
Which wakes grim terror like a flash ?
The ship has struck the pitiless rock,
Beats vainly, quiv'ring with the shock.
Hurled from their berths, now slumberers wake,
    Rush to the deck, bewildered, pale :

    [1] The harbor of Halifax, which all on board thought they
were safely nearing.
    [2] This beacon light was mistaken in the fog by the pilot for
the lighthouse of Sambro.

Some wounded fall; some fall, nor make
   One move—all sounds to rouse them fail !
Out from the ship, up to the skies,
Wild cries and frantic shrieks arise ;
And 'though a storm rolls thunders out,
Far louder frenzied voices shout.
Heaven's golden gates wide open swing ;
   Through them the guardians of the soul
Swiftly, on peerless, pure white wing,
   From Aidenn start, as th' bells of heaven toll !
They come ! they come ! spirits of light,
   From their sweet homes in Paradise !
Tears over their soft cheeks flow bright,
   Issuing from their angel eyes !
Where, where 's the captain this dread hour ?
   He comes ! but strong drink dims his eye—
He 'll save !   Vain hope, no human power
   The doomed can shield—alas ! they die !
Close on the brink of eternity
Weak man braves Heaven continually.
The minute-guns peal forth distress,
   And faster grows the startling boom !
Far caverns mock man's helplessness,
   Re-echoing but the coming doom.
Upon her knees in earnest prayer,
   Her babe clasped to her bosom tight,
A mother cries : "Oh, dear God, spare
   Mine only child, this awful night !"
Each moment, to the sea, a wave
   Sweeps from the tossing ship more lives,
And here and there, e'en o'er his grave,

Still nobly some strong swimmer strives.
Both Fear and Death stalk round, as o'er
    The ship rush mortals to and fro—
Prayers, oaths, and shrieks, with ocean roar,
    Commingle, clash, more frantic grow !
From infancy to hoary age,
Scores, frenzied, war with death here wage.
Child, parent, lover, husband, wife,
Friend, brother, sister, in the strife.
Despairing, raving, many weep,
And others plunge into the deep.
With perfect face and faultless form,
With raven locks tossed by the storm,
With lovely dark eyes wildly gleaming,
So strangely bright her beauty beaming,
She startles in her wild distress
With rich and wondrous loveliness !
In her sad beauty, sweet and pale,
Seeming Heaven's angel on the blast,
Lost, wandering through this dreary vale,
    A woman [1] tied to the icy mast—
High 'mid the rigging firmly lashed—
    Doth seem unto her God to pray !
Unfeeling Death on by her dashed,
    Scaring her timid sprite away !
Beneath the wave, on deck the dead,

---

[1] This beautiful woman, found frozen to death on the mast, high in the rigging, where she had been tied by some kind friend, to prevent her being washed overboard, was the subject of much comment by the many periodicals which chronicled the fearful calamity upon which this poem is founded.

Some shrieking died, some made no moan,
But like each liberated spirit fled
     On phantom wings into th' dread Unknown.
None foil the stern decree of Fate—
     The lowly fall, the great as well,
Alike they yield—some soon—some late—
     All must, when sounds God's fearful knell !
Though number many more the dead,
Yet on the ship the living tread,
And nobly battling for those lives,
     The bark rebels against her fate :
Alas ! for them, in vain she strives,
     And each false hope is desolate !
From highest rigging to the deck
     Now fiercely reigns o 'er all, Despair—
Wild Ruin looks o 'er Hope's sad wreck—
     Strides Horror, shaking her snaky hair.
Oh, for one moment now to save !
     Till the brave [1] may land them on the shore—
That moment 's not.   Beneath the wave,
     Down, down she sinks forevermore,
While through the air where madness jars,
     There goes a wild and frenzied yell
Far to the living, breathing stars,
     Goes up to Heaven, goes down to Hell !
That cry to rouse the corse suffic'd,
     Wake life in its cold flesh and bone ;

[1] C. L. Brady, the third officer of the " Atlantic," and the
Rev. Mr. Ancient, an humble clergyman, who, in utter dis-
regard of their own lives, did all in their power to relieve the
suffering and distressed.

It pierced the bleeding heart of Christ
　And startled Satan on his throne !
Down with the ship sank heroes brave—
　Ne'er nobler souls roamed land or sea ;
They willingly [1] sank 'neath the wave,
　Though told by dearest lips to flee.

　*　　*　　*　　*　　*　　*　　*　　*

O thou pale Niobe of th' deep !
　Now grieving o 'er the ruthless waves,
In thy wild beauty well mayst weep,
　Thy children dead, in deep sea-graves.
And yet 't is well ! for they all are
　Now free from every want and care,
And rest as peaceful as the star
　In heaven's pure, holy bosom there.
Then sleep, ye dead, eternal sleep—
　Sleep on in your unfathomed graves ;
O'er you immortal sea-nymphs weep ;
　O'er you the lovely sea-flower waves.

---

[1] Many of the married men that perished, had they abandoned their wives and families, could have swum to shore and
thus saved themselves, as most of the unmarried men did ;
but, although in many instances urged by their wives to leave,
they nobly remained and heroically died—true martyrs at the
shrine of love.

## MAN.

THE history of the human race
    Is but a tragedy of tears !
Man's life 's a passing breath, I trace,
    Where always jostle hopes and fears.

As bark tossed by the stormy sea,
    High on the foam-capped wave is hung,
One moment more, and lost 't will be,
    Engulfed for aye—by all unsung !

So man each hour stands on death's brink,
    Unto himself a mystery !
An instant stands, then down doth sink,
    Lost in oblivion's sombre sea.

Then boast not of thy power, O man !
    Thou art no more—no more shalt be—
Compared to God, the Mighty, than
    A second to Eternity.

## SONNET TO MATTHEW ARNOLD.

OH, welcome to our shores, great poet, sage !
    Great King of Thought, thou gemm'st the
    sky of time—
We feel twice honored—twice thou 'st come, sublime
With sovereign power ; thrice fame thou 'st won
    this age ;
(Which long shall glow on Truth's immortal page !)
Once as the poet, once as essayest, thou !
Once as the critic, peer of Goethe, now.
That scythe which mows the fairest from the stage,
Will touch thee not, thy fame shall brightly glow
As star from out the midnight sky, etern,
A light above time's ruins, dark and low,
To evermore in deathless beauty burn !
I sing thy praise—had I thy rhythmic might
The saints of Heaven would listen with delight !

## CAPITAL AND LABOR.

MUST Wrong the wide world e'er oppress ?
    Must Truth forever be downtrod ?
Must men unanswered, e'er address
    Their orisons to God ?

Must gold o'er labor ever gloat
    In crimes too dark to be forgiven ?

Must Hell's black banners ever float
  Against the glorious skies of Heaven ?

Not if I read the stars aright—
  The stars of far immensity !
Lo ! morning breaks, and melts the night
  Before the golden days to be !

Progression leads us up and on,
  And Error must his life resign,
While Truth on joyous wings of dawn,
  Immortal, floats to the Divine.

## THE CLOSE OF DAY.

THE moon from out the east doth peep ;
    The sun 's low wheeling o'er the deep ;
The stars are scattered in the sky ;
The mountains rear their heads on high ;
The vale is curtained and asleep ;
The brook and river onward creep ;
The mocking-bird its melody
Is swelling from the hawthorn tree.
Sounds soft and low the tinkling fold ;
Loud barks the watch-dog fierce and bold.
The owlet shrieks far down the brakes,
The frog the drowsy cricket wakes.
There stands the well, and here the stile ,
Where rustics oft their hours beguile ;
But Day hath died—Night mounts the throne,
Reigns o'er the slumbering world alone.

## THE POET'S REVERIE.

THE moon hangs like the fairest lily,
　　Far out above the lucid lake,
Like lesser flowers, stars sweet and stilly,
　　On high, in golden glory wake !

A bard of high and heavenly mood—
　　A poet, hence a mystery—
A being little understood
　　Here, this side eternity—

Stands dreaming 'neath the summer heaven,
　　His heart in sympathy with all.
The poet feels in th' lonely even
　　Death opes the gates o' the jasper wall.

The poet of the beautiful,
　　The poet of the good and pure,
The nightingale hears, dutiful,
　　Like lovely voice of angel wooer.

A golden dream moves through the vale,
　　And down the mount a zephyr comes ;
A whisper breathes through forest swale,
　　Where the pensive night-moth hums.

That beauty seen by poet's eye,
　　Though hid to visions not so bright,
Bespangles earth, air, sea, and sky—
　　Enchanting loveliness—delight !

From ocean foam more stars arise
   And join their sisters of the night—
On mystic wings, from Paradise,
   Lo ! hosts of angels pass in sight !

The poet feels the spell, like sleep,
   The magic spell that floats o'er all,
Across immensity's vast deep—
   The spirits of the blesséd call.

He feels, 'though strange, life 's grand and fair ;
   That beauty springs from the Unknown,
And love ; that we should not despair
   Of hopes we deem forever flown.

---

## THE EVIL SPIRIT OF THE PLAINS.[1]

'TIS midnight on the endless plain,
   The round moon shines upon the slain—
Shines on the white man and the red ;
Two scores are sleeping with the dead—
The Indian warriors number more
Than their pale foemen of the war.
And lo ! excited braves appear,
Conversing of a foe they fear ;
Their dreaded enemy remains—
" The Evil Spirit of the Plains."

[1] W. F. Cody, alias " Buffalo Bill," is known to the Indian tribes of the West, who fear him, as " The Evil Spirit of the Plains."

They fear him as a denizen
Of some far world beyond their ken.
'T would seem that mortal weapons failed
To slay him though a host assailed ;
'T would seem some power, some fiend, or God,
Protected him each path he trod ;
For when the war waxed wild and dread,
He fought around and o'er the dead—
Though scores died in the battle's breath,
He would not fly nor yield to death.
His battle-cry rose o'er the plains,
And e'er their solitudes profanes.
He comes ! they see him—now they fly,
Far onward, 'neath the western sky.
And well they fly—'t is Buffalo Bill,
Who for swift vengeance seeks his fill.

## THE BANDIT CHIEF.

HARK ! 't is a courser's clattering feet !
    That courser madly speeds away—
The midnight moon from her high seat
    Sheds on the earth her brightest ray.

Who comes ?   A rushing steed draws nigh,
    Whose hoofs are sounding far and near !
As swift as though from ghouls he 'd fly,
    He passes forest, plain, and mere.

Perchance some wild fiend crazed with fright,
    Flies on its way from Heaven down hurled !
Perchance some demon of the night,
    Escaped from Hell, rides o'er the world !


Whoe'er he be so fearful near,
    As dread as fiend or demon he,
To followers he rules through fear,
    And leads through crimes to victory.


He nears !   I see his eye of hate !
    'T is gleaming like an evil star ;
He seems th' embodied form of fate
    Swift rushing to the field of war.


On, on, the terror of the sod,
    A tempest in his heart of ire ;
He fears no man, no fiend, no God,
    In his wild, stormy soul of fire.


Ah ! well each follower knew his power ;
    They 'd felt the thunder of his might—
They knew his wrath at any hour
    Was like the awful storm of night.


To him all foes in combat quailed,
    Before his arm and eagle eye—
His life seemed charmed—to him death  paled—
    He swept in power puissant by.

As when in darkness men do mourn,
   And lo ! a star breaks through the night !
That star a mighty genius born,
   Grasps from the gloom immortal light !

So when great hosts had them at bay,
   And his wild clan deemed all were lost,
He led them from the night to day—
   On like the storm-swept holocaust !

Woe ! woe to them he seeks this night,
   For they shall feel his vengeful hand—
They who have robbed,[1] without the right
   From him, the leader of the band !

I see him yet ! and lo ! he 's gone—
   And yet I hear his steed of fire,
Whose steel-clad hoofs still clatter on,
   Swift bearing him and all his ire.

Full twenty years James reigned supreme,
   The monarch of his own desire ;
His will was all the law, 't would seem,
   That marked his mad career of fire.

---

[1] Occasionally some of Jesse James's clan committed robbery unknown to him, in order to cheat him out of his portion of the spoils, which was the lion's share. Then the culprits met with justice at the hands of their irate chief, whose path, sooner or later, they were certain to cross.

And like the great Napoleon,
   He passed in view before man's ken,
A great and strange phenomenon—
   A Titan asking naught of men.

He did what others would not dare—
   His deeds were rampant, fierce, and fell;
Throughout his life, and everywhere,
   He braved each, all—man, Heaven, and Hell.

---

## COROLINDA BLAKE.

SHE stands and combs her long and flowing
   hair,
   Hard by Nature's mirror—the pure, limpid lake—
None could imagine aught so fresh and fair,
   As sweet and lovely Corolinda Blake.

Her eyes are like two gentle stars, that beaming
   Do through the gloom of night, benignly break—-
Her mouth is like a sweet red rose when dreaming
   At morn, 'midst summer, Corolinda Blake.

Now as she combs her flowing tresses dark,
   Lo! that fair hand, how perfect in its make!
Behold that face and form, her beauty mark!
   'T is to enshrine fair Corolinda Blake.

Not e'en the love-enthralling Aphrodite,
    The Queen of Love, for all her beauty's sake,
Could pluck one laurel from her brow ; brightly
    Heaven breathed round her, my Corolinda Blake.

She blushes at her eidolon near her,
    Their thirst for beauty the clear waters slake ;
Is there in Heaven an angel fairer, dearer,
    Than pretty, brown-eyed Corolinda Blake!

## SONNET TO MILTON.

MILTON ! thou Titan of the epic song,
    Majestically thy verse moves on sublime,
Above the wrecks and ruins eld of time ;
In stately numbers, thrilling, grand, and strong,
High o'er the singers of the lower throng.
Reared on the loftiest pinnacle, thy voice
Wakes the wide world, and nations now rejoice !
And weary hearts grow fresh through ages long.
Life's plane is elevated by thy lay—
The world made better by thy poesy,
Which soars so high—thought's radiant rosary.
Before thy mighty march the night gives way,
O minstrel of the glorious epic flame—
O great protagonist on the field of fame !

June 14, 1887.

## A DREAM.

A DREAM I dreamt, the other night—
 When birds of darkness take their flight :
Inwrapp'd I lay, a shadow'd soul,
At midnight hour when spirits stroll,
And howling demons ride the blast—
Strange phantoms from the wasted Past.
I thought I gazed at changeful sky,
And watched the dark clouds floating by,
And lay and saw the pale moon stray
Through Heaven's broad and trackless way—
'Midst stars—mysterious worlds of light—
The flowers of heaven adorning night.
I gazed upon the rolling waves,
Beneath saw Deep's unfathomed caves,
And many a sea-flower waving there,
Round fair mermaids with golden hair ;
Living in love a happy life,
Far from the haunts of mortal strife—
As beautiful as e'er did beam
Ideal in Endymion's dream.
Saw Neptune's calves feed on the shore—
The herd old Proteus guards o'er ;
Then counted the celestial spheres,
Reminding me of absent years—
Of days and deeds, pass'd, vanish'd, gone—
As 'midst the winter summer's dawn,
Like snow which falls on mountain brow

In vale its rippling waters now.
Saw angel acts by sons of God,
Children who e'er the right path trod.
And saw beneath moon's shadow'd sheens
Carousals dark of many fiends,
Low sunk in deepest depths of sin—
The vilest hosts of Pluto's kin.
Upon the Stygian waters tossing,
I saw souls the Cocytus crossing,
Ferried through the mystic dark
By Charon in his phantom bark—
While to and fro along the shore
Roam'd sad ghosts longing to pass o'er.
And all things here which I did see
Bore th' sombre beauty of Hecate.
I heard loud sounds of fiercest might,
Commingled with low moans of Night.
I, too, saw friends I long to see,
In dreamland, who are far from me.
And 'midst those many friends of yore
Saw those who 're lost forevermore—
Though heart may long till mind doth craze,
They 're lost to all save Fancy's gaze.
Thus visions pass, resplendent play,
Like light from Heaven snatched away.
The night pass'd on—bright came day's beam :
I woke to find at last—A DREAM.

## IN MEMORY.

OUR darling left us in the night,
　　She mounted high on golden wings,
And since she left we see the light
　　Of Heaven which a message brings.

She left, and yet she still remains ;
　　We hear her whisperings soft and low ;
At morn, and when the daylight wanes,
　　Her loved light footsteps come and go.

## TO MY WIFE.

I WAKE again the sleeping lyre,
　　To sing once more of beauty bright—
While birds and flowers of spring aspire
　　To lead the young Month to the light.

While lovely music melts around,
　　From God unseen, who all doth see !
I think of her whose thoughts abound
　　With love for poesy and me.

I love her fondly—she 's the star
　　That guides me onward through the wilds—
Through this world's wilderness afar
　　She lights my pathway with her smiles.

Long, long I have enraptured hung
   Upon the beauty of her voice—
For in the music of her tongue
   My heavy heart and soul rejoice.

The gorgeous throne in regal hall
   Without my dear wife by my side,
Would be more desolate than all
   Where woe and penury abide.

The splendid pomp of pæans sung,
   The loftiest meed of poet's bays,
Could not my heart touch, as my young
   Fair wife's sweet, lovely, simple lays.

---

## RICHARD REALF.

O POET with high minstrel power!
   O early Kansas pioneer!
Cut down in manhood's golden hour,
   I weep, though profits not the tear.

Oh waft a song across to me,
   I 'll listen with my spirit ear :
Though parted by a mighty sea,
   Poet, I know that I shall hear !

## BEAUTIFUL WOMAN.

BEAUTIFUL woman, thou art,
  True to womanhood, sweet !
God places in thy heart
  A wealth of love that 's meet.

And why, I cannot tell !
  But oh, thy voice to me
Sounds like some far-off bell
  That wakes sweet memory !

---

## THE OUTLAW.

### I.

IT is the starry hush of night,
  When Hope's sweet madness thrills the heart,
That coming days shall all be bright—
  When happiness comes, ne'er to depart :
With golden, glorious, and immortal beam,
Like radiant light of poet's deathless dream.

### II.

'T is midnight ! and the month of June ;
  The music of the heavenly spheres
Breathes out a sweet and wondrous tune,
  Heard seldom by man's longing ears—

So sweet that listen all the lovely flowers,
And on their way the silent roving hours.


## III.

But vexed in soul, yon man of crime
    Nor heeds nor feels the witching hour,
All beauty and all things sublime
    Upon this wight have lost their power ;
His steed impatient at his long delay,
Hangs on the bit and chafes to flee away.


## IV.

But hark ! from yonder forest dun
    The sound of horses' hoofs are heard !
A hundred clattering racers run !
    The outlaw flies like some swift bird !
But close behind his foes him press full sore,
Their cries of vengeance on the night-winds roar !


## V.

He halts ! the outlaw halts to hear !
    A moment in the stirrup stands—
His soul is centered in his ear,
    O'er his hot brow he draws his hands—
His sinewy hands which oft had choked death
        back,
When foes were close upon his dreaded track.

## VI.

He spurs his steed, and onward flies
  Beneath the stars' and moon's soft light;
Like some swift comet down the skies,
  He passes through the shades of night;
Flies onward toward the yellow sea away,
Where cloud on cloud pavilioned, darkling lay.

## VII.

He spurs his steed, whose sides are wet
  With foam which shames the whitest snow—
His eyes blaze fire, his teeth are set,
  He 's armed and ready for the foe,
As e'er he 'd been, when far and fierce and free,
He roamed a pirate, dreaded, o'er the sea.

## VIII.

Ah! fast and well his foes must run
  To overtake him in his flight;
His courser is the swiftest one
  Whose feet spurn earth's brown breast this
      night—
This night of June, when Nature 's fair and grand,
When summer laughs along the lovely land.

## IX.

His foes knew not the cost of hate
  When hunting down this man of crime—
This son of war, this child of fate,
  Who 'd hurled scores to etern from time;

Whose spirits rose when armies greatest warred,
When blood flowed most and battle loudest roared.


## X.

He long defied both death and time,
　　Though none saw why, how it was so—
For with a boldness rash, sublime,
　　He reckless rushed upon the foe—
He whom some power unknown protected well !
Some power unseen ! some power of Heaven or
　　　　Hell !


## XI.

Lo ! headlong falls the outlaw's horse
　　To rise no more—'t is his last fall !
The outlaw's flight now ends perforce,
　　And he alone must fight them all !
On come the mad, exultant, angry press—
Men come to death ! men die in wild distress !


## XII.

His foes all dead, none now debar
　　The outlaw from his wonted way ;
He stays as though in blood of war
　　His soul exulted mad alway—
But ah ! one foe he slew not, though fivescore ;
Death's iron grasp he can escape no more.

## THE STRIKERS.[1]

WHY harm your brother though you can ?
　　Why roll upon his heart a stone ?
Build temples in your heart, O man !
　　Nor cause one single tear or groan :
Why crush him 'neath your iron tread?
They strike not now for vengeance, but for bread.

The joyous flowers laugh in the vale,
　　The blithesome zephyrs gently sing,
And birds of beauty in the swale,
　　Are haply sailing on the wing—
But man must work, so God hath said :
They strike not now for vengeance, but for bread.

Fate ofttimes harshly rules man here ;
　　Had but the time been spared, some name
Crushed down in death when life was dear,
　　Might now shed far the light of fame !
Man's life is frail, all must be fed—
They strike not now for vengeance, but for bread.

The ghostly cries of children dead,
　　Sweet victims of the greed of men,
Come from the graves of millions fled,
　　On spectral wings, beyond our ken ;
The living die, and live the dead :
They strike not now for vengeance, but for bread.

[1] Written during the recent London bread riot.

Their paths are hedged about with swords—
   Swords wielded by proud tyranny :
Oh let them rise, outnumbering hordes,
   Shake off their shackles and be free
Ere their crushed hearts too long have bled !
They strike not now for vengeance, but for bread.

Amid their sacred altar fires,
   Hyenas of fierce famine prowl,
That cast the shades of funeral pyres,
   And demons from the darkness scowl.—
To what their sorrows lead or led :
They strike not now for vengeance, but for bread.

The speaking stars urge them to rise,
   Assert dear Freedom's rights downtrod
By men who 'd rend the very skies
   And trample o'er the thrones of God !
While all is sad, let it be said—
They strike not now for vengeance, but for bread.

Audible the sounds of discontent,
   The tools of labor laid away ;
That peaceful army only meant
   To strike for justice in their pay,
That wolves of want they need not dread :
They strike not now for vengeance, but for bread.

The great machinery is dumb,
   The locomotive's voice is still—
'T would seem the past again had come
   By some enchanter's potent will !

God grant the day 's not far ahead
When needless it will be to strike for bread.


Look up ! look up ! God calls to you,
 Ye deaf, all heedless of the throng—
Beware ! these selfish deeds you 'll rue,
 For Right will triumph over Wrong,
When there ! up higher ! God has led,
Where souls strike not for vengeance, nor for bread.

---

### MORNING.

THE Day hath chased the Night away,
 Beyond the dim horizon blue ;
The larkspur 's nodding to the lay
 Of turtle-dove, on yonder yew.


The humming-bird flies o'er the heath,
 And sips the sweets from fair wild flowers ;
From off the mount and valley 'neath,
 The smoke from dwellings heavenward towers.


The songsters of the morn have tuned
 Their ready instruments anew,
And have, in melody, communed
 E'er since the sun first peep'd to view.

Fair Nature, rous'd from out her sleep,
   Hath now begun the busy day ;
The glowworm to its hole doth creep,
   .The solemn owl hath hid away.

The nightingale hath ta'en his flight—
   He 's waiting in some forest tree,
For coming sombre shades of night,
   To carol forth his welcome glee.

Off, in " the busy haunts of man,"
   Out on the broad and boundless sea,
All nature and all life but can
   Praise Thee, O great Creator, THEE !

---

## EVENING.

NIGHT'S soft celestials now reveal
   What lurking shadows would conceal ;
The vesper's chime and low of kine,
O'er zephyrs steal, that seem divine.

And music seems to breathe above—
Where cries the plaintive, mournful dove—
And sweetly floats through dim arcades,
And wafts beyond their silent shades.

Down Phœbe smiles ; and starry spheres,
O'er the mutation of the years,

The nightingale, no longer still,
Warbles his wild notes to his fill.

And summer twilight paints the scene—
Woods, mountains, vale, and lake between,
In far moré gorgeous hues than glow
From Titian, Raphael, or Angelo.

The bird of darkness, in its flight,
Oft startles far, the ear of night ;
Then musing—hushed with th' dreamy air,
The soul feels lighten'd of its care.

This is the hour when saints repair,
On bended knees, in humble prayer ;
The soul then seems to own His might,
The God of day, the God of night.

## THE CITY OF THE DEAD.

NIGHT solemnly reign'd, and all was still ;
    The moon shone bright o'er distant hill,
And one by one each modest star
Was glim'ring faintly from afar.
I stood where pensive wanderings led—
'Midst graves of the departed dead,
And thought in meditation deep,
How each had ta'en the awful leap
Into that broad, unfathom'd sea,

Rolling 'twixt time and eternity.
To whose far depths, unseen, unknown,
Millions and millions of earth have flown.
Where are the good that sank to rest?
Are they with Heaven's sweet angels bless'd?
The wicked—where, oh, where are they?
'T is mockery for man to say!
But hark! now falls a distant lay,
Sweet tones that mingle far away!
They 're voices of the hallow'd Night,
Which far hath sped its onward flight.
They rise in anthems on the breeze—
Which from th' South in music flees—
And rushing o'er the glistening lake,
From musings now doth me awake.
From out the grove that 's fair to eye,
Is heard the dove's soft plaintive cry—
Sweet odors borne on Zephyrus' car,
Seem breath of angels from afar.
The loose leaves rustle from their boughs,
And quivering, fall to other mows,
While from the oak's tall leafy shoot,
The solemn owl sends dismal hoot.
Now softly bleat the folded sheep!
The rumbling of the rolling deep
Is wafted o'er the heath to me,
And onward—onward—far and free.
And many sounds both wild and weird
Th' superstitious long have fear'd—
Long on the night-air dwells the roar
Like shrieks from the Plutonian shore!

But ah ! those sleepers slumber still,
Heedless of all things, good and ill :
Are they not better thus by far,
Than those who yet through life do war ?
'T is their last sleep : the morn may break—
From slumber they 'll no more awake,
Until that last and fearful day
When earth and time shall pass away !
From gloomy wolds a solemn blast
Moan'd mournfully as it onward pass'd :
Shuddering cold, while night yet fled,
Hastily I left the slumbering dead.

---

## SONNET TO SAMUEL J. TILDEN.

GREAT man ! great e'en in treacherous defeat—
    By nation's voice selected President ;
For mankind's good thy statesmanship thou lent
Throughout thy life, till thou with death didst meet,
Till thy freed spirit leaped from prison seat,
To upward soar to God, behold His ruth,
To bask beneath the glorious smile of truth !
Loved ones, O Tilden ! will thy coming greet,
And thou wilt be a leader there as here—
Men long shall praise thee, wise and wondrous
        sage,
To men thy memory ever shall be dear,
Far through the corridors of every age ;

Robbed of thy rights, remains thy glorious name,
Thy years round out with honor and with fame.

---

## UNITED 'THOUGH DEATH PARTED.

D AY fled the scene, and Night, serene,
    In white, weird moonshine roams ;
The stars shone bright, like fire by night
On mountains' lofty domes.
A sea roll'd deep, a cliff rose steep ;
Two mortals near, on shore :
A girl sat there, she very fair,
Her lover did adore.
Upon the brink, where sea-birds drink
Sweet odors from the wind,
A flower grew, sweet, fresh, and new,
As reasons childhood's mind.
Oh see, dear heart ! how zephyrs start
The flower that yonder grows ! "
Thus when the maid, admiring said,
She long'd to have the rose,
And from her seat on airy feet,
Glides toward the tempting flower,
Ere her love knew what she 'd in view—
She stood in life's last hour.
He cried, " Forbear ! "   'T was lost on air,
And shades that seaward fall ;
Naught now can save, not e'en the brave—
The cry an empty call.

The cliff, so gray, now gives away!
Her hand the flower retrieves,
In wild suspense, and fear-dumb'd sense,
This scene her lover grieves.
He runs, he flies, where the beach low lies,
He rows from moorings there,
A strong light boat, which bright waves float,
And wildly round doth stare.
He sees her locks 'neath moss-grown rocks—
He draws her to the boat.
Alas! too late! destin'd had fate
The soul unbound should float.
Though lovely she died, and death satisfied,
Her spirit 's living still,
And stands on the wave where her body gave
To death its bloom to kill.
She looks pale, sweet, her phantom feet
Unwet by the watery spray—
She looks as white as heaven-born sprite—
As robes in which angels pray.
When, in surprise, Ionill 'spies
Unharm'd, his own Irene,
Doubting his mind, he soon doth find
'T is the spirit of his queen.
His tried heart broke at one fell stroke,
He looked to heaven above.
Like soft-toned flute, a sweet salute,
Floating as seraphs move,
Her spirit said—a voice from the dead—
Softly, to Ionill:
" List to my voice, wilt thou heed my choice? "

Sadly, he said : " I will."
" Then, please, dear love, my body move
Where my parents rest, I pray,
'Neath willows growing, where waters flowing
A stream, far on to the bay.
Yield not thy breath—at bay keep death—
Haste not from earth for me.
Do not despair ; 'though gone, I 'm there,
In Heaven—I 'll come for thee.
'Though  broken-hearted, we 'll  meet, 'though
    parted ! ' "
Smiling to him she leaves.
Upward doth move like a dream of love.
She wavers—she knows he grieves.
Not as before her way doth she soar
To realms of beauty and bliss,
Heaving a sigh, tears from her eye
Fall from the upper world to this.
Back she came, as ever the same,
And placed on his lips a kiss.
'T was spiritual warm—what a blissful charm !
Turned back from Heaven for this !—
To kiss him solely—where 's aught more holy ?
Then, grieved o'er her lover's woe,
She dropped a tear o'er her own bier,
Her astral eyes, pitying, glow.
She faded from sight in the pale moonlight,
Like the vision of a dream.
In sorrow, Ionill obey'd his love's will,
Though life a curse did seem.
'Midst hope and despair, with tenderest care,

He buried the dust of Irene,
Where silence falls on ghostly palls—
Her own he placed her between.
Months, years have gone—Ionill lives on,
Loving his Irene still.
He travelled on—on—where many suns dawn—
Where nights their missions fill—
Till came unsought, an inspired thought,
A warning while afar :
He must go home, no longer to roam—
With life no longer to war.
Like a spirit of love from the realm above,
The moonlight slept in peace alone ;
The clouds afar aërial mountains are,
Each star on night's soft bosom shone.
List ! list !   Hark ! hark ! a melody mark !
The music that breathes sweetly, cull ;
How ravishing sweet the sounds that greet
The ears ! and how beautiful !
" Irene !—'t is she—" Come ! come ! to me ! "
Cried Ionill—bless'd the while.
A harp holds she, whose melody
Could win to the pure e'en th' vile ;
To him she glides and her voice abides
In strains sweet from above.
" I 've come, love, far, beyond the star,
From Heaven, for thee, my love !
God soon will call !   He 's good to all ;
The angels love him so !
Dost thou feel free to go with me ? "
" I could not answer, no ! "

What joy have I beneath the sky ?
I 've suffer'd many a year !
" 'T is best for thee,—come, haste with me,
God's loving call I hear.! "
Now on the wave where winds talk grave,
A spectre bark they see—
'T was snowy white—as fair and bright,
As sprites are wont to be.
Of those aboard, each did afford
A heavenly instrument—
Some phantom lutes, some phantom flutes,
Some harps in beauty blent.
They were as fair a group as e'er
Leave Heaven for earth awhile.
With friends afloat, they board the boat,—
Each wore an angelic smile.
Ionill's mortal fled, and he of the dead,
Put on immortality.
No longer blighted, forever united,
They sailed the eternal sea.
The bark bore on ; it seemed heaven's dawn,
When flowers sweet whisper to you—
Each waving a hand, that spiritual band
All suddenly sank from view.

## APOTHEOSIS.

DEATH raised the anchor from Time's harbor
      low ;
Your bark has reached the untried shoreless sea
Which we see fit to name Eternity.
But friends will meet you, as you onward go,
With eyes all gladness and with robes of snow —
Those long parted from, you 'll greet again
With smiles, and life will have no pangs of pain ;
There healing streams through sacred valleys flow,
In that bright world bound by no limits there,
Where smoother shores hold calmer waves than
      here,
Where every hour is fraught with danger, care,
Where we must part with those we cherish dear.
Then go your way, above the ills of time,
Where every path leads up toward the sublime.

## THE MANIAC.

THE maniac sprang from off his bed,
  And placed his hand upon his brow.
"I feel within, my soul is dead!"
  His mind is wandering now.—

"Fiend! open the door—unbar! unbar!
  Why am I chained by arm to floor?—
But see, there's one bright, shining star,
  Which kindly guards my prison door!

"It stands a silent sentinel, there;
  With pity looks from its bright eye,
Adown on me in my despair—
  Ah! there's a serpent on the sky!

"It's crawling, like the crawl of Death;
  It coils; now buries in a cloud;
I feel its poisoned, fetid breath!
  It warns me of the burial shroud!

"Hark! hark! I hear, I see in the air,
  Fiends, demons, dragons, and devils!
Why tarry with me in my despair?
  Why not off to their wild revels?

"But still they stay—behold! I see!—
  But this is madness, my keepers tell—
O! from out this prison, free me!
  Why make my living death a hell?"

## THE SILENT HERO—GRANT.

TEN thousand bells toll through the air,
    The toil-worn hero's soul has fled !
The warrior of his time lies there,
    Our statesman of his day is dead !

He loved not blood nor conquest, no !
    He warred that others peace might have ;
He pitied e'en the fallen foe—
    The victor felt for vanquished brave.

Few words were his, but what he said
    Was golden—wisdom grand and free—
He boasted not—by deeds he led
    His followers on to victory.

The silent hero, Grant, has gone
    To that weird land, the great Unknown !
We 'll miss him as we journey on,
    Like some grand star forever flown !

The greatest warrior of his time ;
    He lost no battles, such his power—
In war with wizard art sublime,
    In peace, an unassuming flower.

He rode the tempest of the night—
    The night of war's dread darkness vast,

Directs the storm ! when lo ! 't is light !
  Vanished the storm ! 't is calm at last.

When all lost hope he persevered,
  And led his legions on to war ;
Napoleon-like his self-faith cheered,
  And victory glowed before—a star !

From Belmont to the Wilderness,
  Prolonged, one battle seemed the war ;
One field of carnage, nothing less,
  Which ghastly stretched for miles afar.

From battery to battlement
  The volleying thunder rent the air ;
Wing'd globes of death each way were blent,
  While bravely thousands perished there.

Brave men on both sides, South and North,
  Men clothed in blue, men clothed in gray,
For homes and dear ones each went forth,
  A sacrifice that night be day.

That night of war be day of peace ;
  That sounds which now in conflict blend,
Should hush—and when their sorrow cease
  Men's orisons to God ascend.

Ah ! oft before the ramparts, long,
  Grant stormed the leaguered wall full well ;
But lo ! at length it falls, though strong—
  To him no fort impregnable.

He followed few set rules of war,
   His genius told him what to do ;
Where all was darkness dread before,
   His light came shining 'round and through.


His name is reverenced South and North—
   He hated not the foe he fought ;
As loving parent dealing forth
   Chastisement to a child, he wrought.


When victory crowned his toil at last,
   And Lee wept like a child undone,
He cautioned all his army vast,
   To raise no shout of triumph, none.


When he had crushed the Southern pride,
   And rebels asked : What fate to come ?
He gave them food, clothes, steeds to ride,
   And said : " Obey the laws, go home ! "


Though men a monument may rear
   High as the heavens unto his name,
At Riverside, o'er his sad bier,
   It ne'er can reach his towering fame.


He conquered all the Southern host,
   He served as ruler many years,
The flowers that shroud his grave almost,
   We well may water with our tears.

The plaudits on his funeral day—
  The pomp and pæans to his name—
Men's praise—the poet's deathless lay—
  Meet guerdon that to save he came.

His name shall live in future lore,
  And history shall his fame prolong ;
When kings and empires are no more,
  His fame shall live in immortal song.

------

## FORGIVE THIS TEAR.

FORGIVE ! forgive ! this burning tear,
  Now wrung in memory from my heart—
In memory of the past, so dear,
  That far hath gone from me—a part

Of heaven I 'll see on earth no more—
  A long'd-for joy forever flown,
Like some fair phantom we adore,
  It mocks me with a glimpse alone.

I trust the golden days we lose,
  Will bloom in beauty once again ;
I trust that past, on which I muse,
  Beyond will live, no more to wane.

## LITTLE VIDIE.[1]

LITTLE Vidie ! (O the sorrow !
　　O the cruel things of time,
Where we ever, ever borrow
　　From our hope and faith sublime !)

She has gone ! the little maiden
　　Who came from Heaven to us awhile—
And our hearts are heavy laden,
　　And we nevermore can smile

With the happy, happy gladness
　　Of the days that are no more ;
And our world is like the madness
　　Of a sea without a shore.

O we cannot bear to leave her
　　In the cold, damp earth alone—
Where, O where, is her retriever,
　　Though her spirit now hath flown !

Ah ! the only thing we borrow
　　From Hope's garland brow, is this :
That we meet her on the morrow,
　　Over where all life is bliss.

[1] The niece of the author, a precocious child, beautiful, good, and affectionate, died June 7, 1883, in her eighth year, of a malignant form of diphtheria.

## TO LITTLE AUBREY.[1]

O WELCOME ! welcome, little stranger,
 Unto our happy home and thine ;
Art thou mortal, or a ranger
 From a distant world divine ?

O little angel ! tell me, tell me,
 What is thy mission, sweet and good ?
Wilt thou remain, or wilt thou flee
 To summer lands beyond the wood ?

My little son, could I but teach thee
 That which we only learn through time,
No cloud should harm, that ofttimes reach me ;
 Thy life with peace should be sublime.

May thy soul be ever lifted
 On white wings above earth's sod ;
May thy mind be ever gifted
 With the purest thoughts from God.

----

## TO IDA.

THOU 'rt absent, Ida, and I pensive feel
 The blow as keen as woe e'er gives to weal !
'Though I 've not known thee long, nor thou
 known'st me,

[1] The author's first child (a boy), born August 17, 1883.

Thy loss me sorrow brings, and misery.
Think'st thou why shouldst thy absence thus me
    move ?
Because in that short time I 've learn'd to love !
The flowers of hope are growing sad and sere,
The world seems gloomy—all is dark and drear.
As some bright, beauteous star, lost in the night,
Leaves all in darkness where once all was light,
Since thou 'rt gone, thus my sad heart feels the
    pain,
Tho' Hope faintly whispers : " You 'll meet again ! "
Ah, when and where !—when shall I greet thee !
    oh !
What joy to clasp thy fair hand—fair as snow !
And hear in silvery melody flow
Thy voice, that thrilled the sweet, sweet long ago !
But why should I feel sad ?   'T is well with thee,
E'en though in absence thou art far from me !
When thou, so fair, so lovely, and so good,
Still bloomest sweet in the beauty of womanhood !
And friends who dearly love, whom thou lov'st dear,
Do cluster 'round, thy winsome voice to hear !
To gaze on thee—on thy rich beauty, rare
And peerless, for where 's she that 's half so fair !
There ! through the corridors of memory
I hear thy merry laugh ring gay and free !
I see thy dark eyes ! lovely eyes of th' South !
And thy sweet, rich, warm, cherry, wine-kissed
    mouth !
Thy sweet, perfect face, and thy form, too, bless !—
Joy ! 't is thee ! complete in thy loveliness !

And beautiful girl, thy bright vision seems
Far sweeter to me than all other dreams,
And fairer than the fairest forest flower,
Blushing unharmed in its woodland bower ;
More lovely than the brightest diamond star,
Breathing its beauty from high heaven, afar ;
And of all things cherished, pure, fair, and free,
There is naught so dear unto memory ;
And my sad, sick soul freely drinks, I vow,
From th' sparkling fountain of thy beauty now !
Refresh'd, refin'd, and filled with hope and love,
As th' wretch revives on whom smiles God above.

## REVERIE.

THE picturesque, wild, and glorious, I love,—
 Plains, vales, and mountains, in fair Nature's
  dress.
The universe, round, below, and above ;
 Where the breeze seems an angel's soft caress—
 Some spirit friend, whose mission is to bless
And inspire ; to dwell on themes for reverie
 And speculation, I love ; and to express
The thoughts which fancy wakes ; when I dream
  free,
Be we what we may, beyond we learn life's mystery !

That maiden fair, we see, with many a charm,
 May once have been a pearl beneath the sea,

Where she was shielded from the great gulf, Harm,
    Which flows through Time unto Eternity.
    Ah, Love ! who hath not been thy votary
In Youth's fond hour, when pleasure joys on high !
    Lives start 'mid beauty, love, and melody,
But Disappointment's clouds oft fret their sky—
Where rang the light and joyous laugh there sounds
        the heavy sigh.


Then what 's all beauty but a tempter's bait ?
    It 'lures us on, it leaves us all alone,
To muse upon the unforeseen of fate—
    To feel, where'er we live, in whate'er zone,
    We live for what we know not : then atone
For present thoughts, do we ; to meditate
    Anew : till lost 'midst wilds of gloom, unknown,
We deem our lives too early or too late—
Till Hope drives off Despair, when life seems sweet
        and great.


Oh ! what is life to man ? and what is man ?
    Immortal ? or th' mere shadow of an hour ?
Is earth all ? or has life a broader span—
    Beyond time, reaching with eternal power ?
    The star high hanging in heaven's tower
May once have been a drop pearled on a rose !
    Then if a star is but th' essence of a flower,
Will not man, far the greatest life earth grows,
Live on beyond the grave, and find naught to
        oppose ?

Yon mignonette, upon the river brink,
  May be the germ of life, the future brings,
Of one who drank o' earth's fountains, and will
      drink
  From those of far, far greater, purer springs !
  E'en now methinks I hear an angel's wings
In mid-air ! guardian of this only link
  Which holds the mortal to immortal things—
For were it lost, a soul thereby would sink
Down in oblivion's slime, and perish in its rink.


Thou, ocean, who dost seem, for evermore,
  One vast live heart that beats its sides afar,
What mission 's thine ? what God dost thou adore ?
  At times, as peaceful as heaven's tranquil star ;
  At times, with th' Eternal thou dost seem to war.
Great deep ! where mysteries ever endless seem
  In each unchecked, upheaving, foaming scaur—
Where bright, the stars, behold their mirror'd beam,
'Neath heaven's projecting power, tell me thy
      cherish'd dream !


Full well, old giant ! far from the first hast thou
  Thy secrets kept through time's long flight and
      dread,
Through many ages past, on, on till now,
  When thou entomb'd the lost, th' remember'd fled;
  Mysterious flow, where wild sea monsters wed,
I read in thy weird face, as in the stars :
  That earth 's not all to th' living nor the dead.

Thus Heaven in mercy unto man unbars
Tokens of life eternal, beyond time's wars.

When we look through the gloom of misty years,
   Th' past seems a world lost we mourn and admire,
'Though the now be night, day yonder appears !
   And hope—all we most ardently desire—
Illum'd by the glory of her unquench'd fire.    ˇ
Aye, Hope 's a sylph to whom all beauty is given ;
A perfect being whereto we should aspire ;
She comes at twilight, at morn, noon and even,
Breathing from her bright robes the sweet perfumes
      of heaven.

  1876.

---

## LOVE.

THERE 's love that 's like the meteor—
    Endearing while its lasts—
That flashes, and for evermore
   Dies—darkness then o'ercasts.

Yet, like th' sweet, fix'd star of night,
   A love far, far more dear, I see !'
Pure, beautiful, and grand, and bright !
   Glowing ever—eternally !

## A SECRET OF THE SEA.

THE god of day had sunk to rest,
　　Afar in his hesperian bed,
And night walk'd forth in darkness dress'd—
　　A mourner for bright hours now dead.

Dark clouds came o'er the deep, profound,
　　The wild winds moan'd a solemn lay,
And ghosts that nightly wander round,
　　Pass'd sadly on their restless way.

The honest wrecker of Laclare,
　　To ocean gazing, o'er the lea,
Shudder'd, while breathing forth a prayer
　　For the stranger far out at sea.

Great bolts of thunder loudly crash'd,
　　And living lightning ran the sky,
And here and there it angry flash'd,
　　Like some fierce demon's vengeful eye.

Time wing's his constant flight—now wan,
　　The blast strays homeward o'er the deep,
The weary clouds move slowly on,
　　In his deep cave the storm doth sleep.

Far on the sea, with broken spars,
　　Where mad waves beat the lurid sky,
There toss'd a corse beneath the stars,
　　Under the wild moon's redden'd eye.

And here, 't is said, e'er since at night,
    Rises a fearful, frenzied cry,
When e'en the bravest wake in fright,
    And gaze at th' distant, shadowy sky,

Where pale and sad, far on the sea,
    A ghastly ghost glides slowly by,
Shrieking aloud and mournfully
    For a boon which Heaven seems to deny.

Oh ! what unhappy wretch was he
    Who braved e'en ocean, Heaven, and Hell—
When night had veil'd in shades the sea,
    And loos'd the angry storm as well !

Ah ! who that one remains to be
    A tale untold by star or wave—
But shrouded in deep mystery
    The secret of the sea's deep grave.

---

## THE CHILD TO ITS MOTHER.

MOTHER ! 't is thee, thy erring child,
    Would thank for thy past deeds of love :
Thou cared'st for me till reason smil'd,
    Like morning in the deeps above !

Like astral fire which lights the vault
　Of heaven, when sad Night mourning wears,
Though others frown'd, thou saw'st no fault :
　If so, then e'en that fault was theirs.


Thy friendship 's number'd by no hour,
　But years will ever find it true ;
It lives like the immortal flower,
　As ever fragrant, fair and new.


And he who guides the eagle's flight
　Where man's short sight doth blindly fail,
Will thee reward in world of light,
　Beyond this dark and dreary vale.


Mother ! the name is sweet to me—
　A light on silent memory's shore,
Which beacons from my infancy
　Along life's wandering path before !


## ADMONISHED.

### A PHANTASY.

IN the wonderful realm of Thought,
　On the shores of a mystical stream,
I once for pure happiness sought—
　The happiness of which we dream.

There I sought in pensive sadness,
　For the lov'd and beautiful dead ;
I was well-nigh unto madness,
　When thinking, " Where hath she fled ? "

The stream to a tarn in the wold—
　To a tarn of grandeur and gloom—
Led me—where the air was cold,
　And where echoed a sound of doom.

" Where ! where ! is the beautiful dead ? "
　I shrieked in the ear of Night—
But my voice and its echo fled ;
　I trembled with feeling of fright.

" Alethea, sweet being of Truth,
　Come, come to my longing eyes !
O come ! for thou hast feelings of ruth ;
　Come down from thy home in the skies ! "

Hush ! hark ! a sound ! a low, soft sound,
　As though a zephyr breathed close by !
And instantly I turned around,
　To meet Alethea's loving eye.

" How heavenly fair thy form and face !
　When of the earth—yes !—thou wast mine !
And still thou art ! for I can trace
　That love so beautiful—divine."

" Follow ! " she breathes—I do—she moves
　Like a dream that floats at eventide,
O'er that sweet bower where dwell the loves,
　Far from the world and its hollow pride.

A sound as when the air is hush'd,
    Rises a sudden, sullen blast ;
Now rose, as down the river rush'd,
    A hideous throng of phantoms past.

Alethea cried—her voice a tome :
    " Love ! see the danger thou wast in !
'T is ever thus with those who roam
    The pathways of the world of sin !

" Be good ! " she said ; a smile she wore—
    Then floated upward to that world
Where bloom Love's flowers forevermore,
    And Supernal Beauty is impearl'd.
1876.

---

## ON THE MOONLIT WAVE.

OUT on the moonlit wave joyously we sail,
    My love and I, she fondly by my side ;
Our cheeks are fann'd by the gently-breathing gale,
    As onward softly, sweetly now we glide.

As a young bud dreams of the future flower,
    Thus happy we dream as onward we roam,
While 'neath the bright awning of Hope's sweet
        bower,
    We on are wafting to our happy home.

As when Cupid, aërial passing on,
    Whispers of love in a beauty's pink ear,
While she lies asleep in the early dawn,
    Wreathes a smile on her lips with thoughts so
        dear ;

With astral eyes, lustrous, scintillant, dark,
    Thus my darling smiles to whate'er I say,
For love sweetly guides our moving bark,
    And Hope points the bright and beauteous way !

---

### A BEAUTIFUL MYSTERY [1]

WHAT beautiful being was this
        Afloat in the welkin there ?—
An angel from the realm of bliss,
    Come down to a world of care ?

[1] RIPLEY, OHIO, October 30, 1874.

Yesterday evening, between ten and eleven o'clock, there
appeared suspended between heaven and earth almost a fac-
simile of one of Raphael's angels, white as alabaster.  The
wings were outspread imploringly, and its evolutions were as
rapid and as beautiful as a bird circling in mid-air.  Over
150 of our best citizens, ladies and gentlemen, were eye-
witnesses of this singular spectacle, and gazed with admiration and awe. *—Cincinnati Gazette.*

Did it come of its own will, free,
  Cheerfully down to this drear clime ?
Or, lost on the waves of Eternity,
  Was it wash'd to the shores of time ?


It came and vanish'd like a tone
  Of melody we hear in dreams,
On summer eves, when not one lone
  Cold breath blows o'er the happy streams.


Favor'd were they who caught a glance
  Of this fair child of mystery,
As beautiful as the nymphs that dance.
  At night on the moonlit sea.

---

## VENNOVA.

ONCE, on as bright and fair a day
    As ever mortal eyes behold,
When Nature to her God did pray
    Her thanks for mercies manifold,


Fair Vennova and I both moved
  Beneath the clear cerulean heaven ;
Beside the crystal lake we roved—
  To love both our fond hearts were given.

Around the lake on every side,
  Mystical shadows veil'd the air ;
Some cherish'd secret seemed to hide
  In mystery eternal there.

Until Eve in her beauty was born ;
  With veil of twilight o'er her face ;
We seemed as happy as fair young Morn,
  When smiling to view from her hiding-place.

Swiftly, sorrowfully, then a sadness,
  Fell on our raptured souls, so light,
That eftsoons nigh unto madness
  Led with melancholy blight.

"Seest thou yon star so lovely bright ? "
  Pensively, Vennova to me said.
" Yes ! dear one ! but why so sad to-night ? "
  I whisper'd—she droop'd her lovely head.

As tears from her soul-rapturing eyes,
  Fell like the melting dews of even—
" Farewell ! my love beyond the skies,
  When that star wanes, I 'll be in heaven ! "

The star grew dim—my lov'd one pale,
  She by the loveliest beauty bless'd !
I curs'd high Heaven with frantic wail ;
  She meekly passed from earth to rest.

## THE CHICAGO FIRE.

CHICAGO ! great city of the West !
   All that wealth, all that power invest ;
Thou sprang'st like magic from the sand,
As touch'd by the magician's wand,
On Michigan's surf-beaten shore,
Where dashing waves and wild winds roar.
Where that which Nature's wilds obscured,
When found great enterprise allured,
And soon the wilderness of the plains,
Gave place to civilized domains.
Where roamed the savage, wild bedight,
There settled wealth, and power, and might.
Improvements on improvements grew ;
Excelled by none, thy equals few,
Thou stood'st a monument of what
Real enterprise and worth had wrought.
Alas for man ! his works are frail,
Uncertain as the fitful gale ;
To thee came an insidious hour,
Which swept away with fiendish power
The gather'd wealth of many years,
Leaving sad hearts and bitter tears.
The fire-fiends, with hell-born delight,

---

[1] The great Chicago fire began late on Sunday evening, October 8, 1871, and terminated the following Wednesday ; destroying in the meantime many million dollars of property, and many lives.

Did marshal up their hosted might,
And fiercer grew, and called for more,
And wider spread with deaf'ning roar.
The flame, a wild and fierce simoon,
And now a raging mad typhoon,
Destroy'd the buildings with a breath
Of his hot breathings—breathing death !
With cottages, gray, white, and brown,
Palatial mansions crumbled down
And melted, as the hot fires won,
Like snow beneath a torrid sun.
With all the rest, did perish there
. A mine of all the fine arts rare ;
Releas'd from prison-house, of clay,
Too, many a soul winged its far way.
The living flame, leap'd high, afar,
As though the vault of heaven 't would mar !
Now madly sweeps with angry glare.
Salvation ! where art thou ? Oh ! where ?
Fair women, who had ne'er known want,
Now see the Wolf,[1] grim, gray, and gaunt ;
And she who ne'er had felt a care,
Runs here and there in wild despair.
The merchant, once the millionaire,
Needy and maniacal stare.
Everywhere the hot flame heats ;
All grades of mortals fill the streets :
Here pass'd the maiden, chaste and pure,
There some wild rake's fair paramour ;
Here, sad the man of fortune's wreck,

[1] Poverty.

There culprits writh'd and hung by neck ;
And here forlorn a wretch, now crazed,
Sought peace and rest where Death but gazed.
Another, frenzied, ran through flame,
Loudly shrieking some lov'd one's name.
The broad lake bore, in wild distress,
Brave men and women's loveliness.
For days and nights the fire-fiends raged,
No mortal means their force assuaged.
Destruction did no atom wane,
Till Heaven, in pity, sent the rain.
'T was then it waver'd and grew less—
Then, then, for man his God to bless.
Now gird thy loins, the demons rest,
Thou Garden City of the West ;
Thou hast been—thou again shalt be
The goal of all—'t is thine, in thee :
A Phœnix, in thy ashes, thou
Shalt spring in glory from the now.

## THE RESTLESS WANDERER.[1]

THE Morn is up, in all her fair array ;
　There 's on the breeze a floating murmur
　　borne ;
Now Nature weeps her silent tears away,
　And hands to Night the mantle she has worn.
　The lark 's aroused, and sweet his winging horn !

Far in the East, the morning star appears !
　The mist fades from the yellow fields of corn,
As Phœbus brightly comes ; the hearts he cheers
Are many : Darkness hath flown from the foe he
　　fears.

Eve comes ! now slumbers sweet the curtain'd Vale :
　In Nature's bosom, th' Lake is hushed in sleep,
The owl hoots to the moon a melancholy tale.

[1] Morning and evening. A night storm. The seeming
promise of happiness associated with a beautiful morning,
is felt by all who have an innate love for the æsthetic. But
as time passes on only to bring, as it often does, misfortune,
we look back to see that this very beauty was a mask, as it
were, for misery to come.

Chalporth, a man of powerful intellect, a sensitive and
sympathetic nature, with a great love, in the highest sense, for
the perfect in the beautiful, wandered over the world in dili-
gent search of the genial spirit he hoped at first to find. At
length, after spending a lifetime of fruitless search for his
ideal, he despaired ; abandoned his undertaking, when his
liberated soul soared to the arms of the Eternal.

'Twixt leaves of trees, dews o' twilight softly
  seep—
The Breeze oft soaring lowly now doth creep ;
The Storm is resting in the forest cave,
  There husbands strength, to future ruin reap ;
The Wind is softly whispering to the Wave—-
The Blast is hushed, but erelong he will madly rave.

It later grows ! and Night now reigns supreme !
  Stars silently come, and lovingly they meet.
Forth Luna walks : hark ! 't is the night-bird's
  scream.
  There softly floats along one cloudy sheet—
  I hear the sad sea dirging low and sweet !
A wondrous lay—a grand, pathetic tune.
  Now spirits hover near lov'd hearts that beat
On earth to guard their sleep. 'T is now night's
  noon !
When Fairies dance on clouds and Peris greet the
  moon.

Fair Dian wanes—a cloud obscures her face—
  The mutt'ring Thunder growls his savage threats.
A mighty storm is coming, and apace
  Each element of Nature more power begets.
  Now lightning sparkles in bright zigzag jets ;
Cloudy phantoms grimly dance 'neath heaven's bar.
  The rain, once dropping, now a torrent sets—
Now lightning, chain'd and fork'd, shoots near and
  far,
And living storms fling thunderbolts from star to
  star.

Both night and storm hath fled ! the sleeping wake !
　And hand in hand now forth come Love and
　　Joy !
The songsters sweetly carol from the brake,
　And all seems beautiful !. But to decoy,
　Now Misery comes fair Happiness to destroy.
Star-soul'd Chalporth fell victim t' misery's bane,
　When young, a man in mind e'en when a boy :
A pilgrim from his birth, Nature his fane—
He seeks, but seeks in vain, while his years on-
　　ward wane.

He sought a genial soul, but none could find ;
　His spirit from the loftiest life had sprung ;
Expecting more than those he met enshrin'd.
　Like him, all such, whate'er the sex among,
　Are led to mania, if they die not young,
For flesh and spirit ever are at war.
　No pen can truly write, nor tell no tongue,
The gloom that shrouds that life, full sore,
That saw each flower o' hope decay when scarce a
　　blush it bore.

Chalporth had travel'd much, through many lands ;
　Imbibed from Pleasure's sweetest founts, to lose
The phantom following ; then tried wedlock's
　　bands ;—
　But all these failed happiness to infuse.
　While 'midst life's darkest shadows he did muse,
Alone, one came, an angel from afar,
　To minister to him, now a recluse ;

To aid him mount to Heaven's celestial bar—
'Midst life's dark clouds the faint, 'though soli-
    tary star !


Her stay was short : for jealous eyes did spy
    Them hidden in the bower with fair love fraught.
The demon, Darkness, hover'd in the sky,
    His damp wings flapp'd despair and Hope was
        naught ;
    All her scintillations his fierce jaws caught—
He swallow'd as new and tender snow-flakes
    Are swallow'd by th' remorseless Sea.  Thus
        wrought
The fiend—o'er ruins chuckling ; as in wakes
Of shipwrecks, Death laughs at shivering ghosts he
    sportive makes.


His spirit weep'd within for his sad heart's
    Deep misery, which well knew that Hope had
        fled.
A desert waste man's life, when she departs.
    Much of life's path is through a wood where
        dread,
    Grim ogres rise to flee before the tread,
Of many, far ; while others do despair,
    And feel that hope is number'd with the dead.
But lo ! in heaven, behold that angel there !
Who cries : " Beyond, Hope still lives, in perfec-
    tion fair ! "

Behold the Pyramids ! relics of long ago ;
   Each towering toward heaven a glist'ning head.
Where fleecy clouds dream round, above, below—
   Peacefully slumbering in soft aërial bed,
   Ere called by Nature their bright tears to shed.
The Pyramids ! monuments of mummied kings,
   Where the imprison'd blast howls o'er the dead,
And melancholy ghosts whom Misery stings—
Each earth-spent, wasted life, on memory's track
     he flings.

Chalporth had seen the Pyramids sublime,
   Seen Nature's mighty wonders throughout th'
     world—
In every nation, country, land, and clime,
   Had wander'd where'er Time hath wings un-
     furled :
   Had watch'd the mighty avalanche, as it hurl'd
Down in the flowery vale—when in its maw,
   Went all the loveliness that once impearl'd,
Or fell a shapeless mass 'neath its demon paw :
Thus swiftly pass earth's fruits away.  The Alps
     he saw.

Saw the Rocky and other mountains.  Vast forms,
   Rising, like giant phantoms, man to fright ;
Triumphant conquerors of mightiest storms—
   Storms cloth'd in the armor of day and night,
   Which with great thunderbolts do vainly fight.
Here Nature shames the greatest works of art,
   In all that 's grand and sublime unto the sight—

Which to the soul ambition doth impart,
Inspiring it to fulfill the dictates of the heart.


" A man may smile and be a villain still,"
   A truth experience often calls to mind :
The belle's proud breast an aching heart may fill,
   E'en while she reigns the queen of beauty ;
      kind
She may be, but ah ! too vain.  Thus we find
Th' Wanderer—th' proud victim of circumstance—
   Within his heart his ideal he enshrin'd ;
Cherishing a wish he hid from every glance,
Though roaming plains or mountains, or in the
      fane or dance.


One other thing also would make him bless'd,
   He thought ; and yet that this could ever be
He little hoped ; and still that wish his rest,
   His soul disturbed, as mighty storm the sea.
   He long'd from all restraints existence free,
To be a real plurality, and, clear
   Retain his individuality,
So that with each and all his friends held dear,
He could be e'er, at once, though miles did in-
      terfere.


'Though he loved Nature long, thus time did kill,
   With whom his being moved with impulse free ;
Yet she tired his soul when it drank its fill,
   As the alluring charms of revelry
   Did satiate—a honey-laden bee.

Not so a genial soul—that presence bright—
   Then earth-life 's a dream of heaven, fair to see !
Of which sun, moon, stars are concentered light,
Without which mortal's world  would ever  be in
     night.

And Chalporth wearied of the world and fled
   'I' Solitude, which he his companion made ;
Sought Nature out and on her grandeur fed ;
   But all her pleasures like the rest did fade—
   Of heaven's bliss earth's joys are but the shade ;
Such the Almighty's will.   By His bequeath
    Chalporth reach'd th' land where life in love 's
      array'd ;
A land where sorrow 's not, nor doubt, nor death ;
A land fairer than " Love's  young dream," sweeter
    than th' rose's breath.
   1875.

---

### THE HAUNTED LAKE.

Ere Heavenly Phœbus wakes the morn
With amber rays in beauty born,
While yet the zephyrs bear along
The sweetest notes of night-birds' song,
While Cynthia rides in glowing car
Past fleecy cloud and lovely star,
Fair Mabel rising from her bed,
Flushed with sweet dreams now scarcely fled,

Trips lightly through her marble halls —
Whilst th' nightingale his love-mate calls,
Out where the starlight gently falls.
Her auburn tresses long are streaming—
Her sweet eyes tell her spirit's dreaming.
The connoisseur her form approves ;
With the carriage of a Grace she moves ;
The brightest intellect all trace,
In her pure, sweet, and beauteous face—
Her charms do rival love's own queen,
Her beauty e'en Psyche's, I ween.
Noble as th' looks of this sweet lass,
Their peerlessness doth not surpass
The love and sympathy she bears
For those that suffer woes and cares :
Her hand e'er reached to the distressed,
Her beauty is her soul expressed.
O'er th' lawn she glides, a sprite of bliss,
Blushing, feeling the zephyr's kiss ;
Her ruby lips are wreathed in smiles,
Pure—innocent—all void of guiles.
Through eglantine and asphodel,
Where soft th' fountain water fell ;
Her friend, the Breeze, a gallant true,
The shrubbery parts as she moves through.
Her eyes as blue as heaven above,
Mirror her heart in beams of love ;
She stops at the lake whose bosom still
Reflects star, moon, and mighty hill—
Romantic mirror marked with trace
Of Nature's God and Nature's face.

Why leaves the beauty her soft pillow !
Why seeks the lakelet's mimic billow,
Ere Day has come on wings of light !
While Silence walks the paths of night !—
Why loves she at such hour to rove,
Morn still dreams in her bower above !
Onward impell'd by mystic power,
She seeks the lake at this lone hour.
Her vows to keep, oh, sacred duty !
This lovely girl with wealth and beauty—
Next morn the peerless bride to be
Of one she worships to idolatry—
Wishes to feel the mystic powers
Which Nature wields in these soft hours—
The hours that give, while fair Faith reigns,
Fond Fancy's sweet Æolian strains—
The hours of night Death's brother, Sleep,
Doth best his faith with Nature keep—
When th' silent slumberer's spirit roams,
To study Nature's ancient tomes,
Or whisper fondly in the ear
Of some far distant one that 's dear—
When e'en the forest round the lake
A living presence seems to take,
And in its whisperings seems to tell
That round our very being dwell
Spirits of th' dear departed, true.
Near by in the breeze that sips the dew—
Angels of light from homes above,
Whose presence tells their yearning love.
The Lake which oft in childhood's hours,

Saw Mabel cull its shore's wild flowers,
Beholds her now 'neath th' starry sheen,
In her fond prime, sweet beauty's queen ;
Out from the past she blooms this hour,
A bud developed to the lovely flower.
A sigh of love, heav'd deep and dear,
Oft sweetly melts into a tear,
Which brightly glows through flowing tress—
Tresses that do the lips caress ;
Conflicting feelings in her breast
Disturb her thus though she is bless'd—
Hush ! soft ! a sound breaks on her ear !—
Hath angel like her aught to fear ?
A knight and steed come into view
Just where the flowers their petals strew.
It is ! oh ! can it be of all
He whose presence e'er doth call
Up joy, and wakes, her looks confess,
Her world to one of happiness !—
Where dearest wish is gratified,
And hope is ever by her side !
'T is he ! and ne'er 'mid weal or woe,
Did braver knight than Don Raldo,
For Beauty's claim combat the foe.
He, too, awakens in the night,
Nor waits the tarrying day-god's light,
But mounts his steed and rides away
'Neath the pale stars and Dian's ray ;
And though he hath no place in mind
To journey to, he rides to find
Relief from feelings, restless, ill,

While bright the 'luring vale and hill
Are lit by moon and stars, as dawn—
His heart leads him, unconscious, on
Where doth abide without a peer,
The reigning belle both far and near—
She who, when few short hours have died,
Will be his young and beauteous bride.
They meet—these two who love so well—
Life breathes of heaven and cares dispel ·
And they, apace, within a boat
On lake's broad bosom sweetly float ;
Contentment dwells in their warm souls,
And joy her pleasures now unfolds.
But see ! dark clouds are threatening war,
And dimly glows each red-lit star
From heaven's dark vault ; the thunder growls,
Fierce coming on the tempest howls.
At last ! to th' happy two comes care—
Their danger 's known too late.　Despair
Assails the boat from stern to prow.
Where, where is she, sweet Mercy, now ?
The bark is o'erturned by a wave—
Now lightning licks its watery grave—
Beautiful Mabel and Don Raldo
Float o'er the waves—the storm doth grow—
They struggle well—O Heaven them save !—
They vanish, and beneath a wave !

　　*　　*　　*　　*　　*　　*

Ere from the skies the stars have flown,
While nymphs to rove 'neath moon are prone,

And wood-fays in the leafy boughs
In secret plight their sweetest vows,
And Halcyon broods o'er the wave,
And Echo whispers from the cave,
Before Day doth on Darkness break,
Two phantom lovers sail the lake.

---

## ARION.[1]

SWEET songster of the olden time,
　　Thy lyre was tuned to lovely lays,
Thy rapturing melody and rhyme
　　Was grandest of the bygone days.

When 'midst the corsairs on the wave,
　　Who for the gold thou didst possess
Destin'd thee to a watery grave,
　　How sweetly did thy song-powers bless!

But one request thou madest of them—
　　Who could refuse that simple boon?—
To play, ere they to death condemn,
　　One only, lovely, farewell tune.

[1] A poet and musician of Methymna, in Lesbos, said to have
lived in the reign of Periander, ruler of Corinth, about 600
B.C.

Thou play'd'st, and all were charmed around,
    As though with harps were angels near;
And trusting to that heavenly sound,
    Far out thou sprang'st to disappear

Beneath the wave—to rise again—
    By charmèd dolphin borne along ;
Well, thou didst worship at the fane,
    The sweet enchanting fane of song.

---

## BETHLEHEM'S STAR.

### A SONNET.

THIS is the happy month and merry morn,
    When Bethlehem's bright star so sweetly
        came,
And shed throughout the world a wondrous flame,
Which banished shadows from the earth forlorn.
Peace, peace to men, the Infant Christ is born !
The gonfalon of glories of the skies,
All evil things of every world defies.
No longer need the lowest wretch now mourn ;
Hope promises the thing the soul desires,
And death is shorn of all its terrors dread.
Death means a change—man ne'er himself expires.
The good are safe with God, and Death is dead.
No more the trump of doom disturbs men's sleep,
By awful bellowing through the troubled deep !
    1887.

•

## FALSE GINEVRA.

O GINEVRA, Ginevra! your smiles are bright,
But your heart is fickle—to me untrue ;
You are not the star I hailed with delight
In the morn of the past that's vanished from view.

---

## UNSEEN.

L IFE'S dreary plants are in our sight,
We catch but a breath of the unseen flowers—
O God ! in the depths of the infinite,
Yield man a glimpse of the Unknown Powers !

---

## CHRIST'S LOVE.

I SING the love of the Nazarene ;
Who taught along the Galilee—
A light by every wanderer seen
Through time and through eternity !

His love is more than woman's, friend !
Though strong her love, it bears the mould

Of vanity, as when ores blend,
　When mix alloy and virgin gold.

Christ's love is as a morning joy,
　As spring perennial, fair and bright—
It is not wavering, transient, coy,
　'T is the one fixed star o'er lonesome night !

Like to a sea bound by no shore,
　His love extends, deep, far and wide ;
From earliest dawn till evermore
　It flows one mighty, endless tide.

----

## LINES ON THE DEATH OF AN INFANT.

DEAR little babe, few were his days,
　In this sad world, we call the earth,
Lo ! far beyond, with poet's gaze,
　I see ! he found a second birth !

Wrapped in his infant, spirit-clothes,
　With friends ; no longer him bewail ;
Beyond the reach of earthly woes
　No more shall death his life assail.

How sweet to pass from earth so pure,
　Before vile contact soils the soul ;
As sinless as our Lord, secure,
　Your babe has reached a glorious goal.

## "IT IS I, BE NOT AFRAID!"

GOD'S beauty, grand, supernal,
　　Far in the starry depths unfurls !
God's glory lives eternal
　　Above the crash of mighty worlds !
Wafts o'er the grave's abysmal shade :
" It is I, be not afraid ! "

O Conqueror of Death ! O Light !
　　The stars that seem to speak in ruth,
Unto Thy radiance are but night—
　　But froth and foam on sea of Truth !
Christ calls to all—to Peter said :
" It is I, be not afraid ! "

The night passed on—the fourth watch came—
　　Christ glorious walked the troubled wave ;
They saw him coming like a flame,
　　And cried for fear a ghost to brave ;
" Be of good cheer ! " their dear Lord said ;
" It is I, be not afraid ! "

I hear the courser's thundering tread !
　　The shouting of the armèd foe !
I saw the vanquished as they fled
　　In their sad misery and woe—
But hark ! a voice their sorrows stayed :
" It is I, be not afraid ! "

Though ships are tossing on the sea,
    Though winds are running wild and high,
Though fishermen on Galilee
    Are fearful when the storm is nigh—
O deep His meaning! more than said:
"It is I, be not afraid!"

---

## SONNET TO RICHARD HENRY STOD-
### DARD.

(On receiving from him one of his autographic poems.)

I 'VE heard the music of a friend's regard,
    Which touched my heart and waked sweet
        memory, dear,
That slept 'neath waters of the Past's veiled mere,
To feel life's burdens were not half so hard;
Above the thorns enhaled the rose and nard—
As though some wizard's power did now repay,
And reared me temples on the shores of day.
O Critic thou! and thou, O tuneful Bard!
Now comes thy song, with beauties none deny.
Thy fame is builded on two mountains high,
The mount of song, the mount of censor free,
Pinnacled in golden clouds that kiss the sky.
O Bard, accept these grateful lines from me!
To thank thee for thy song I speak in poesy.

## MY LOST GEM

I MOURN the gem I might have had,
   I saw it erst in crystal wave ;
I touched it not, my heart was glad,
   'T was mine whene'er I wished to have.

For long, long years, 't was only mine,
   For me God kindly placed it there ;
I took it not—it was divine,
   For mortal hand it was too fair !

One who had looked on it with me,
   And knew 't was mine, oft said : " So fair,
I e'er would leave it in the sea,
   'T is far too bright for man to wear ! "

I said, e'en while my heart did doubt :
   " Yes ! yes ! I will ! I 'll leave it there : "
A broken spell—he snatched it out !
   And I am wild in my despair.

## IN MEMORY OF THOMAS WILLIAM PEA-COCK.[1]

" AFTER life's fitful fever," now
        In peace, rest, father ! free from care,
E'en while we mourn that o'er thy brow
    Death waves his fearful banner there !

O thou didst fight a noble fight—
    Most would have lost hope's star ere thou :
But, guided by a sense of right,
    Not e'en to mountains wouldst thou bow.

Thy mind was great, thy will was strong,
    But thy soul's mansion time made weak,
And, too, disease did thee a wrong,
    And vexed thy generous spirit meek.

Thou didst aid men who e'er were blind
    To that true honest faith of thine ;
'Though thou gav'st them thy years, I find,
    Alas ! thou didst " cast pearls to swine."

Though some would teach thou distant are,
    And though I would each good revere,
I deem that thou art not afar—
    I feel, I know that thou art near !

---

[1] Father of the author.   He died June 2, 1880, in his sixty-fifth year.

For why should one so good and wise
  Desert us in the hour of care !
Why mount at once beyond the skies
  And leave us in our sad despair !

––––––

## MORE LIGHT.

O WILDERNESS of worlds ! ye stars !
    Could man but read you once aright,
The mystery that ever mars
    Our hopes would clear––lo ! God and Light !

––––––

## THE SUNSET IN VICTORY.[1]

L IFE is a mystery and a dream ;
    Man like the stars we fathom never ;
We glide adown Time's flowing stream
    From cradle to the grave, forever.

[1] This poem is written as a slight tribute of appreciation of
the honor conferred on my friend, Hon. S. S. Cox, of New
York, in the way of the presentation of a floral device (the
Maltese Cross) with the inscription, "Sun Set in Victory,"
by a host of friends, on the occasion of his late re-election to
Congress, 1884.

Some live and fail to rise above
    The common herd ; a few we see,
That, like the star of eve and love,
    Soar far beyond the wave and lea.


Thus by his intellectual power,
    Brave Cox all odds hath overcome—
The sweet bud blossoms—lo ! the flower
    On Fame's high mountain is at home !


The highest honor unto man,
    The Maltese Cross, looms gloriously !
High up the heavens, Cox leads the van,
    His " Sun hath set in Victory ! '


---


## CRUEL, CRUEL DEATH ! [1]

OH, bear me from the battle-field !
    I 'm wounded with earth's sorrow—strife !
I 'll try to rest.   Pray, friend, me shield !
    Oh, sad and dismal is this life !


[1] Lines wrung from my heart by grief on hearing of the sad
death of my beloved brother, William Carson Peacock, M.D.,
who died suddenly on his thirty-ninth birthday, Monday,
September 14, 1885, at Prairieville, Kaufman County,
Texas.

O God ! where wast Thou on that night
   My lonely brother Carson died ?
Couldst Thou not back death-cruel fight
   Until I reached his suffering side ?


Oh that I might have held his head !
   Wet, feverish face, though life must wane ;
It drives me mad to think him dead,
   And I not near to ease his pain !


He died ! no kindred love was nigh !
   Alas ! why was it thus to be,
When, had we known he was to die,
   For him we 'd cross'd the wildest sea !


Oft, oft he called us in his pain !
   His cries on selfish winds did die !
Alas ! alas ! he called in vain—
   Blind ! blind ! short-sighted wretch am I !


O God ! what sacrifice ! what boon
   Dost Thou demand to call him back !
He died too young ! he died too soon !
   O hideous monster Death, alack !


Forgive me, God ! I know Thou 'rt good,
   That Thou wilt help us carefully o'er
The darkest and the angriest flood
   Which flows fore'er from shore to shore.

A friend unto the friendless poor,
    He healed their sick and asked no pay.
Oh ! God remembers, and His door
    To such is open night and day.

His love was as a gentle dream
    Which makes us happy till we wake ;
In darkness died that tranquil beam !
    My aching, wounded heart must break.

The years he lived were beauteous years,
    Made beauteous by his life so fair ;
For him I 'll e'er weep sorrow's tears—
    He died ! my bright sky 's dark with care.

But hush ! steals softly on my ear
    A well-known voice from out the air :
Weep not ! I live ! and I am near !
    Cheer up ! take hope ! why, why despair ?

He is not dead ! but gone before,
    To live that life that never ends—
We soon shall meet ! a few days more,
    We 'll greet him and his heavenly friends.

---

## SONNET TO DR. OLIVER W. HOLMES.

YOUR letter came across the world to me,
    O Poet, you of rich and mystic song !—
And crows that perched and cawed till all was
    wrong,

Flew to the woods that frowned beyond the lea ;
The low'ring storm is banished from life's sea.
'T is sweet, the light, when all is dark as death ;
'T is sweet, when sick, to breathe one unbound
     breath ;
'T is sweet to know of immortality :
Your words of praise are welcome quite as these,
And came to me, how sweet ! as in the night
Voices of unknown, wondrous melodies,
Shed on the world a pure and hallowed light !
Time kinder deals with you than most of men,
So bright your mind at threescore years and ten.

## SPRING.

'T IS spring ! the birds are singing everywhere ;
    The trees the lovely blush of promise bear,
And sweetly o'er the land, from sea to sea,
The infant bud dreams of the flower to be ;
And vale and mount, alike in vernal green,
Bloom forth in beauty, gorgeous and serene ;
The silvery stream goes dancing on its way ;
The fisherman hides from the sun's warm ray,
Beneath the foliage of the sycamore,
And waits to see what luck 's for him in store ;
The gentle kine graze on the meadow grass,
The flocks search high up in the mountain pass ;
The plover pipes upon the prairie way,
From early morn until the close of day.

When lovely Luna hangs her horn on high
Far in the eastern watch-tower of the sky,
Above the fleckless fleecy clouds of grace,
Hovering o'er, in the vastiness of space ;
Far down, the stars from their high, saintly rest,
View themselves tremulous imaged in the breast
Of a lovely lake in th' solemn, dreamy wold—
A lake of beauty, wondrous to behold !
Yet, whilst we gaze, its grandeur doth improve ;
The waves awake ! the scene grows sweet as love—
As she, who far too proud to e'er be vain,
Though near and far the one belle she doth reign,
Adds to her loveliness a charm, and rare,
When blushing she beholds herself mirrored fair !
All these breathe of spring—of gentle spring begun,
When sweet and dear, life, love, youth, hope are one :
Not only of this world, and things of this,
But of the sweet forevermore, where life eternal is.

---

## AUTUMN.

WHILE gently fall the leaves,
    The pensive boughs o'erhead
Are mournfully singing low,
    A requiem of the dead.

The flowers, too, have faded,
    And Time has conquered all—
Has changed the summer zephyrs
    To rushing winds of fall.

The harvest season 's over,
　And numbered with the past ;
All nature 's sad and dreary,　　·
　As roars the autumn blast.

The barren hills and valleys
　Are records of the changes,
With spring-birds' absent warblings
　Along the mountain ranges.

But where are they, the dear ones,
　Who, far past summer's life,
Should, in the year's autumnal,
　With hoary age be rife ?

They well-nigh all have perished,
　As did the fragrant rose,
But unlike will again appear
　Where no autumn doth oppose.

Each spring to autumn hastens,
　Each youth transforms to age,
Each genius leaves a record
　On Time's historic page.

## DEPARTED.

### A FRIEND.

DEAR friend, companion lov'd, forsooth,
  Can it be so that thou art gone?
Alas! it is the mournful truth,
  Thou died'st in manhood's early dawn.
In spring-time, when the wild flowers wave
  Their perfumes o'er thy hallowed bed,
They'll mutely speak from off thy grave
  To passers by : " A soul hath fled."

## FUTURITY.

IN future far, I see the goal ;
  There! there! I see the darkness lit,
Where now each earth-departed soul,
  Goes soaring toward the Infinite ;
Anear the dear, momentous hour,
  When it shall rest beyond the skies :
I see each spirit-bud a flower
  Bloom sweetly there in Paradise !

## THE HALL OF VALHALLA.[1]

HARK! on the ear there is toss'd
   Sweet martial melody wild;
It comes like the sob of a lost,
   Yet loved and beautiful child.
From Valhalla's Hall it doth come,
   Where Odin the great god is.
Good tidings his ravens brought home,
   And to-night is a revel o'er this.
Phantoms feast on the viands of the god,
   And they fight the battles of yore—
Fierce shades of heroes under the sod,
   Oft fight their wild battles o'er;
Alternately, they feast and fight,
   'Neath the smiles of their mighty god,
Who watches, and when all is right,
   Doth render an approving nod.
Th' Valkyrior virgins recruit o'er the corse,
   From the battle-field of the slain—
More phantoms to aid Odin's force—
   An army of ghosts to retain;
Till arrives that hour so drear,
   When the great dread battle 's to fight,
Which gods and Titans do fear—
   When one race will vanish in night.

---

[1] The abode of the god Odin.—[Scandinavian mythology.]

## ASLEEP.

SHE sleeps! the beauty of the vale!
 Her brow is calm, her cheeks are pale,
Lips slightly ope, as though would stray
Her thoughts upon the wind away.
She one of perfect health doth seem,
In whom love's noblest feelings teem.
She sleeps in an Arcadian bower,
Where perfume from the forest flower,
Breathing around her wild-wood bed,
And through locks of her lovely head,
Enhances restless, wanton breeze,
Which stirs the leaves upon the trees,
And now and then, in ruder blow,
Exposes breasts of virgin snow;
A hand as perfect and as fair
As hopes that swim in happy air;
A foot as light and comely made
As e'er possess'd by nymph or naiad;
A limb as perfect as the roe's,
That swiftly through the forest goes.
With beauty which to homage pay,
That th' many crowned her "Queen of May,"
With Diana's virtue, Sappho's soul,
Her presence made an Eden goal.
And though the whispers of the wind,
With voices of the trees combined,
Oft rise above, oft lowly creep,

Still doth the " Queen of Beauty " sleep.
But lo ! she stirs ! gaze on her brow !
Hush ! hush ! draw near ! Great God, e'en now,
E'en while we spoke of her fair charms,
Death subtlely our darling harms.
Each breath in weaker volume flows,
Each rise of bosom slower grows.
Wake ! wake her, and we 'll death oppose !
Why should she die ? this sweet spring rose !
Already she hath woke above,
And with pure angels' sacred love
Is shielded from all pain and harm on high,
And finds that rest for which the weary sigh.

---

## IMPROVISED.[1]

W HO, who art thou, fair nameless friend,
  That wishes me so great a boon ?
Why not with thy good wish, too, send
  To me thy hidden name as soon ?

A merry Christmas, happy year,
  You write you wish me, from afar ;
How sensitive to wish, yet fear
  To tell me who you really are.

---

[1] On receiving a newspaper, dated December 19, 1874, from a distance, with the following sentence written on the margin, in a lady's hand, without a signature : " I wish you a merry Christmas and a happy New Year."

Although thy name incog. remains,
    And even though I knew thee not,
Yet comes thy wish as on the plains
    Heaven's aid to a wretch by man forgot.

Methinks I know thee, though thy name
    Thou hast withheld through modest fears ;
The past comes back, more sweet than fame,
    Across the weary waste of years.

Oh ! dear to me the nevermore !
    I would that dream might ever last—
The golden days, the days of yore,
    The past that is forever past !

Since thou hast given no address,
    'T is meet to thank thee, thus, I deem :
May Heaven thy eon ever bless—
    Thy life one sweet, unbroken dream.

-----

## IN MEMORY OF EUGENE COLE.

YES ! he, Eugene, has to the blast
    Of fate bow'd early in life's spring,
As each and all, in turn, at last,
    Must fade beneath Death's sombre wing.
Promethean fires, warm, beauteously,
    The chambers of his soul illumed ·
A votary of Parnassus, free
    The flowers of his muse have bloomed.

Gone ! as a dream we fondly cherish
   Yet lose alas ! forevermore !
And oh ! must our friendship perish
   With that loved one whom we adore ?
No ! no ! for while his vanish'd form
   Shall brightly live on memory's page,
Haunting fore'er life's calm and storm—
   Like some sweet bird freed from its cage,
As fair as love beyond the blue,
   Where morning never veils her form,
The soul will soar high heaven through,
   Above time's ruins, death, and storm.
1875.

## MURDER.[1]

WHEN rampant Murder earth stalks o'er,
   Breathing death-blighting far and nigh,
Hills, wolds, all things, the wound feel sore
   And in distress to th' Eternal cry.
Wild Anger rises from his rest,
   Shakes off the drowsy web of sleep ;
Now fiercest passions him invest,
   And o'er his swollen body creep.
And Vengeance dons his robes blood-red,
   Calls to clouds which sympathetic be,
That, moving on, mourn for the dead—
   Souls hurl'd from time to eternity.

[1] Composed at Independence, Kansas, when first hearing of the horrible murders by the fiendish Bender family.

Are th' midnight, crime-stained deeds of woe,
　Of wandering fiends which naught appease,
Are Hell's dark nameless deeds more low
　Than th' Drum Creek Bender tragedies?
The moon grieves o'er the silent dead,
　In pity gazes th' sad-eyed star;
Where deep death-cries the wild air fed,
　With silence they yet seem to war.
The spirit o'er the grave doth weep,
　For its dead body hidden there.
Shrouds rustle! 'gainst death's untim'd sleep
　Rebelling, moves the corse in its despair!
Whoe'er struck much the harmless flint
　And brought not forth the venom'd fire?
Just Nemesis! arise, nor stint
　The vengeance of thy fatal ire!

----

## THE CHASE.

MORN in her orient chamber wakes,
　And the blast of the hunter's horn
Startles the stillness, as it breaks
　The sleep of all to whom 't is borne.

Brave knights uprise, and ladies fair,
　And call for their steeds—a noble race:
Each anxious hound runs here and there,
　Eagerly panting for the chase.

A stag is loosed from his pent rest,
  Where he has fattened for the chase ;
Of all the deer he is the best—
  The largest, swiftest of his race.


The horses plunge, nor urging need—
  Of the excitement they partake ;
Away they bound, o'er fence and mead,
  And through the leafy umbrage break.


Through gloomy cypress wolds they flee—
  Past many a wild Idalian bower—
They hear the booming of the sea,
  They breathe the perfume of the flower.


The deer bounds on his headlong way,
  Swift rushing from the foes he fears—
The ope-mouthed bloodhound's baleful bay
  Comes like a death-knell to his ears.


With eager haste the hunters urge
  Their steeds, and test their fleetest powers ;
Now from the woods they do emerge—
  Far o'er the plain the swift deer scours !


But lo ! the lord of many a waste
  Now pauses, gazing wildly back !
Far better for him on to haste—
  He falls ! and to the rifle's crack.

Night's shadows fall on all below—
   The queenly moon comes forth, no less
The radiant stars, that ever glow
   In their eternal silences.

A-weary with the long-liv'd chase,
   The knights and winsome ladies fair,
Their jaded steeds turn, and retrace
   To castle and refreshments there.

---

## THE PRAYER OF THE UNIVERSE.

THOU, ocean ! in thy restlessness,
   Speak'st of the Throne on high,
And in thy heavings thou dost bless
   The God whom men deny.

O thou, bright Sun ! whose golden rays
   Dispel the darkest night,
Thy prayers are many as the days
   Thou usherest into light.

Sweet Cynthia ! thou pale orb of night,
   Whom Hesper guards, serene—
Thou ! who in thy bless'd realm of Light
   Rulest starry subjects, queen.

In beauty, thou obeisance payest,
  To Him who thee afar,
Plac'd there where thou enraptured stayest,
  Thy diadem a star.


And you, ye glittering starry spheres !—
  A million Argus eyes—
Your very presence life endears ;
  The poetry of the skies.


In modesty's sweet loveliness,
  The sacramental cup
Ye fill and drink ; by hope no less,
  Ye bid the soul look up.


Sweet Bow ! thy prayers are great, thou art,
  Thou joyest in the happy sky,
Thou givest hope to every heart
  Through ages passing by.


The mountains by their lofty flights
  The rivers by their flow,
The forests by the pure delights,
  They offer and bestow.


Thus Nature ever freely gives,
  Devout, her prayers o'er earth ;
True to herself she nobly lives
  As destined at her birth.

## EGERIA.

THOUGH years have come and years have gone
　　Since I beneath thy magic smile
Basked—like the glad earth in the dawn,
　　When hope and joy the hours beguile—

As some fair, pure, and tranquil star
　　Seems to embody all we crave,
And though it sweetly shines afar,
　　Still keeps our hopes beyond the grave,

Sweet Undine of the deep blue wave—
　　Lov'd houri of Utopian Heaven—
Thus dearest thoughts to thee I gave,
　　Thus in memory they are given.

The stars forevermore enshrin'd
　　In their high homes far o'er the sea—
In their dear beauty, me remind,
　　Egeria ! darling one, of thee !

Ah, yes ! methinks I see thee now,
　　In all thy wealth of beauty, sweet,
With bright tiaras on thy brow,
　　And flowing tresses to thy feet.

Dark eyes of wondrous loveliness—
　　A Peri's figure ere its fall—
Supernal beauty—nothing less—
　　Thine, darling, dearest one of all.

## PURITY.

A N angel she looked in her robe of white ;
　　A spirit stepped out from its earthly shroud,
A being of Light in a world of Night,
　The brightest of stars 'mid the darkening cloud.

She knelt, poured forth her soul in prayer,
　And meekly asked to be forgiven ;
Each word was borne from earth with care,
　And entered in the book of Heaven—

By angels borne, whose missions are
　To descend and ascend from birth,
From world to world, past cloud and star—
　God's messengers, 'twixt Heaven and earth.

---

## DRIFTING.

I N our boat we are on the sea
　　Lying now so calm and still,
The world seems full of melody,
　And fragrance seems the air to fill.

Fair Rosamond is by my side—
　In all her loveliness so fair,
She oft wounds many a beauty's pride—
　Awakening pangs of jealous care.

The night is one of loveliness—
  A night when in our hearts we feel
That angels, in the homes they bless,
  Behold all human woe and weal.


While o'er the waters wide we roam,
  Across the wave the sea-bird calls ;
We 're drifting on, a league from home—
  O'er vasty deep the moonlight falls.


The breeze which whispers 'round our sail
  Seems to breathe of another world,
Near by, just there beyond the pale
  Blue, dreamy clouds, that float unfurl'd.


A radiant world of peace and love,
  That freely yields all the warm heart craves.
On, like a lovely dream, we move,
  Far o'er the bosoms of the waves—


That are floating, gently ever,
  Upon their far Eternity—
And like the longing Peri, never
  Find the goal they wish to see.


I gaze in Rosamond's sweet face,
  Thinking : death ends all can science show—
Ah ! how can sightless science trace
  The unseen spirit free to go ?

## ESCAPED.

THE moonbeams do the waters lave,
   And shimmering dance on many a bower,
On land and far across the wave,
   The air is fragrant from the flower.
The distant Pleiades seem to be,
   There, gazing from their far-off coasts,
Born angels of Eternity,
   Or mortals' wise, departed ghosts.
Afar upon the dark-blue wave
   A beauteous bark bears o'er the sea,
A sea that seems beyond the grave—
   The ocean of Eternity.
On deck, behold ! 'neath awning shade,
   A noble maid and cavalier ;
The damsel looks as though afraid
   Of dangers on the deep, anear.
Still onward like a bird, the boat
   Now swiftly glides the sea afar—
To what safe haven doth she float ?
   To yon serene and heavenly star ?
The lovely maiden Isabella,
   The daughter fair of Don Valdorn,
Who vow'd that she must wed Garella,
   His friend, a rich hidalgo born.
But one she loved most passionately,
   Who equally loved her as well—
To reach a home beyond the sea,

Was heaven to them beyond a hell.
So, to pursue the heart's dictate,
    The heart wherein love was enshrined,
They trusted all to hope and fate,
    And left their foes and Spain behind.
But lo ! again the god of light
    Illumes the world beneath his smile,
And heaven erst sweet with stars bedight,
    Now dons the veil of blue the while.
" O ! haste thee, dearest Fabian ! speak !
    Are we safe from my father's wrath ? "
The maid look'd to the strong man, weak—
    " O haste thee on our ocean path ! "
" Forget thy fears, smile as of yore,
    Art thou not mine, and I with thee ?
Am I not thine ? and what is more—
    With this armed ship we shall be free."
She smil'd, yet paler grew her cheeks,
    " But lo ! yon coming ship ! " she cries ;
" E'en now my sire, my foe, me seeks ! "
    She looks the unhappiest 'neath the skies ;
She swooned from fright ; and well she feared,
    For he who claimed to be her sire,
When balk'd, was like a tiger speared—
    As mad as murder in desire.
Don Fabian caught the one he loved
    And placed her in the cabin, then
Quick looked, where o'er the sea there moved
    A vessel teeming with armed men.
" Now, by the heavenly saints, I swear,
    I 'll make yon foeman rue the hour

When first they thought my rights to dare
  And make me to their wishes cower.
What ho ! Bernardo ! load the gun !
  The gun on the forecastle there,
And when thou this thing well hast done,
  To those on yon craft say, ' Beware ! ' "
Upon the deck the sailor sprang,
  And quick obeyed the order given,
And soon the cannon loudly rang,
  Like Triton's mighty trumpet, even.
Boom ! boom ! the enemy replies,
  And now the battle opens well ;
Each ship the other one defies,
  And Anger wears the front of Hell.
Each vessel sheers close in the fight,
  And small-arms now begin to play,
And on apace draws darkling Night ;
  The Day, aggriev'd, hath hid away.
The vessels feel the wounds of fight,
  And still approach ; each larboard bow
Beats boldly 'gainst each other quite ;
  Each boarder draws his cutlass.  Now
Fate wills, and upon dark Death calls,
  Who doffs the cumb'rous robe of sleep ;
He wakes to hear Time's swift foot-falls—
  Knows his dread harvest is to reap.
Heavens ! what means this strange commotion !
  The very air is trembling now !
And near and far the living ocean
  The blow feels on his massive brow !
One ship up like a rocket rose,
  Amid a wild and deafening roar !

The other backward helpless goes,
  Feeling the fearful shock full sore.
Now wakes in her high orient tower,
  The lovely, sweet, and gentle Dawn,
Who, gazing from her beauteous bower,
  A horrid direful scene looks on.
The bark that once had held Valdorn
  And his bold crew of sunny Spain,
Now was a ruin ; and forlorn,
  Each one aboard had felt the bane.
A spark had reached the magazine
  Of Valdorn's ship, GITANO ; dread
The ghastly, wild, and fearful scene
  When that bark hurl'd up with her dead.
From where she battling sheers her course,
  Back ! the HABANA, Fabian's vessel,
Was heav'd like some light cork, perforce,
  And with the wilder waves did wrestle !
          *       *       *       *       *       *
Days, weeks, and months have come and gone
  Since Death worked havoc on the sea—
And on an island fair as dawn,
  Don Fabian and his bride are free
To live and love—she bonny fair,
  So fair that like her there are few ;
And he with Bayard would compare,
  So brave, so chivalrous, and true.
As spring's soft breath the sweet buds ope,
  And flowers bloom fair where all was blight,
These two now view the star of Hope,
  Dispelling night with its glad light.

## PROOF OF MAN'S IMMORTALITY.

MAN'S lofty thoughts immortal, never
    Perish, though time may mountains strew ;
When his creations live forever,
    Shall man not, their creator, too ?
The seed placed in the ground soon dies
    To live again—a tree or flower :
Then man, the noblest 'neath the skies,
    O'er grave must own the victor's power.
Were earth all that exists for man,
    A tamer mind he would be given,
And not those mighty powers that scan
    All save the sacred rights of Heaven !
'T is th' lot of mortal to lament,
    And naught will change this wise decree—
'T is the striving of the spirit pent
    Within the body to be free.
Outside of Bible, dogma, creed,
    We see it in the restless sea ;
In blast, in zephyr, we can read :
    Man's life goes on eternally.
Why should sweet music so touch hearts,
    That e'en when vanish'd to the ear
There is a something ne'er departs—
    Its soul enrapturing still is near ?
Why do we in our hearts e'er find
    A friend whom we do prize so dear,
Grows more within our souls enshrin'd

As life's last parting hour draws near ?
Does man fore'er through life aspire
    To soar above his lot for naught ?—
Like some proud bird, its course e'er higher,
    Why do we rise on wings of thought ?
These ! these are proofs within themselves
    Of that bright life we ever crave ;
Our every nature, too, rebels
    Against annihilation's grave.
We long for Heaven-born sympathy,
    This in life, in death, we cherish ;
That we would live beyond time's sea,
    Proves that we shall never perish !
Those spectral ones that come and flee
    Like fair eidolons haunting dreams—
Like glimpses fair earth's favor'd see
    Of Heaven's few, short minute gleams—
Teach us, e'en while their loss we mourn—
    Fair ones to every impulse dear,—
To dry our tears, for they are borne
    To Light where Hope has naught to fear.
With angels they now sweetly soar,
    Where all 's revealed in one grand truth,
Where fair flowers bloom forevermore,
    Enthron'd in life's perpetual youth.
Along the whole dark way of life,
    With being th' angel Hope is fraught,
And there before, all through earth's strife,
    It sweetly floats the ocean Thought !
And in life's glorious twilight even
    We see the golden clouds unroll,

Where this fair angel looks from Heaven,
   And beckons to the lovely goal.
And we feel Heaven's gates are wide swinging,
   Ever open to children of sin—
By angels open'd, who are singing
   To welcome the wanderer in.
The skeptic may cry : " No proof I find
   Beyond the grave there 's woe or weal ! "
So there are those who 're color-blind :
   Still the beautiful shades are just as real.
For all desires, save one, there be
   A panacea on earth for it :
Must our craving for immortality
   Not have a goal as real, as fit ?

---

## THE DECREE OF FATE.

IN an imperial valley glade,
   Where every thing was fair
With beauty-gifts that round were laid
   On earth and hung in air,
A castle held a maiden fair,
   Who dwelt 'midst all that wealth could buy,
A youth in a lonely cottage, there
   In the lovely vale lived nigh.
Affection sprang in their hearts warm—
   O'er the gulf that beneath them lay,
A beauteous bridge kind Love did form,
   Which Fate's dark waves destroy'd for aye.

As th' day-god in his golden car,
  Rode over the western wave,
And twilight flung each sparkling star
  Into the sky which beauty gave,
That maid lay sickened unto death ;
  Wan was her lovely classic brow,
And slower came each painful breath
  Which mocked life's passing moments now.
Now bending o'er that one so fair,
  From which the rose of health hath fled,
Is he who loves—despair—despair,
  The one he fondly loves is dead !
Oh ! thus it is on earth :  we find
  A glow of holy transient light,
Absorbing heart, and soul, and mind,
  To see it vanish in death's night.
Oft wandering in solitude,
  He felt and he saw in the breeze,
Her spirit, so pure, haunting the wood
  Of the vale with its whispering trees.

---

## TO A FAIR ONE.

THOU art so fair, so radiant fair,
    That beauty, love, and melody,
Are far more precious everywhere—
    Because they are adorned by thee !

Adorn'd by thee, as roses are
  By th' gentle perfume, sweet as love,
As heaven's eternal glowing star,
  By th' mystery clothing it, above.

Thy face is like a fair spring morn,
  Thy eyes are like the depths of heaven—
So deep they reach beyond this bourne,
  So distant deep their meaning, even.

Thy hands are like fair glows of light
  Snowy receptacles for flowers—
As beautiful as spotless white
  As clustering pearls in sea-nymphs' bowers.

Thy voice thrills round like golden bells
  Bless'd fairies ring near eventide,
When singing birds in happy dells,
  Tell Spring comes like a blushing bride.

---

## ANGEL VOICES.

WITH fragrant odors on the air,
  Which zephyrs to my windows bear,
There comes to me a sweet refrain,
Seeming from off yon dewy plain !
Angel voices sweetly swelling ;
Wafting by the arbor, telling :

"Above we sympathize with thee,
O man ! in thy deep misery !
And here in Heaven we ever pray
For thee, a being far astray—
Whom Hope now lights, whom now Despair
Shows all is dark, where once 't was fair.
But why shouldst thou despond on Earth
When Heaven for thee hath other birth—
A tranquil life, a life oft sought
In vain by man's best searching thought—
Beyond the star, so sweet and bright,
Glowing on distant shore of night,
Where there 's no need of Lethe's waves—
Heed ! Heaven yields all the soul e'er craves !"
The voices vanish—sweetly wane—
And meditation now doth reign.

----

## MAN'S LIMITED KNOWLEDGE.

MAN'S vision is short—confined to a sphere
    Which little reveals and leaves him to doubt
Much that 's beyond the lower world here—
    The mysteries speculated about.

A singer, a nation may win by her lay,
    A beauty entrance by her charms a whole race :
But do these prevent other nations away,
    From equalling the voice, and the beautiful face ?

Worlds may exist with fair beings as great
  Or greater by far than Earth ever bore—
Some stars be the abode of creatures elate,
  Other stars mighty shades long gone before.

Great worlds of beauty, with temples of joy,
  May roll beyond space's invisible sea,
Where love is love without any alloy—
  The stars the outposts of Heaven may be—

Light-houses to illume the spirit's dark way
  To Heaven when from Earth's bondage set free—
To keep it from wandering far astray,
  And perishing ingloriously !

Perchance the link between Heaven and Earth—
  Man's only sight of Eternity—
O mortal ! wilt thou e'er know their worth ?
  They are a beautiful mystery !

The sun may borrow its light from God's throne
  As borrows th' moon from the sun sublime ;
A mystical light has ever shone
  Down from the life etern to time.

-----

## TROPICAL.

WHAT a joyous thing to wake,
    In a lovely summer clime,
Where orioles sing from tree and brake,
  And nightingales join the chime.

Where dark-eyed girls with raven hair,
   More lovely than a goddess, even,
Dwell in all their radiance fair,
   Real houris in an earthly heaven.
What glories there the day unfolds—
   What rapturous charm of scenery !
In sea, in streams—mounts, vales, and wolds,
   E'er green in flowers that bloom so free.
How fair to see that land when dead
   Is day, and night makes good the loss :
Behold, o'er wave, on aërial bed,
   Asleep the floating albatross !
Behold that moon, that mingles light
   With all the stars that blaze and burn—
Eve's blooming flowers.—By day or night
   The eye sweet beauty doth discern.
Oh, constant I 'll be to the maiden
   I know in that tropical land,
For my heart with love is o'er-laden
   For Lorena, my soul's deodand !
And oft as Eve's fairest star, yonder,
   Doth serene light in loveliness dole,
Then steals on my sense the sweet wonder
   Of her loving and beautiful soul.

1875.

## REST.

OH ! we shall rest—forever rest—
   At home, beyond yon dreamy sky
Fast growing purple in the west,
   'Neath Day's all-seeing, glorious eye.
Where all do live as clear from stain,
   As o'er the earth yon glowing star,
Reflecting from the liquid main,
   Its image taintless, free and far.
Where life is long, and hope is real,
   Undimm'd by shades that mock us here ;
Where that crav'd vainly here, we feel
   In radiant beauty, thrilling near—
There each and all shall happy be,
   By time's annihilation wrought ;
Each life now pent will be as free,
   As soaring as unshackl'd thought.
Then look ! nor veil in tears the eye,
   Beyond 's no vestige of despair—
Behold ! afar on Being's sky,
   Fair Hope's bright sceptre stirs the air !

## A VISION.

THIS vision strange transported me
   Far, far beyond the rolling sea,
Where 'mid sweet scenes which ever bless,
Live Love and Beauty in happiness.

The golden hours in peace roam there,
By sparkling rills so pure and fair ;
They seem as they gently lave th' brink,
The fountains where sweet spirits drink.
There day e'er flees through golden light,
There e'er in beauty roams the Night ;
There with a peerless orient maid,
In that elysian land I staid,
For months and months this boon was mine :
A votary at the fairest shrine.
How fair she was to look upon !
As beauteous as the infant dawn
Of summer with its flowers and streams—
A golden dream of lovely dreams.
Her rich lips through which song flowed free,
Are like the past, a memory—
Her lovely person so admired,
Like a fair flower bloomed and expired.
Expired on earth in Heaven to be—
Beyond those beauteous stars we see,
O'er yonder dreamy mountain wold,
Where fleckless clouds their beauty hold.
No flower of Heaven can breathe more rare,
A beauty than her presence there—
When called from earth, which sighed to give,
She went to God—fore'er to live.
'Mid feelings which awaken care,
I wander back, in memory, there,
A fair loved angel looks from Heaven,
Above the starry orb at even.
1875.

## POETRY.

POETRY is that higher, better life—
  A poem a gather'd ray of it ;
As a flower to its perfume, rife,
  A poet to his poems writ.

The Universe is a poem sublime—
  The greatest poem that man can trace—
God is the poet : He wrote it one time,
  On the great blank scroll of space.

All poetry erst is radiant pure,
  Since up in Heaven it hath its birth—
And all its parts that stains endure
  Come from their contact with the earth.

In Heaven are poems, so wondrous divine,
  That none comprehend them aright
Save God, and the mystical ones at his shrine,
  Yet man in time may read with delight.

## THE HERO.[1]

THE train with the speed of lightning flees on—
  On—on—like the flight of the shooting-stars—
Over miles and miles that come and are gone
  'Neath the whirling wheels of the rushing cars.
The train is as swift as some mighty bird,
  And seems to possess an immortal soul—
With depths of feeling could it be heard,
  Which would startle the world from pole to pole!
Lo! what's on the track so small and so frail?
  'T is a living thing, for it moves around!
The engineer whistles down brakes—'t will fail!
  No one can respond in time to the sound!
"'T is a child!" cried Jack Evans, the engineer,
  In an instant more 't will be crushed to death!
Not e'en a moment impeded by fear,
  Jack springs, e'er drawing another breath,
Swiftly in front of the breathing smoke-stack!
  In time, and no more—he grasps the fair child,
Springs forward and just in time from the track,
  To see th' joy'd mother; who gratefully smil'd.
Though praised by th' mother for the brave deed
      done,
  Jack merely said, when she thanked him and
      Heaven:

[1] Founded on the heroic act of one Jack Evans in saving the life of a child, in the spring of 1874. He was at the time an engineer on the Chicago, Burlington & Quincy Railway. Published in the *Inter-Ocean.*

" You had better take care of that young one ! "
   As he gave her the child—advice well given.
Jack Evans, although unknown to the world,
   Is as great a hero as fame ever knew ;
'Though time has a number of heroes impearl'd,
   This brave deed of Jack's belongs to the few.

## WILL YOU REMEMBER ME?

WHEN I am gone, and friends of thine
      Who may be near and dear to thee,
Are gathered round thyself divine,
   Will you, fair friend, remember me ?

When Morn light to the world doth bring,
   When birds pour forth their melody,
Awakening from her sleep sweet Spring,
   Will you, fair one, remember me ?

When Spring hath gone, and Summer sweet
   Beholds the blooming flower and thee,
And Heaven once more seems Earth to greet,
   Will you, e'en then, remember me ?

When Autumn comes, with her decay—
   When brown and sere each towering tree—
And I am absent, far away,
   Oh, say ! will you remember me ?

When winter shakes his hoary locks,
    And life seems but a mockery;
When th' blast the moaning forest rocks,
    Undimm'd, will you remember me?

When twilight comes at eventide,
    And Luna walks in beauty free,
O'er fields of ether, endless wide,
    Will you still, still remember me?

---

## IRENE.

OH! What! is she a child of earth?
    She ever must have been divine;
Such loveliness could ne'er had birth
    Save at Heaven's sweet glorious shrine.

"T was thus I thought when first I gazed
    Upon the beauty of Irene;
Her wondrous wealth of charms amazed
    Where'er she moved, in beauty, queen.

The glory of her perfect face!
    There's naught with which to it compare;
Nor light reveals one radiant grace
    More sweet, nor gloom one veils more fair.

It was the fount of all things good
    Springing from out the soul and heart,
As rare books breathe intellectual food—
    Love, knowledge, science, poetry, and art.

When she deign'd to come, though last or first,
  To mingle at the fane or ball,
'T was like when through the darkness burst
  The glorious sun, illuming all.

1875.

---

## METAPHYSICAL.

ONCE, lately, weary with the world,
    Myself, and all mankind, I roved,
And chanc'd to wander where impearl'd
    That, by all, save the soulless, loved—
That beauty which enthralls the heart,
    Creating love both pure and deep,
That haunts us when we from it part,
    Like some fair phantom in our sleep.
A stream went murmuring on its way,
    O'ergrown with flowers of every hue,
All blooming fresh as showers of May,
    As sweet as Hybla's honey dew,
A fairy-land hid in the vale,
    Far from the world's hypocrisy ;
It seemed to be where none could fail
    From Nature learn to wiser be.
Tree, bush and flower to breeze did nod—
    To breeze that gently whisper'd nigh,
And like fair Messengers of God
    The white-winged clouds went gliding by.
Perplexed with doubt which filled the night,
    Like evil things that haunt the air,

Beyond the stars and moon for light,
  I sent to God an earnest prayer.
O'er me the waken'd trees sigh'd even,
  Or seemed to sigh at my distress—
With fervent sympathy, high Heaven,
  It seemed, looked down as if to bless.
The breeze that murmured, solemnly,
  By me in solitude, alone,
Did suddenly seem unto me,
  A whisper from the Great Unknown!

—

## TIME'S MOMENTOUS FLIGHT.

TIME ever passes on his way
    Mowing with unswerving scythe;
He stops not for the sad nor gay—
    Not for the blighted heart nor blithe.

'T is wise not to forget, therefore,
  When joy dissolves our bitter care,
That many souls are sorrow-sore—
  That throbbing hearts well-nigh despair.

The coming hour which Time creates,
  May be the last to us or them—
So dark, mysterious are the fates—
  So closely doth the Unknown hem!
1876.

## TRUE FRIENDS.

OH, you were loving friends to me,
   When other friends I numbered few—
A haven in life's stormy sea
   I freely found with yours and you.

I 'm sailing, as the clouds go by,
   And see the port my bark would gain ;
The sun shines brighter in the sky,
   And clearer grows the flowery main !

---

## TO THE Y. L. M. S. OF TOPEKA.

O SISTERS, in a noble work,
   You 're building for Eternity ;
No thieves around your treasures lurk,
   In temples safe above the sea.

Your souls grow whiter from your deeds,
   Your hearts more tender day by day ;
Ye rise above the clouds of creeds,
   And bask within God's brightest ray.

## THE GARDEN OF THE MIND.

OH, weed the weeds unsightly
    From the garden of the mind,
That flowers of thought bloom brightly
    In beauty fair enshrined.

That the fragrance of those flowers
    Waft in glory o'er the earth,
And forever through the hours
    Lead to better, brighter birth.

That the angels, all immortal,
    In their purity and grace,
Smile adown from Heaven's portal
    On the wondrous human race.

---

## DEATH AND IMMORTALITY.

SHE lies upon her dying pillow,
    Her spirit struggling to be free,
Which hears that sea's eternal billow
    Speaking of Immortality !

And still it lingers (fearing danger),
    In leaving home upon the earth ;
It hesitates to go, a stranger,
    To world beyond its coming birth.

Her spirit's cry went out afar,
  To one o'er which time's no restraint :
It pierced beyond the outmost star,
  To spirit that had grown a saint.

He heard her in his heavenly mansion
  Afar, remote from earth and time,
That cry had bridged the wide expansion
  With mighty spirit power sublime.

As thought, quick through immensity,
  He passed and reached her lowly bed,
Where she lies dying, soon to be
  A bright immortal, from the dead.

---

## IN A WEARY LAND.

YEARS ago, in a weary land,
  I roamed from my native shore,
Through forests wide, o'er torrid sand,
  A land where ne'er I'd been before.

Here mountains towering against the sky,
  Above the clouds and thunders' roar,
Frowned at the crouching shadows nigh,
  Which lay like fierce death at the door.

From out the earth grew a radiant flower,
  Out of that flower a star arose,
And upward ascended every hour,
  Till in heaven it sweetly glows.

It gave my heart a brighter ray,
   It warmed my veins like generous wine ;
It seemed like a thought conceived at day,
   By a peerless spirit divine.

Though long I 've hated, still do hate,
   That land with its dreary story,
Yet blest I feel, I there dared fate,
   When I think of that star of glory.

My soul still roams to the regions vast,
   Of which it is rash to be proud,
For a sweet face looks from out the past
   Like an angel from an inky cloud.

# THE VENDETTA.

A TRAGIC ROMANTIC POEM.

IN FIVE CANTOS.

The peculiar custom of retaliation denominated Vendetta, sanctioned by the superstitious religion of the Corsicans, is the theme on which this poem is founded. Years ago two certain Corsican families became very hostile toward each other, through a fierce quarrel arising between two individuals, members of the respective families, ending in murder. Glenore Gonzails, the leading character of this poem, and the last surviving member of one of these families, was compelled to fly from his country for safety. Having been outlawed, he became an independent sea-rover, in order to accomplish the fulfilment of his Vendetta vow, since that mode of life seemed to offer the surest and most available means ; in which capacity his aim was accomplished by his slaying all of the remaining connections of the opposing Vendetta ; and he soon afterward obliterated his own—*felo de se*.

# DEDICATION.

FRIENDS! whom I meet as time speeds swift
    away,
Creating flowers that bloom and then decay ;
Friends ! whom hitherto I 've met at fane and fête,
In thought I 'm wandering o'er sweet Memory's
    track
With you, through yest of Time's o'erchanging
    date,
While vista visions fondly tempt me back.
Though pain 's allied with pleasure of this beam,
If with the thorns the flowers yet living seem,
Wherefore should I complain of life's strange
    dream !
Oh ! breathes one spot, man's home, remote or near,
One spot more beautiful than earth elsewhere,
Where joy doth ever make that home most dear—
Where never come the mourners, Misery and Care ?
Dear friends, if such a land of beauty smiles,
May Heaven direct that there your future whiles.
In fondest love for you—old friends and new,—
With wish your hopes may have no bitter sting.
But that each life may be one long sweet spring,
This metrical romance I sing to you.

# THE VENDETTA.

## CANTO THE FIRST.

WHEN stars are peeping through day's gloam-
ing glow,
In ocean reflecting, in billowy flow,
At twilight, when no grim shadow of night,
Like ghouls, have stalked in wake of the light,
Gently, the soul feels that soft pensive care,
Mingle so sweetly, love, hope, and despair—
Which melancholy doth so fairly define,
That th' poet breathes in pathos divine !—
Rise thoughts of the dead, the absent, and lost,
Which crowding on, are o'er memory toss'd ;
Though some through the vortex of misery gleam,
Which best were dropped in Lethe's sweet stream,
Pleasures and pains of the past gliding by,
A tribute claim though it be but a sigh.
Such now is the hour—far out on the sea,
Where wild waves roll calm—then toss boundlessly,
Unfetter'd—unhamper'd—brook no control,
Like one who, though kind, has a lofty soul—
Then placid, breathe low, like the pensive sigh
Of some restless spirit, on, passing by,—
A bark bears on with looming sails and shrouds—
A phantom ship floats shadowy in th' clouds.

She seems so white—so weird each spreading sail—
High o'er the wave, unruffled by the gale.
As Bellerophon's far, aërial flight
Through realms of Phœbus—o'er regions of Night—
In ascent through space, by ambition driven
Astride of Pegasus, into high Heaven—
Fleeting onward—upward—swiftly now flies
Past Iris' beautiful home in the skies—
Striving vainly toward Mount Olympus afar,
Where dwell the mystical gods of war.
How beautiful this bark bearing away
O'er the blue wave, through the sparkling spray !
Is there aught more perfect beneath the sky ?
Trust not too far the wisdom of the eye :
Th' flower in looks superb may have no fragrant part;
The lovely girl may be without a heart ;
Yon vessel blessed with such fair outward show,
To all she meets brings but the greatest woe.
A buccaneer, she swiftly wings the wave,
Which e'er to meet, is but to meet the grave,
And to acknowledge Death's superior power ;
No petty ruler of the fleeting hour
Does she allegiance or alliance owe,
Nor her fierce crew that naught of mercy know—
'T is death to each—to all—to every foe.
That scarlet banner [1] flying to the breeze,
Would make in all the warmest heart-blood freeze,
Could each discern with closest scrutiny
The signs [2] she bears of brute ferocity.

\*   \*   \*   \*   \*   \*

[1] The pirate flag.　　[2] The skull and cross-bones.

Sad was the soul of the chieftain, Gonzails,
Lost on his ears were the ocean's wild wails ;
He stood on the deck like a lofty rock
Amid the wild hurricane's wrathful shock —
A vacant stare slept down deep in his eye—
Soul distant th' body as earth to the sky ;
Yet plain to friend, and foe, and passer-by,
There crouched a sleeping demon in his eye,
Which when aroused, the wildest, fiercest shocks
Of nature's wrath feebly his anger mocks.
As plainly to the view he now doth stand,
The last on earth of Vinci's large proud band,
'T is clear to see how looks the corsair brave,
The chieftain of the rovers of the wave ;
His large athletic form commands respect
Through fear ; his eyes the midnight storm reflect ;
Like mountain lion he would ne'er retreat,
But dare e'en death.    From head unto his feet
A model of great strength is he 't is plain !
His fierce black eyes grow soft, then fierce again.
Wild his looks—face handsome, yet one to fear,—
He seems a god down fallen from his sphere ;
His dress is plain—a cloth suit raven black ;
'Round him belted, of trusty arms no lack.
His dark hair dangles wanton in the wind ;
High and broad his brow—his no common mind.
He moves the true embodiment of grace—
His heart masked by a proud and haughty face.
Had he not been th' victim of others' wrong,
He would have shown a great light 'midst the
    throng.

A noble spirit naturally was his,
But warp'd by crime and harden'd by it ; this,
And taught from childhood that for him it was
Revenge to seek for his religion's cause,
Had changed him, made him what we see him here,
The wicked, brave, and hapless chief all fear.
Then judge him not too quickly in his sin :
Put in his place, know you what you 'd have been ?

The TIGER[1] fled on through yeast of waves,
Leaving foam in her wake each soft ripple laves.
"Land ho!" shrieks th' look-out far up in the
    shrouds ;
A phantom he looks—a ghost in the clouds.
A moment scarce fled since th' cry, when on lee
Of th' deck rose pirates like fiends from the sea.
Each in his hat wore an ebon black plume,
The heart's reflection :—to death do we doom !
They seek a glimpse of their green island home,
Where they find peace in Nepenthe's dark tome.
The wine-cup yielding relief to the soul—
Forgetfulness found in flow of the bowl ;
Intemperance to them the speedy resource,
A Lethe to drown pain, grief, and remorse ;
A dear-bought boon, for with tenfold power,
Gaunt Misery comes to haunt the hour—
As wealth the miser gets, though Heaven the cost,
Who gains what murders Happiness fearfully hath
    lost,
As Man did Woman gain, her price a future Hell !

        [1] The rover's ship.

Is it not told in sacred writ, that man by woman
    fell ?

   \*       \*       \*       \*       \*       \*

Fair Cynthia blushing bids th' earth adieu,
Now Phœbus walks the azure heavens anew ;
The isle they near grows plainer to the sight,
And shows the cannon, ope-mouth'd for the fight—
Prepared for battle should a battle call—
Defiance breathing from the beetling wall.
And too with bold ensign, the blood-red flag
Floats proudly out from its rocky crag,
Reflecting Hades mirrored in its glare,
And reads no mercy, but to all despair.
From ship to shore, from shore to ship, a cheer
Pays back the donor with a voice as clear,
When shout on shout by these approaching friends
Re-echoes o'er the mountains, through the glens.
Behold the joy ! call'd forth on time's face-track,
Which 'lures the wanderer in memory back !
The crowd on shore, the guard, bold men who
    dare—
Women's soft presence also welcomes there,
Their sweet joy embittered with tort'rous pain,
As wildly o'er the ship their dark eyes strain !
For husbands, lovers, friends ! came each again !
'Gainst hope they fear ! for doth not each corsair
His life, his earth, his Heaven doubly dare !
Lo ! hope hath won and vanquished every fear—
The cruise each rover liv'd, and now is here !
The smile, the kiss, the fond caress returning,

Each happy couple now hymeneal yearning,
Soon seek the flowery grove's sequester'd shade,
A perfumed bower for love—love long delay'd ;
We leave to them fond Cupid's sylvan bower,
Where love and passion rule the cytherean hour.

　　*　　*　　*　　*　　*　　*

But where is he, Gonzails ? had he no one
'Midst all the fair whom he could call his own ?
Ah, yes ! he loved and was beloved by one,
A peerless beauty of the burning sun,
Whose love was pure as heaven's clearest streams ;
She loved him as the Poet loves his dreams !
The chief one was she of her island sex,
Not her wish but his who lovingly decks
Her snowy neck and arms with jewels rare,
Who lessen'd sadness—sooth'd each pensive care.
From those that pass'd their time in revelry,
With some loved servants of her own sex, she
Lived in a tower old, looming gray and high
Far o'er the earth, whose turret frets the sky ;
And long this castle, dim in shadows strewn,
Had towering nodded to the queenly moon—
The moon, who in her bower beyond the earth
Beholds each beauteous infant star at birth,
From the tower had heard the plaint of mortals sad,
And the fierce watch-dog, baying hoarse and mad,
For many long, long years of weal and woe ;
And ofttimes heard when loud the wild winds blow,
And angry tempest blacks the scowling sky,
The waking eaglets' wild and startled cry,
High nestled in the tower, midway from the storm,

Feeling the damp air which chills each naked form.
Erected by some misanthrope of old,
The castle warred with time and heat and cold
For ages long—generations had flown,
While owl, bat, and spider held it their own.
Chance led the bold pirate to the lone isle
Deserted by man, though wreathed nature's smile.
As shields a mother with the fondest care,
From earth's unprincipled votaries there,
Her daughter, beautiful, lovely, and chaste,
So nature hid the isle in ocean's wide waste.
A spot of earth in the tropical clime—
A spot unchang'd to all save restless Time—
Nameless and unknown to the world ; though
  sweet
To those who called it the " Corsair's Retreat ! "
'T was here the lovely Peris whilom said,
Soft Night with ebon Darkness ne'er had fled,
Than loving Nature's music sweetly borne,
Floated around, while bright tears freely shed
The wondrous beauteous eyes of weeping Morn—
And peerless though in falling tears so sad ;
Herself is Beauty, whether gay or mad !
Are these the flowing tears of joy or grief
Which add new charms to blooming flower and
  leaf ?
They both commingle fondly, sweetly there,
Thus genially with soul of happiness or care,
Hope guides the bark of life, tho' at the helm De-
  spair.
The island bloom'd, in fragrance rich and rare ;

Long each crystal stream, prolific there,
In gorgeous splendor flourish'd sweet parterre ;
Here 'midst this beauty, the castle rose in air.
Here, where the tall tower's high turret broke
The sky, Gonzails' love lived ; there her sweet voice
    'woke
The silence of the twilight hour, between
Day's golden reign and Night's more sombre scene,
When sweet stars come and greet their silent queen.
Thus sang the Beauty, in her bower, unseen :
" Though thou dost, chaste Diana ! come !
Though thou, sweet star, in beauty roam !
You have no charms, no charms for me,
Who craves the absent lov'd to see !
Thou mayest come in glory, Light !
And thou in robes imperial, Night !
For e'er the same, thy children, Time !
My life, my love, is true, sublime ! "
A sad and plaintive lay for that one far away,
Amid the storm of battle, or wind's fitful play ;
One chain'd unto a crime—the fetters link'd by
    Fate,
Death only could unbind Ate's red chain of hate !
The hour of birth saw his destiny on his brow ;
Stern Fate he could not 'scape—to him each, all do
    bow !—
An oath religious bound, cemented by a vow.
Then judge him not in pride, in hasty, thoughtless
    scorn,
Nor she who clung to him in the tie of passion's
    morn,

Proud Beauty by chance to wealth wedded and
    born.
Since Fate decreed, she for love had freely given
Her all on earth to him, and risk'd her claims for
    Heaven.
While thus she sang she felt the gloomy painful
    fear :
" Will I e'er meet again him whom my heart holds
    dear ? "
Thus ne'er do love's sweet pangs sway mortal's
    heart,
Than watchful Nature the mixture doth instill
Of fear and misery, where Cupid's dreamy dart
Hath pierced, leaving the wretch in agony to
    smart—
Afraid earth's temporal pleasures may so fill
Enamoured heart and soul, all else forgot,
The soul too far will stray from Heaven, its destin'd
    lot.
Peerless in her beauty, Inez, fair of face and form,
Loving the chief, Gonzails, with passions deep and
    warm,
If her life fail'd perfection—alas ! whose earth
    lives are ?
There glow'd, as through the darkness at midnight
    glows a star,
One priceless virtue from her faults, too precious
    to be bought—
Charity ! that virtue—pure as an angel's thought—
Her lovely mirror eyes, of beauty's sweetest mould,
Reflecting her pure spirit's wondrous image told—

As kiss of wandering zephyr on the hidden bloom
Its sweets abroad doth scatter, th' hills and vales
    perfume.

## CANTO THE SECOND.

A H ! here 's what allures, here 's what entices,
    Leads man to virtue or deep into vices ;
Nor sylph nor nymph more graceful than is she,
Fair Inez, th' beautiful " Pearl of the Sea,"
With soul as spotless as fresh-fallen snow,
Ere mixed with impure of earth down below ;
With charms of person so wondrously fair
That the loveliest belle might well despair
To rival the beauty that was enshrined
In her form and face, which both combined.
A pearl she was, if perfection implies,
With carmine lips and her dark lustrous eyes,
And brow as fair as the pale lily white,
Or airy snow-flake on th' far mountain height ;
With tresses flowing luxuriantly to view,
Of shade 'twixt raven's plume and hyacinthine hue ;
Cheek damask, teeth of pearl, a smile of purest
    love,
She looked a sacred being fresh from God above ;
Whom sweet false hopes did down to sinful earth
    entice,
Heaven's sweetest one misled by fate from Para-
    dise.
Like a pearl she was ta'en from the dark rolling sea,
The only one saved from the wreck of the BEE,

Which, ere it went down, nobly struggled the wave;
Like a soul it seemed to beg Heaven to save.
As though in its vitals was buried a knife,
The vessel plunged wildly—a creature of life.
Lash'd to a spar by the lov'd ones who 'd given
Her life, she was kissed, with a prayer to Heaven:
" Save our child from the deep! shield her delicate
form !
Save "—The voice was lost in the shriek of the
storm.

\* \* \* \* \* \*

The TIGER sailed on toward the corsair's isle,
Each rippling wave lit by a sunbeam's smile.
'Mid the flapping shrouds Gonzails sat on high;
Hard by his old pilot he view'd the sky
And the wave where the storm had been so late;
And he sighed, when he thought, this child of fate,
Of those that perished in the deep, perforce;
Saying : " Would t' God they 'd lived, not I "—re-
morse
For his life he felt—but lo ! his eyes keen,
Now some strange object in the sea have seen.
Swift he goes to th' deck and mans a boat,
And soon he takes from the sea, afloat,
With his own hands, a lovely girl, so fair,
He thought her some immortal child of air.
Inez was the jewel cast up by th' storm,
Snatched out of Death's jaws life fluttered back
warm.
Gonzails lov'd her, and swore to shield her from
harm,

Though it took the last drop from his good right
    arm.
So radiant and so beautiful was she,
Found on th' wave, he named her " Pearl of the
    Sea."

   *      *      *      *      *      *

What is that which oft lures the wanderer on,
When vanished and lost, life's pleasures are gone?
'T is Hope, who comes like the smile of the spring,
And sweet is that life where waves her bright
    wing.
As the seaman becalm'd feels his cheeks warmer
    grow,
When first breathes the monsoon in whisperings
    low,
Despair cries: " In vain ! "—life's burdensome
    song ;
Hope whispers : " Thou 'lt conquer ! with Faith go
    along ! "
In visions e'en is felt this wondrous power ;
When lost to reason, Somnus claims the hour.
'T is night ! wild, deep, black, dread, profound,
One floats the air, now flies the ground ;
A stranger to himself he seems,
His brain with vagaries wildly teems ;
He nears a gulf of Horrors, flees,
And more imagines than he sees ;
For soon Hell opens to the gaze,
Where sights and sounds the senses craze.
Hell's minions—ghastly grinning crew
Now burst in terror on the view ;

And Satan claims his victim even—
But lo ! from open'd cloud of heaven,
Almighty God appears, profoundly saith :
" I will thee save ! Hope thou ! In Me have
    faith ! "
Like wolves when foiled of prey for which they
    prowl,
Th' Satanic host, each face a malignant scowl,
Now disappears with dismal, baffled howl.
Hope wins ; the sleeper smiles in joy once more ;
Night leaves the soul, and Light illumes before.
The days and nights Inez pass'd in the tower,
Alone she liv'd in her secluded bower,
Like some sweet, solitary forest flower
Breathing unseen—the loveliest 'neath the sky—
Too fair to meet the rude world's vulgar eye.
As the fond wretch, to misery given,
Longs for the elysian bliss of Heaven,
This sybaritic syren sighs and pines
For the ecstatic bliss she only finds—
A passionate joy that soothes and charms—
In the warm embrace of her lover's arms.
Thus even as she longs, Gonzails, as warm,
Is hastening to clasp her melting form.

    *     *     *     *     *     *

'Midst Inez's sorrow, Hope's light dimmer grows—
Till morn of joy breaks sweetly on her woes !
She 's happy ! he comes ! her lover ! 't is bliss
To see him ! O life ! that ye ever were this—
As blissful as the bliss the angels feel

When the soul—thought lost—to high Heaven doth
    kneel !
Fierce Fear hath vanish'd—now Joy takes her rôle,
And lifts the dark cloud from off Inez's soul,
Revealing the long-hidden smiles that trace
And illume the bright beauty of her face,
As the rose which Winter doth long oppress,
Comes forth in its beauty at Spring's caress—
Its tender sweetness for a time unseen
Hath but increased tenfold more I ween !
Oh, Joy ! the light of her young life doth dawn !
Inez, enraptured, smiles happy, 't is one
Of all on earth, that claims each tear, each sigh—
'T is life to welcome—'t is death to bid good-bye.
How truly very fond, how fondly true
The love of the beauty that glides to view,
Is evinced in actions—in glances thrown
Toward him swift coming o'er the meadow mown,
As hast'ning meets 'neath the mistletoe bough,
That one—her lover—where pledg'd was their vow.
No less he return'd her passion so warm—
She th' star of his night—the calm in life's storm.

    \*      \*      \*      \*      \*      \*

As th' snow-flake lives in ocean, life lives in the
    sea of Time,
Man lives, dies soon, and sinks in ages' oblivious
    slime.
In nation's storm, a flash !—in ages' night, a
    dawn !—
Life on waves of ages rises, a bubble that bursts—
    is gone !

The good and bad alike fall to oblivious graves !—
While through Eternity roll the ages' passing waves.

### CANTO THE THIRD.

H ARK ! hark ! what tocsin breaks upon the
ear !
Wild cry of merriment, and yell, and cheer !
Sounds of the revel in the outlaw's cave,
O'er wines and treasures—the spoils of the wave.
Strong libations from golden goblets pour ;
Bacchanalian songs mix with ocean's roar !
The silvery peal of the siren's laugh
Comes wafting on the breezes' balmy quaff,
From where Passion's ardent love-lit glance
Is flung o'er revellers in the mazy dance ;
Where eyes drink love from eyes with mutual
powers,
As sips each other's sweets, Night's fragrant flowers,
While outlaws and their lemans, clasp'd in love's
embrace,
Whirl through th' mazy dance to music's measured
pace.
The sparkling wine, the drunken glee,
Tell of their wild hilarity.
By sybaritic pleasures time 's beguiled ;
A carnival feast, a banquet wild :
Carousals that drown th' nightmare of thought,
Nepenthe of mind, the Lethe oft sought.
Guitar and lute combined and met
In sweet, wild tones, the castanet ;
In chorus the music rose and fell,

Through vaulted caverns with ocean's swell.
The voluptuous tune, th' seducing waltz,
Show'd grace and beauty, and hid the faults.
Here are Aglaia, Thalia, and Euphrosyne ;
Here rosy-lipped Bacchus, the worship'd deity
To whom the outlaws their libations pour,
The god whom their wild savage souls adore.

    \*     \*     \*     \*     \*     \*

Far, far from earth and all the spheres,
Etern, throughout Eternal years
Is changeless ; where Time's hand doth touch,
Is seen mutation great and much.
The sweetest moments of life fly past,
And helpless wither in death at last ;
Never should mortal this thought forget :
'Mid many that enhance the minuet,
E'en in her happiest hour, elate,
The beauty bows to blast of Fate,
Though the most beautiful one is she,
Where all are beautiful, remarkably !
Alas ! that the lovely and beautiful should fade !
Yet Fate decrees that Death shall reign unstay'd,
Till fleeting time hath ended, nevermore to be,
And voices now heard blending, blithe and free,
Shall ever sweetly echo throughout Eternity !
Without the fair scene nature is,
No revelry, more of Heaven than this.
Here flows the lucid, sparkling stream,
Beneath the hot sun's scorching beam,
O'er rocks of porph'ry, beds of sand,
Goes winding, gliding through the land ;

At length flows from its channel's bed,
And, like an apparition, fled,
Is lost in ocean's vasty bed.
The forest bows before the breeze,
Where wild birds sing their melodies ;
And others flutter through the trees,
Which oft do ope their foliage green,
Where frightened deer has fled between.
Here myrtle with the ivy vine,
In clinging tendrils amorous twine,
And here and there wild flowers, serene,
Fling soft their beauty o'er the scene.
Here, lost, the mountain streamlet stray'd
Through meadows green and forest glade ;
Now winding east, now winding west,
As fearful where, which course the best,
Like pain of thought which love inspires,
A soul still fluttering 'twixt two desires.
And here and there, of rarest kind,
The wild flower dances to the wind
Merrily, until tired with this,
She sleeps—then wakens to the bliss
Of listening to her lover's voice,
Which makes her gentle heart rejoice ;
And blushes rise when he caresses—
Thus, in sweet confusion, she confesses
'T is he alone her heart so blesses—
'T is he alone commands her sighs :
As oft the loving wind replies
That she has all his sympathy.
Here frowning cliffs o'erhang the sea—

There, far beneath, the waters flee,
Where skyward towering, mammoth rocks,
That firmly stand the mighty shocks
Fierce ocean heaves in wrath, still fret
The heavens as looms mosque's minaret.
Though round about the storm may sweep—
Far from the shore—high o'er the deep—
Seeming like ghosts from giant tombs,
There, warning of approaching dooms,
Each mammoth monster upward looms.
Here flows the tide, with fruitless toil,
To move a petrean bar from soil,
Which ages will its progress foil—
Here and there o'er sweet halcyon spots,
Come whispering voices from hidden grots :
As Nature speaks from earth or sky
Fond Echo ever doth reply.
Pale shadows flitting o'er the streams,
Weird phantoms, seem, of restless dreams.
The owlet shrieks from shaded perch,
Th' squirrel gay, dances on the birch ;
Fiercely laughing th' hyena growls—
Answering th' prowling jackal's howls.
The frightened dewdrop doth retreat
Between th' wild flower's petals sweet.
The timid zephyr, startled—driven
On a sunbeam seeks its home in Heaven.
A cadence, far out o'er the bay,
Is chanted by the wild winds' play,
And ripples laughing at the tide,
Thrown back by breakers on its side,

Seem merry as the new-made bride.
The zephyr's sigh on rock-bound shore
Commingles with the wild waves' roar.
Here where the bay wide 'gins to grow,
And stops the course of streamlet's flow,
And flow and ebb of tide to hem,
Sparkles the hyacinthian gem.
Where waves kiss shore as oft they 've met,
There nods the sweet wild mignonette
To gentle zephyr floating nigh,
Or breath of Heaven when passing by.
As in their homes th' Peris of the sky,
Lament that fate did steal them from on High,
In voices sweet, but ah ! too sad to cloy
Fond Beauty's breast, which should o'erflow with
    joy,
Or wailing tunes of dying year,
Æolian harps sound far and near ;
Sweet melodies that seem to tell
Of a fond bower in fragrant dell,
Where Love and Beauty sweetly dwell ;
A spot profuse with Beauty's sheen
As Tempe's fair, delightful scene—
As home of Israfel, where free
Flows sweet, exquisite melody.
From vale to mountain-top, that looms,
The loveliest growth of Nature blooms.
The light of Day once more well-nigh has fled,
Sol sleepy hangs o'er his hesperian bed ;
While slow, with laurels, fades departing Light,
Bright stars of beauty bind the brow of Night !

Here, man, entranc'd, fore'er might live, I ween,
Drinking the wondrous beauty of the scene.
In such suggestive spots, the wide world o'er,
Live knowledge mines, most precious to explore—
Where mystic lore is drank from all around,
By one who has a mind and soul profound—
One wise and thoughtful—one who delves his best
For secrets hidden deep in Nature's breast—
And feels at heart, that yet the hour will be
When he will learn life's strange, strange mystery !
Oft clouds flit o'er the chaste moon's light,
And far into the dreamy night,
Where Will-o'-wisps in marshes, oft do leave,
Th' deluded followers lost, they 'lure but to de-
    ceive—
As in chaste robes by preacher worn and priest,
Th' fawning knave and hypocrite may feast ;
As oft th' sigh, the blush and fallen lid beguiles,
And hides the aim of the designing woman's wiles.
Close in the breezes seeming dwelt,
Like viewless symphony, heard and felt,
The spirits of departed friends—
Now near, now far, as Fancy lends :
High o'er those mystic lamps of night,
Hanging to Heaven's vaulted height,
'Neath which the twilight hour oft whiles—
To th' lover basking in love's smiles—
To all ! thus all false Time beguiles !
Afar upon the deep blue sea,
Fair Nereids dancé right merrily,
To Nature's strains borne o'er the deep,

From lyres her airy fingers sweep ;
Where waves in limpid beauty blent,
Reflect the starry firmament.
Now sweetly in the twilight air
Floats bright form of an angel there ;
Th' Omnipotent, in the azure sky,
Is mirror'd faint to mortal's eye.
Now shadowy veils the peerless moon,
Lo ! forth in silvery sheen ! and soon
Behind another cloud she 's flown,
Th' imperious coquette's heart is shown.
And now fair Luna's glances glow,
In modesty from lake below,
Nestled beneath the sylvan shade—
The home of dryad, gnome, and naiad—
And many stars in heaven pending
Unto the lake its beauty lending.
Now cloudy phantoms race afar,
And swiftly flit 'neath pale lit star,
And fly across the moon as fast
As thistle-down before the blast ;
Thus proudly they through upper deep,
Speed on to death—to wail and weep.
'T is late ! O'er th' nervous one's quick mind
Steals th' thought : a spectre's in the wind ;
Who, next in superstitious fright,
Hears some dark demon chuckle from the night.

&ast; &ast; &ast; &ast; &ast; &ast;

'T is sweet on ocean's shore in solitude to be,
And hear the sad waves murmuring sweet and
    pensively.

'T is sweet to linger there on the wild and lonely
    shore,
And listen to the music of its sad and sullen roar ;
To the eternal monotone of restless sea and breeze,
Of Nature's many voices, wooing hard to please.
Thus e'er in all things grand and dear to mortal,
    free,
Nature speaks her praise of God's profound sub-
    limity.
'T is sweet with friends to wander on the pebbly
    beach,
And to, alone, read what Nature's book can teach,
E'er open—and there invade the realm of Thought,
    where sing
The Bards ; high soaring on fond imagination's
    wing.
'T is sweet when lovely Morn her orient light distils,
And gladdens with her voice, plains, forests, vales,
    and hills,
To find night's horrors gone, which near-by seemed
    to be—
Laughed off by happy joy—a nightmare's phantasy.
'T is sweet at noon, when Sol rides 'midway over-
    head,
To weave a future bright—past disappointments
    fled.
'T is sweet on summer's eve t' seek the cool, se-
    questered bower,
And while away with one we love the swiftly fleet-
    ing hour,
When sweet affection's tendrils lovingly do bind

Two trusting hearts and souls in one united mind ;
And in the sylvan shade, far hid from all we shun,
To linger and caress that lovely, loving one ;
Who readily returns each sympathetic sigh
Untarnish'd by the world's cold, calculating eye.
But, sweeter far than all—to soul most purely dear—
Is an unselfish heart and conscience that is clear ;
Then all is well, for Truth hath banish'd Error's
    woes,
Though beauteous Dawn awakes—though Twilight
    seeks repose
Within the gossamer folds of her voluptuous bed,
With Night's soft mantle lightly and gently o'er her
    spread.
Though life be sweet to us, and sweet hope's cher-
    ished dream
While floating on like driftwood adown the fatal
    stream,
We are that which we are, but what we can but
    deem—
We know not, but we bravely trust immortal as we
    seem.

### CANTO THE FOURTH.

IN th' solitary dell, where wild winds sadly weep,
    The isle a mystery kept, as sometimes secrets
    keep.
Oft there sounded afar an unearthly yell,
As if souls were struggling on the brink of Hell ;
This yell arising o'er sea, mist and gale,
Seem'd a stern warning to th' wicked in its wail.

That cry at midnight rose, and, in the gloom,
Uneasy spirits shriek'd madly their doom
With fiendish horror ; and e'er at night's noon
In darkness Erebus, or 'neath the pale moon,
The island shook at the terrible roar.
In the cave were many spell-bound to the floor
Till died each demoniac yell on the wind.
And reason returned to the half-frenzied mind.
Save he, Gonzails, who 'd have brav'd th' hosts of
    Hell
In all their fury—fiendish, fierce, and fell,
Not even would the boldest outlaw dare
The sombre dell—the weird gloom ever there—
Where howls and shrieks of misery, death, despair,
Came floating on the dismal midnight air.
As, close on Crime's track, of dark face and form,
Fierce, gory Vengeance rides the rolling storm.
'Though none had proof, suspicion darkling fell,
With spectres weird the corsair chieftain talked ;
Holding communion in the haunted dell ;
At night-tide he alone with phantoms walked.
'T was all they dared, for they no questions asked ;
His face they feared, a face forever masked.

   *      *      *      *      *      *

'T was rumor'd that a bloody massacre had led
To the lost spirits of the murder'd, restless dead,
Hovering over corses whose blood a foul foe shed.
And too, with many a shudder, 't was breath'd, in
    dread,
They were not ghosts in th' dell that shrieked so
    startling there ;

But th' fiendish laugh of ten thousand demons on
    th' air—
Ten thousand demons mocking man in his despair.

    \*      \*      \*      \*      \*      \*

Thou spirit of Eternity's darkened space,
That giv'st no hope of thy shadowy race,
Canst thou no solace find ? no secret spell ?
Lost wanderer o'er earth, through gloomy walks of
    Hell ?
Debarr'd from Heaven, is there no rest ?—no Lethe
    for thy woe ?
Dost thou, strange being, not some blest nepenthe
    know ?
" Lost ! lost ! lost ! "  A voice from the tomb !
" Lost ! lost ! lost ! "  It speaks of its doom !
Why should I thus so madly question thee !
'T was ever thus—is now !  Oh ! will it ever be ?

    \*      \*      \*      \*      \*      \*

With thought's strange, subtle, mysterious power,
We silently enter the lone gray tower !


[GLENORE GONZAILS *and* INEZ GALVO *in their
favorite room in the tower.*]

INEZ.—O dear Glenore !  I 've an unpleasant
    dream
To tell thee of thyself—though it may be
Distasteful, I trust thou wilt overlook
My fault, if fault it be in me to tell !
I hope—O fervently I hope 't is false !
Thou 'lt not chide me for what I feel through love ?

GONZAILS.—A dream thou 'd tell ?  Of course a
    woful one—
About my being slain, or plunged into th' deep
At night asleep on deck.  Were it not thou
I would not hear ; proceed—tell me my fate !


INEZ.—'T was eve !  I wander'd on a lonely shore ;
As oft I 've heard its voice, the sea sobbed low ;
Immerged in water half, with wild white face,
On thy back reclining, 't was a dreary spot,
Thy locks toss'd by the wind, alas !  I saw
Thee dead !   O God !  my heart, in misery bled—
A melancholy spirit and alone
I seem'd—wandering in the breezes by the sea.


GONZAILS.—Thou, e'er solicitous for my welfare,
Hast felt dear one, th' result of all thy fears
In slumbers—'t was an incubus—     •


INEZ.—The nightmare ?
Alas !  no !  dear Glenore, it seem'd not to be—
I fear 't was a warning and a prophecy !


GONZAILS.—Forget this dream, for it can only sadden
Our lives and yield no good.


INEZ.—(With an affectionate caress.)
Thy heart I' d gladden !
Content thyself—I 'll tune my good guitar ;
Together we 'll sing of lone Trafalgar—

GONZAILS.—Thanks, but my voice has grown rough
 like the sea.
Excuse me from singing—please sing to me
The song you love best, my Pearl of the Sea !
With a voice which would rival Israfel's own,
Pathetic and grand was her lay and her tone.
Whate'er each other's pleasures such each craves,
Thus Cupid binds his not unwilling slaves.

 \*  \*  \*  \*  \*  \*

The days were many to those on the isle,
In luxurious ease the swift hours while.
Earth's pleasures must end, as end must its pain,
The pirate's heart sighed once more for the main,
The wine was consum'd, the brandy was gone,
They wish'd a fair change on th' wide waters wan ;
Ne'er long a wanderer finds a peaceful home,
Some far delusion ever whispers : " Roam."
The love of Inez was deep as the sea,
And fearing to part with her idol, she
Oft asked to go with Gonzails when he cruised :
That danger to her the outlaw refused.
She tried to persuade him to give up the sea
For the love she would yield, abundant and free,
With all the power of her beautiful charms,
And tried the force of her dreams' dire alarms ;
When all else failed in the depths of her fears,
She tried woman's last strong resource, her tears,
Which smote her lover with puissant force,
He nigh repented in his soul his course ;
Reluctant to go in that moment of bliss,
While sealing his love in that lingering kiss—

Hark ! hark ! the crack of gun and cannon's
    boom !
And on the shore the clouds of battle loom !
Glenore Gonzails hath heard that sound before.
Loud rolls each crash—the thundering peals of
    war—
The guard's quick shout—the vidette's hoarse wild
    cry—
Tell of surprise, and tell of death or victory !
Now thick and fast on th' chieftain's restless soul,
Past wars in all their ghastly horrors roll,
As gathering clouds beneath the moon rush o'er,
Grim phantoms hast'ning to a mighty war,
That shriek o'er tempest thunder shouts afar ;
With shrieks breathe lightning from their fiery
    throats,
When shakes in terror each lone living star—
Till over all, Death, the triumphant, gloats.

     *       *       *       *       *       *

The lovers part with battle's first wild knell :
" Good-bye, dear Pearl ! " were words that fondly
    fell
To her sad ears who kiss'd and dared not tell
The ominous thought embodied in adieu, farewell.
Now sadly this Cytherean Beauty feels
The loss which Fear, awaken'd from her, steals.
And, one by one, tears mount her lovely eyes—
Wrench'd from her heart—o'er each cheek slowly
    trails,
No longer she her lover's form descries,
She knows th' danger that awaits Gonzails ;

For ne'er would he yield the battle to foes,
Though enemies desp'rate and many oppose.

&ast; &ast; &ast; &ast; &ast; &ast;

Gonzails apace dash'd on to the front
Of battle's dread ranks, and there bore its brunt,
Where foemen thick and most, alive and dead.
" His sable plumage nodded o'er his head "—
Fiercely he cheered his comrades on to fight—
E'en though 't was wrong, he thought he battled
  right.
The enemy came like the deadly simoom,
Twelve Moslem war ships the pirates to doom,
Mohammedan warriors sent out to th' field,
To conquer a foe that never would yield ;
For scores of times their foes had vainly striven
To take the isle at night, morn, noon, and even.
Though ne'er before surprised, the island guard,
Pick'd men, whose prowess to o'ercome was hard,
Saw their dark foes, a squadron, making way,
Over th' ramparts, from out the island bay.
Then their alarm resounded on the coasts—
These foes had risen silently as ghosts ;
Strong men, these Moors that scaled, and used to
  war,
And ere 'neath foes they fell to rise no more,
Fought like fierce fiends upon the bloody shore.

&ast; &ast; &ast; &ast; &ast; &ast;

With cannon, gun, and cimetar,
And other implements of war,
The Moors attempt to waken fear
In th' bosom of the buccaneer—

With battering rams they beat the side
Of wall high towering o'er the tide,
In vain to dash it from the bank :
As well might they have storm'd Mont Blanc.
When climbing 'gainst the pirate's fire
Of missiles of destruction dire,
These fearful squadrons ere they die,
Oft to Allah and th' Prophet cry,
To help them scale the desperate flights
Of frowning ramparts' towering heights—
But soon they fall, drench'd in their gore,
'Neath death's fierce thunder-bolts of war ;
Hurl'd like snow-flakes down from the clouds,
They 're soon enwrapped in watery shrouds.
On deck, on land, all 'round, death's pall !
With many wounds bold warriors fall,
And shrieks the wild demoniac blast
Of dread war madly howling past
The dead and dying everywhere,
Whose blood by thirsty sea, earth, air,
Is drunk from them in their despair.
Through opening of the fatal wound,
Souls forth emerge, unseen around,
And from each ghastly corse, death's prey
Its fierce wild ghost now glides away,
Unwilling toward those dismal wolds,
Where swift the dark Styx ever rolls.
Ah ! none may know, when Sleep's twin-brother
    Death,
Is hovering o'er with his foul poison'd breath.

     *     *     *     *     *     *

Bravely each outlaw battles through the strife ;
He fights for his all, his home and his life.
Perforce, the chieftain falls, 'midst those he hates,
Who war with the wrath of the furies and the fates.
He falls to the ground 'neath armor and shield,
While a shout goes up from his foes on the field.
A wounded lion, he renews the fight,
And looks in his ire like the storm of night.
The star of their hope in darkness doth wane—
His path on the field is heaped with their slain.
Though valiant the Moors, and veterans of war,
They vanquished, now yield, as foes oft before.
When 'midst confusion the enemy are flying,
The chief again falls 'midst dead and th' dying.
But ere Gonzails, the outlaw, fell once more,
His sword piled high the Moslem on the shore.


Inez from the tower sees, where th' smoke has parted,
Her lover fall, and dies—aye ! broken-hearted,
Too young she dies, Count Galvo's peerless child,
A hapless waif on earth's cold, cruel wild.
In life all that is beautiful astray,
She yet, in death, a lovely ruin lay.
Had not stern fate decreed to do her wrong,
A beauteous light above the lower throng
She would have won some radiant wondrous goal,
A height reached not save by the noblest soul.
The poor would e'er have blessed her with their love,
As some sweet angel down from Heaven above.
Thus does the dread environment of fate
Make lives of beauty lone and desolate.

E'en now in name of truth, fair Astræa,' like a
    star,
Beholds my Muse's flight with anxious eyes afar.

    \*     \*     \*     \*     \*     \*

Ye who have felt the fierce and bitter pain,
When death bears off those whom ye dearly love—
When desolate see ye a dear one lain
In gloomy shroud entomb'd, no more to rove—
Will know the feelings of the corsair chief,
Whose heart was broken—buried in his grief—
At sight of Inez dying ; as falls the sweet spring
    flower,
Killed by the frosty blast that breathes in its lovely
    bower.

    \*     \*     \*     \*     \*     \*

Thou Chastity that long hath held
The world in virtue's modest check,
Man owes to thee in heart, joy-knell'd,
For th' little pure saved from Vice's wreck—
Warm thanks to surface ever gurgling up,
As o'erflows Nature's sparkling chaldron cup.

    \*     \*     \*     \*     \*     \*

The chief is sad and alone in the tower,
A bleeding stem bereft of every flower.

[GONZAILS' *soliloquy over the corse of* INEZ.]

" 'Till now in this world I have wished to rove—
Till now I had one in this wide waste to love,
Whose trusting heart, of gentle, sweet desire,
Kindled my soul with unquenchable fire.

            ' Daughter of Justice.

Alas! Love 's gone—Life from Hate's fountain
    drinks!
Accurs'd be the chain which e'er to Ate links.
The great and damning curse on earth to me,
E'er has been the Vinci chain of Destiny—
A chain that 's slowly rusted, link by link,
And I, the last, am hovering on the brink!
Could I but lie in death by that dear form,
All would be calm—no more of this life's storm!
One hour with thee, beloved! would be divine!
Vanish'd in death that hour will ne'er be mine!"
The outlaw gazed on his dead leman's bier,
While sadly flowed from his eyes, the pent tear.
" Far through the shades of years—strife—havoc—
    war—
Thou hast been my only bright and tranquil star."
While gazing on th' corse of her whom he loved,
His heart and his soul's best impulses moved;
On her pallid brow he now placed a kiss—
No agony ever was more keen than this,
It held for him th' last Hybla of bliss!
There crept through his soul, a dread—a nameless
    fear—
He gave to the dead—'t was all he could—a tear.
From youngest infancy—from year to year—
His life at once centred in that scalding tear.
" I will seek again th' gloomy haunted dell—
From those weird ghosts oft mingling wildly there,
By that power resistless—the Vendetta spell—
I 'll rend the unseen future from them bare!
While she lived I hoped this dark life to outgrow—

While she lived I loved, but now all is woe !"
As one whose fond wishes gone ever unheard,
At length dies a victim to hope long deferred.
Tenderly lifting his loved one so dear,
Gonzails placed her in her tomb, dark and drear,
Where nought could disturb her long restful sleep—
From haunts of living things, in her sacred keep ;
Then kissed her saying : " Thy only fault was
    loving me !
Farewell ! farewell !" His voice died out in agony.


## CANTO THE FIFTH.

[GONZAILS *in the haunted dell— Time, near midnight.*]

GONZAILS.—By that which binds us !—By Fate's
    deep power ! By th' Vendetta vow !
By th' conjuror's spell and magic power ! By all !
    I now
Call ye ! spirits of Vinci's band ! to harken unto
    me !
E'en though afar, come from th' air, th' clouds, and
    night !—come from th' sea !—
Come from th' realms Invisible ! speak and harken
    ye !"

[*Sulphurous odors impregnate the air, and immedi-
ately afterwards several puffs of flame and smoke are
seen, accompanied by a rumbling, sullen sound—Spirits appear—Gonzails shudders.*]

SPIRITS.—Short-sighted mortal ! what wouldst thou
  With spirits ? Child of clay !

We 've come—we dare not break our vow !
　What wouldst thou with us say ?

GONZAILS.—I 'd know how long my soul must bat-
　tle in the flesh—
How long I 'm to be linked to th' accursed Ven-
　detta vow ?
Impelling me on through dark labyrinthian mesh,
When shall I rest fore'er in sleep this aching
　brow ?

SPIRITS.—What meanest thou, rash mortal ?
Think not to cross death's portal,
Whilst thou hast such great cause to live !—
In thee our only hopes survive !
Religion's vow told us on Earth—
Instill'd in us from very birth—
That long as blood of foes survived,
Of Heaven we would be yet deprived !—
We know the changes on man's sphere,
But we have found no knowledge here
Of our Vendetta ; nought of Heaven's bliss,
A longing for it, this and only this—
And yet we feel too well ! too well !
We near th' dreadful gulf of Hell !
E'er at th' solemn hour of midnight drear,
Hell yawns and shows us much to fear !
Thou ! only thou our course can stay,
And to high Heaven open the way !
Alone on Earth of our Vendetta !
Beware the offspring of Roletta !
For five of his cursed blood remain !

List ! shouldst thou leave Earth ere all 're slain,
We all are lost !—a broken spell !—
Eternally we 'll creep through Hell !

[*Spirits exeunt.*]

GONZAILS.—Back ! by our Vendetta vow, its power,
    return ! beware !
Or by high Heaven this knife shall blast your
    hopes fore'er ! fore'er !

[*Holding a poniard in his hand high over his head,
ready to drive it to his heart.*]

[*Spirits reappear and rapidly speak.*]

" Hold ! rash mortal ! wouldst thou prove indeed
A fiend ! what ? wouldst thou leave us here ?—
    Proceed !
Slay thyself and thy own woe as dread
As ours will be ! If number'd with the dead
E'er all our foes, we 're lost !—Send them before,
And thou and we are blessed forevermore ! "

GONZAILS.—Then hasten ye, and tell me all I wish
    ye to unfold !
Why thus in ignorance leave me ? Ye have not as
    yet told
Where one of these ill-fated five are by me to be
    found !
I might seek in vain from pole to pole and earth
    around !
It seems to me I 've slain enough to satisfy
Fierce Death himself, and yet ye say five more must
    die !

A SPIRIT.—One lives in Venice, a Venetian count ;
With him two sisters—

[*A pause.*]

GONZAILS.—Which do three amount—

SPIRIT.—This night a mother dies, a child 's born
    to weep,
'Neath th' arching bow [1]—not that of upper deep—
But where 'midst vales the Alpine torrents creep.
The fifth and last in one respect 's like thee ;
He roams the wide, deep waters of the sea—
His ship 's a licensed merchantman, and he
A lawful trader of fair Italy.
List ! Our Vendetta heed ! The Vinci vow !
And all 's well ! Our sufferings all shalt thou
Escape ; and thus thou 'lt raise us out of woe !
Then heed ! heed, mortal ! We go ! We go !—

GONZAILS.—Hold ! hold ! I invoke ye ! I command
    ye ! I adjure !

Their names ! their names ! or I can no longer
    endure

This red horror of blood—this continuous night-
    mare !

Reveal e'er night's noon wakens th' cries of de-
    spair !

ANOTHER SPIRIT.—The Royal Venetian
Is the Count Orsini,
His sisters patrician
Husbands wedded, of power ;
Their husbands too soon died—

---

[1] A phenomenon seen among the Alps.

Bloody victims of our
Vendetta they all fell—
The twin brothers Bembo,
In the wild Bernese dell.
The child of the mother
A moment since adead,
Hath th' surname, mortal brother,
Strozzi, whose given name
To tell we forward press,
By mortals it 's unknown—
'T will be this nothingness :
The name Agostino !
Sforza makes th' five—woe
Should the five outlive thee !
Mortal, heed ! heed ! we go !
To thy mission ! hence ! hence !

GONZAILS.—Hold ! Unveil the dark future ? O
    when from earth shall I be free ?
When sail I from th' sea of Time into th' ocean of
    Eternity ?

ALL THE SPIRITS.—We 'll answer not, 'though ask'd
    by thee !
We 're not permitted to relate !
Nor Life nor Death swerve Heaven's decree !—
Knowledge cannot change Fate !

[*Spirits vanish in space.* GONZAILS *gazes at va-
cancy, where the souls of the departed were last seen,
muttering :*]
" I care not to call ye back from your hell beyond
    the tomb !

O God ! that I was certain of some less fearful
    doom ! "

[ *The corsair chief slowly leaves the dell, and with no
signs of the bitterness of his heart, appears before his
band, who welcome with the cry :* "*Long live our brave
captain,* GLENORE GONZAILS ! "]

    *      *      *      *      *      *

From wounds, which ever are with war allied,
Where Life and Death, austere, are side by side,
On Mars' red field, where ghouls are wont to roam,
Rose up, save those who 'd gone to their long home,
Th' pirate band, and which their chief praised well ;
Brave had it fought, and bravely many fell !

    *      *      *      *      *      *

Gonzails and his outlaw crew slowly now embark ;
In deepest gloom the great chief's soul—no night
    as dark.
The TIGER leaves her moorings, swiftly speeds her
    flight,
While sweetly smiles afar the peerless Queen of
    Night,
From off her gorgeous throne, amid the spheres so
    bright,
Each sphere a light-house seems that pitying an-
    gels light.
While shines the lamp of day Gonzails is loth to
    leave
The resting-place of her his heart and soul do
    grieve.
Ever of the past he thinks, ever pensively,
Ever of the loved and lost, this mournful reverie :

" Ne'er shall I return to gaze on this lonely shore,
Nor as in other days, wander the island o'er,
Doubtless beneath the sea where Ruin dwells, alone,
To drown and perish there, unseen, unwept, un-
    known.
My love hath no response, Hope, like a bird hath
    flown—
Vengeance, I live for thee, and live for thee alone !
When thou art satisfied, I 've lived my wretched life ;
That hour I trust is nigh, when ends my days of
    strife.
O better far the evils Death may hound on me,
Than this most woful life !—Fate, I shall trust in
    thee ! "
And now upon his eyes while memory seems to
    mock,
Dies one by one the visage of each dim island rock.

    *      \*      \*      \*      \*      \*

Afar upon th' main, like a bird that is free,
Flies th' TIGER proudly, 'neath th' blue canopy.
She tosses her head like a haughty belle,
As onward she floats o'er the ocean-swell—
Over ocean, where fiercely the wild winds sweep,
Or lull'd in silence with calm waves sleep.
Behold ! sinks the day-god down to his rest,
And o'er the wide waters smiles out of the west !
And he sheds in his beam a weird red light,
Till veiled into slumber by shades of th' night.
'T is night on the waters, and dark as the doom
That waits the murd'rer, though gone to his tomb !
'T is night ! moon and stars are hid from the view

Of th' children of earth, of th' TIGER's fierce crew.
How silent it is !—there 's a flash in the sky !—
It seems the red glare of a mad wizard's eye !
Hark ! loud breaks the thunder ! startling the
    crash !
Looms far and anear the red lightning's flash !
Now rumbling rolls one continuous roar—
From Heaven's wide floodgates the high waters
    pour.
Now here, and now there, amid the great storm,
The TIGER high rears and dips her proud form—
Ah ! will she fill a dark and sunless grave ?
Or toss triumphant o'er the howling wave ?
Mad lightnings wildly shooting far and near,
Cause the unseen aërial ones to fear.
Well may they fear—for means the flash and roar,
The mightiest elements are at fiercest war !
The angry storms fling huge destructive shafts—
In deepest scorn each warrior hoarsely laughs,
And martial'd far around in densest crowds,
Live thunders swiftly leap from clouds to clouds,
Hurling their deadly massive bolts afar—
Hitting the very vault of distant Heaven !
Which jars each high-hung planet star,
And shakes the earth to its foundation, even !—
The mighty demons of the deep abyss,
Rous'd wondering, trembling, with awe, gazing see,
E'en the hosts of Heaven, amidst peace and bliss,
Beholding ! stand amaz'd in Eternity !

    *     *     *     *     *     *

The loud chuckling genii that revell'd o'er the wave,

A kindred spirit met in th' corsair chieftain brave :
Upon the TIGER's prow, which well the waters
 walked,
Gonzails fearless sat, and with the thunder laughed
 and talked.
His wild and stormy soul could such grand scenes
 enjoy ;
His nature thus inured up from a prattling boy.
While others trembled, pale, 'midst such surround-
 ings drear,
He coolly eyed the scene, for Fate had murdered
 Fear.
For years in safety through all strife, all danger
 borne,
And fearless, he well might laugh even Death to
 scorn.
Of real joy in his laugh there was a painful dearth—
Something akin to madness mingled in his mirth—
Disgust of life and every thing of earth apart,
Since now but misery's breakers broke upon his
 heart.

  *  *  *  *  *  *

In the distant sky vanish the skirts of Night !
The Morn comes forth !—her lamp is glowing
 bright !
Sweet odors borne upon the passing breeze,
Waft from far shores of fragrant flowers and trees.
Aroused from slumbers sweet, the morning star
Shines softly bright from Heaven's celestial bar.
As though his holy image man might keep,
Th' Eternal now seems mirrored on the Deep !

The morning brings to view a noble-looking brig,
Which moves th' outlaw's soul as wind the tender
    twig.
He thinks of the plunder that may soon be his
    own—
By the right of his might, and his victim's death
    groan.
Aboard the TIGER, one, though sins stain'd soul
    and brow,
Had ne'er shed blood for gold—an outlaw forced
    by vow—
Of robbery he is free,—it never him could tempt—
Though dyed with many crimes, Gonzails of that 's
    exempt.
A pirate he was named because of his fierce crew—
With the guilty th' guiltless must ofttimes suffer too.
    \*       \*       \*       \*       \*       \*
A year since last the TIGER fled her island home.
Swiftly the DOGE OF VENICE o'er the deep doth
    roam.
The bark is but ten leagues off India's burning
    shore,
The stars smile on the deep and 'lume the wide sea
    o'er.
Alone upon her deck a man stands 'neath her sails,
One glance his visage reads ; 't is the corsair chief,
    Gonzails !
Unconscious and adrift, he had one day before,
Been found, pick'd up, a waif the sea-waves on-
    ward bore :
His ship, the TIGER, and her fierce, desperate crew,

While battle roared the loudest, with foes had sunk
    from view.
Gonzails alone survived when death alone he cher-
    ished,
His friends and foes from Time's moorings all had
    perished.
Like a storm-swept leaf he was hurled from off the
    deck
By the falling mast of his vessel's sinking wreck.
Entangled in the sails that parted from the mast,
At Heaven's tender mercy, he floated the ocean
    vast.
When neither Fate nor Vengeance forced him with
    time t' strive,
When his Vendetta vow's fulfilled, he would not
    longer live.
He springs far o'er the bow, he strikes upon the
    wave,
And for a moment floats above his cheerless grave.
Adown in the sea he sinks, bubbling not a groan,
Restless as his soul the waves that o'er him dirges
    moan.
Far, on a rock-bound shore, his body floats to
    mould,
As that dead dreamer's dream, in life had long fore-
    told.
In this, her prophecy fulfilled, why doubt the rest,
Which told that he here dead by her presence would
    be bless'd ?
Then who 'll not believe in the soft wind whisper-
    ing by,

O'er him the angel spirit of Inez hover'd nigh?
From that far-distant realm beyond the fields of air,
All sinless and forgiven by Him who reigneth there.

# THE STAR OF THE EAST.

## A METRICAL ROMANCE.

## Argument.

The incidents portrayed in this poem are founded on well-authenticated events in the history of Circassia. Centuries ago the two wealthiest and most powerful princes of Circassia lived near the Black Sea. The elder one, Prince Agra, was a widower, having but one living child, his beautiful daughter Zalumna, who was dearer to her father than all other possessions. The other, Prince Bravello, was young and handsome, living quite alone, if we except his retinue of servants, he being the only remaining one living of his family.

Notwithstanding that these two princes were the greatest by far of all the petty rulers, and that their principalities joined, yet they lived in harmony and peace. Why should they not, when Prince Bravello was the affianced husband of the beautiful Zalumna, the Star of the East? Her beauty was acknowledged far and near. This rare and remarkable attraction, however, was the cause of great trouble to its innocent possessor.

Circassia, as the reader is aware, has long been subjected to invasions from the warlike Russians and licentious Turks.

The then ruling Sultan of Turkey was Kafar, and was to Circassia its greatest curse, owing to the many raids he made in that section of the country for spoils and new inmates for his harem.

Having heard of the great beauty of the renowned Zalumna, he determined to possess her at all hazards. In this undertaking a fierce battle ensued between the forces of the Turkish monarch and those of Prince Agra, in which the former was triumphant, the prince slain, and his daughter stolen.

Prince Bravello being fond of the chase, passed a considerable portion of his time in this manner. At the time of the descent of the Saracen horde on the Agra castle the young prince was absent on one of these hunting expeditions. Evil forebodings of some unseen danger lurking near his friends induced him to leave the chase for the home of those dear to him. He arrived only in time to see the result of the horrible deeds committed in his absence by the bold marauders. He soon discovered who the principal participant in this dastardly outrage was, and on him made a vow to avenge the wrongs of his friends.

The poem reveals how that vow was kept.

# THE STAR OF THE EAST.

### PART FIRST

A S young lovers in their new-born bliss,
  Lo ! day and night each other fondly kiss !—
Roseate Diana blushes in the east !
Sings  now  the  nightingale—all  other  birds  have
    ceased.
In their high homes the stars their vigils keep,
And far below are mirror'd in the deep.
Hark ! from yon castle, looming o'er the trees,
The lute's sweet tones are borne upon the breeze !
Here dwells Kafar, who ruthless rules the Turks—
The Sultan King, and evil are his works !
In dread, as all should dread degrading sin,
His subjects all his favor work to win.


" My harem fails to interest,
    Its inmates now to me are old ;
My harem soon I will divest ;
    These women must and shall be sold !
Circassia I will soon invade—
.  I 'll sweep her soil by land and sea,
And make this swift and bold crusade
    One of sweet satisfaction be !

The creatures in my harem now
    Have justly served their time and me—
I 'll cast them out for those, I trow,
    More beautiful and fair to see ! "


Thus spoke the monarch of the Turks, and swore
By Mohammed, the prophet of his lore,
That thus it soon should be ; and then apace,
A fiendish smile broke o'er his savage face.
He strode through rooms and halls of gorgeous
        make ;
'Midst many luxuries lived this kingly rake—
With finest carpets from rich Persian looms
Were velvet ottomans in satin rooms.
Here sparkled jewels of pure ray serene,
To world unknown, by all unseen :
Pearls, diamonds, amethysts, rubies, and gold,
Great wealth had this king, unseen and untold.


### PART SECOND.

HARD by the Black Sea's weird and sombre
        waters
Lives one of earth's fairest and loveliest daughters,
With her sire—a prince—and to his soul as dear
As Heaven's forgiving voice unto the Peri's ear
Is his beloved child—who bright, a Hebe looks—
As fair as Venus—as nymph of ocean nooks ;
So peerlessly perfect that even she seems
The belle of the angels haunting our dreams !—
Caring for the needy all over the world,

Her personal beauty her spirit impearl'd !
And she, the sweet spirit, the beauteous and good,
Lov'd her dear sire from child to womanhood.
The theme of her beauty had so far increased,
That she was by all named " The Star of the East."
This beautiful, lovely, and peerless young girl,
With conscience as pure as an unsullied pearl ;
With health, and with every thing riches can buy—
Yet mourn'd she that which the world can't supply :
A mother beloved—a saint now above.
Ah ! what can compare with a fond mother's love ?
They dwelt near the lovely, sweet village of Kale ;
They liv'd all alone in a sweet winning vale,
Where wild flowers grew and beautiful trees ;
Where wafted the breezes from three rolling seas.[1]
Zalumna's soft glances and lustrous dark eye,
Hinted the secret revealed by the sigh
That heav'd the pure bosom of Agra's sweet
     daughter :
One other she lov'd—ah ! Cupid had taught her !

&ast; &ast; &ast; &ast; &ast; &ast;

She loved to rove the forest wild—
The loveliest flower that nature smil'd—
There seek and find in silent dells
Lilies, roses, and pimpernels,
Till weary in this happy lot ;
Then pause on some enchanting spot,
In some sweet grove of chaparral,
To sit and weave a coronal,

[1] Mediterranean, Black, and Caspian seas.

To carry to her secret bower,
Where oft she whiled away the hour.
There rested, ramble home returning,
From Nature's tome its mystery learning—
List'ning to wild birds' silvery song,
Now soaring as she moves along ;
While flits the bat in winding course,
And sounds the owl's voice, deep and hoarse,
From silent, dense, and gloomy woods—
A solemn world in its solitudes.
Out from the wolds she roams the plain,
Spreading onward to the main ;
And breathes the aromatic breath
Of spring, that blooms from winter's death.
And oft in silence now doth brood,
Whilst straying where'er points her mood,
O'er her brave lover, Prince Bravello,
Who, by sunlight, or moon's pale yellow,
Far over rugged mountain goes,
Through vales of lily, vales of rose,
And other fragrance-breathing flowers,
All heedless of the passing hours ;
On track of fleeing buck and doe,
Escaping from their dreaded foe.
From covert starting timid hare,
And savage beast from thicket lair.
Zalumna thought with childlike glee,
A thought endeared to memory,
Of a near, new, and blushing morn,
When life for her would change—be born—
Which Heaven's divinest laws allow—

The life assured by marriage vow ;
A sphere of life both sweet and true,
And pure, thought she, as mountain dew ;
As crystal liquid of the fount,
Which doth on high, in beauty, mount
To Heaven's dreamy sapphire scope—
Her vision bright, full bright her hope.


PART THIRD.

THE day orb sinking in the west,
   Seems like a golden realm of rest,
Till light takes wings and flies away ;
Then Darkness comes on earth to prey,
Save where the bright-eyed sprites, on high,
Reveal close objects to the eye.
Scarce one lone hour, down in the west,
Had red-robed Sol gone to his rest,
When sounds of cant'ring, prancing steeds,
Afar but clear, o'er wolds and meads,
Awake the stillness of the hour.
The steeds draw nearer, onward scour,
Until they halt beside the tower,
When men's fierce voices on the air,
Reach ears of Agra's daughter fair,
While resting 'neath the arbor vines,
Where each long shoot in labyrinth winds.
She hears the sounds first in a dream
And fancies some wild panther's scream.
Then, wakening to a conscious state,
She sees dark forms come through the gate ;

The sight of troopers' glittering spears
Awakens all her sleeping fears.
Of this, her dear sire to apprise,
She swiftly to the castle hies,
But vain her mission now at most ;
Through doors and elsewhere through a host
Intrude, and in their bearings show
They are a bold and savage foe.
Prince Agra hearing foes draw nigh,
Well knew some bold and treacherous spy
Had foiled the warders at their posts,
And oped the gates to foreign hosts.
"Arm ! arm !" he cries ; " our foes are near !
Rouse ye ! my warriors ! " They appear,
With javelin, sword, and axe, and spear.
" Charge ! charge ! or, gods, 't will be too late !
Fight ! fight ! and yield to naught but fate ! "
The battle fiercely now began—
Each foeman fought—each man to man.
Steel shone in light of chandelier,
And dim the forms that battled here—
Still dimmer those in outer dark,
Where targets foemen faintly mark.
Then what th' Circassians' woe or weal,
As loud there dwelt one constant peal
Of cries for mercy—or oaths scream'd,
And frantic yells—one sound it seem'd,
The sounds that rent the air within—
A fierce uninterrupted din—
Commingled with the sounds without,
Where roar'd War's messengers about.

Like howling storm when raging best,
Like cries of spirits seeking rest,
Through darkness shrieking, "lost ! lost ! lost !"
Which floats at midnight o'er the frost ;
And like ere dawns the morning gray,
Wild hosts of midnight fiends at bay,
Arose and echoed one loud roar
From turret to foundation floor ;
A sound that seemed to reach the sky
And mingle with the clouds on high,
That rushed o'er sea, o'er wild moorland,
Whilst ebb'd with blood life's shifting sand.
As foemen fell 'midst blood and dust,
From nerveless hands fell swords to rust ;
While Moslem and Circassian bled,
Peacefully slept the fallen dead,
Unconscious of the angry strife
That robbed each warrior of his life.
Yet 'mid the corses of the slain
The living fought the field to gain.

\*　　\*　　\*　　\*　　\*　　\*

The battle now began to wane,
As thunder after storm and rain—
The clansmen dead on every side,
Their blood in streams one ebbing tide,—
Circassia's army, but tenth size
Of foes they fought became their prize.
The prince was pinioned in a chair,
And then they sought his daughter fair :
Beneath the turret's roof concealed,
Her hiding-place the search revealed.

In fright she saw their cause forsaken,
And next by Saracens she 's taken
Before their savage barb'rous chief,
Who well had won the name of thief.
The sight of one with charms so rare,
Soon caused the Turks to rudely stare.
Their monarch stopp'd it with a glance,
And toward Zalumna did advance,
Thus saying :　" Thou ! Circassian maid,
Alone art worth my Northern raid,
And I will vouch, no doubts retain,
Thou art the gem of this domain."
Insulting words, so thought the sire,
And wildly woke his slumbering ire.
Without a token's faint alarm,
He deftly loos'd each fettered arm,
And sword unscabbar'd, with a spring
Swift as the bolts the mad gods fling,
To avenge in blood the insult made,
In th' monarch's side plunged his bright blade.
This madden'd thrust, to shield his child,
By foes undreampt, was rash, was wild,
For ere he had breathed another breath,
He lay in silent ghastly death !
Thus fell proud Agra's prince to Moslem hate,
And wither'd—all must—to the blast of Fate !
With anguish cry, which spoke her wild despair,
Zalumna fainted, and her raven hair,
In flowing tresses veiled her ashen brow—
Unconscious, she knows no misery now.
As though in fear of hidden danger nigh,

With captive maids and captive warriors by,
And wounded king, the fierce and brutal Turk,
Swift from the scene, where ghosts of dead men
    lurk,
Departed through the dark and gloomy wold,
While yet Night in her glitt'ring dress of gold,
Walked forth in all her pensive loveliness,
Grieving for man's sins, his misery, and distress.

### PART FOURTH.

WHERE zephyrs stray, where breezes sleep,
    Where fountains play, where cascades leap,
Bravello braved the chase afâr,
While nothing seemed his life to mar.
A life of dreams and visions dear,
Pass'd with a being of beauty near ;
Whose heart o'erflowed for him with love,
A heart as pure as saints above.
When wandering he paused from tire,
Or, passing beauty to admire,
The lone, wild spots beneath his views—
Romantic scenes invoked the muse.
His verse did oft discourse in story,
Of haunted ruins, wild and hoary,
Combin'd with Cupid's beauteous bowers,
O'ergrown with fair and fragrant flowers.
He wrote—the famous nine inspired—
Who read, by ardent love was fired,
Translated to a realm of bliss,
Undimm'd by shades that darkle this.

One moon he pass'd where roamed the deer—
Until arose a growing fear,
Which grew until it woke to steal
All thoughts save those that sorrow feel.
Why did he feel this sudden fear?
He asked himself, in accents drear :
Could aught, had aught, of harm befell
Her, whom he fondly loved so well?
She whom he loved with such devotion
That e'en all wealth of land and ocean
Could purchase not one single hair
That round her sweet self floated there.
Bravello ! image of Apollo,
Did swiftly flight of Cupid follow—
And onward hasten'd, till he rode
Beside his loved one's gray abode.
He met not now one to retard,
Or one to challenge—a trusty guard.
Now, swiftly he ran through the gate's widened wall,
O horror of horrors ! most dreadful of all !
The simoon of death had swept dark o'er the land.
The proof of its visit everywhere lay at hand—
The ground was now strewn with men still and
    stark,
And ghastly each face ! no life-telling spark.
Here lay a pale rider and there lay a steed,
In silence, in blood, 'neath the tall waving reed ;
Circassian and Turk, who warred in life's pride,
Now, peacefully lay, in death, side by side.
Bravello awoke from the trance he was in ;
He sought for his love, he sought for her kin.

No sweet reward met his eyes' longing strain—
For those whom he sought, he sought for in vain !
Not on th' domain was the breath of a sound,
Wolves in the distance broke the stillness profound !
Lo ! Turks on the ground and down in th' moat !
His woe had been wrought by the Sultan cut-throat !
Behold ! while cold starts the sweat from each pore,
On his back Prince Agra welter'd in gore,
Silent in death, with a gash deep and wide,
Lay the father of her he loved as his bride.
O'er his dead friend he loudly and silently wept,
Ere he entombed him where his ancestors slept.
The mystery is cleared ! no deception lurks now:
From quiv'ring pale lips, through his teeth a fierce
    vow
He hissed like the snake that hisses at bay ;
It wafted on breeze, o'er dead, and away
Did float 'neath the veil of the vine arcades,
And grew in the gloom of the silent shades,
Which wakened the souls of the listening trees,
That now far around sighed their deep sympathies.
Vengeance looks from his eyes : Ah ! new th' light
    now,
The clammy cold sweat on his pale classic brow,
Remain'd and settled where first it oozed forth.
He wildly gazed round, south, east, west, and north:
But little he linger'd—no time was there lost—
Next boldly he plung'd, through the night, and the
    frost.

### PART FIFTH.

THE night was departing, and coming the morn,
　　When loudly a blast, from the shrill bugle-
　　　horn,
Full many awake afar and anear,
Creating a panic of frenzy and fear,
In the bosom of all ; who looked for the sword
Of the minions of Turkey's tyrannical lord.
'T was Prince Bravello who,'midst silence, profound,
Had wakened the slumberers by the bugle's sound.
The poor and needy of the village of Kale,
Now knowing the cause, in deep sorrows bewail.
Widows and orphans all over the land,
Owed many a comfort to Zalumna's fair hand,
And many owed safety from the roving brigand
To her good brave father and his trusty band.
As soon as his countrymen knew the desire
That raged in the breast of Bravello like fire,
To wreak swiftest vengeance upon the foul foe,
They eagerly cried : " We are ready to go
To th' ends of the earth ! south, north, east, and
　　west !
And will willingly start when thou dost request ! "

　　　*　　　*　　　*　　　*　　　*　　　*

Sol, suddenly 'rous'd, peer'd from th' east, and
　　espied
Ten thousand horsemen, that swiftly now ride
Toward land of the Turks—a nation of foes,
That e'er had created the deepest of woes.

Ah ! dark were the brows and fierce were the eyes
Of each of that band—" Revenge ! " their loud
    cries.
O'er many wild moors—through dark shaded
    wood—
O'er streams—and past ruins, which ages had stood
Deserted by man ; though owls held their posts,
With goblins and ghouls and uneasy ghosts.
By light of the sun from the first peep of day,
At night by the stars and the moon's misty ray,
Swiftly onward they ride, toward their foul foes afar,
Each avenger dashed on—each bold, fierce hussar.

      \*     \*     \*     \*     \*     \*

The king of the Turks sits at home—the day
    wanes—
He heeds not the twilight, his wounds, or his pains.
In soft mellow lights that illume like the dawn,
His eyes now one hundred fair captives feast on—
Georgia's brunettes and Circassia's fair blondes,
And almond-eyed houris from Orient dawns.
But hark ! what 's that sound, that strange rum-
    bling sound,
That seems like a storm in the night air around ?
And why are those cries so savage the while,
Bursting now forth from the mountain defile ?
And why do the guards give back from their posts,
Shrieking : " Allah ! our foes, they 're here in
    great hosts ! "
But hark ! the sound ! 't is the clashing of steel,
Far thundering on, one roaring, loud peal !
The Sultan now look'd in the Stygian air,

Met two rolling eyeballs—a slave's frenzied stare.
The doors of the harem now trembled and creaked ;
'T was air of the halls, that swiftly in leaked
From the outer dark air, where war-storm loud
    dinn'd :
With crash fell a door ! through th' house a cold
    wind
Moan'd low and whistled with a sad, mournful
    sound.
The fair are bewildered, the king darkly frown'd,
And wildly he cried to his minions without :
"What ho ! there, slaves—what 's all this about ?
This clash, and this din of tumult, and strife !
Some dark, drunken broil I 'll wager my life ! "
A score or more slaves appeared on the spot—
Their features were wild, perspiring, and hot.
They looked at their king with a cowering stare,
Who yelled in their ears with an angry glare :
"Why stand here speechless like Death o'er his
    spoil ?
What means your leader that he stops not this
    broil
Of harlots a-drunk and wine-bibbing slaves,
Of thieving scoundrels, and dishonest knaves ?
They all shall swing on the scaffold at morn,
For breaking my peace by this racket, I 've
    sworn ! "
"My noble king, the foe invades !—
'T is deep in blood each warrior wades ! "
One loudly now shrieked in the ears of the king,
Like shrieks of a fiend or a phantom on wing,

When lost in the night, some wanderer roams,
Through the drear sombre wolds, where the cata-
ract foams
And roars from th' mountain, when on rolls the
storm,—
When lightning's flash shows a tall spectre-form,
Walking pensive alone in the deep solitudes,
Seen ghastly 'midst trees of th' dark, dreary woods!
The Sultan frowned darkly and gnash'd his teeth—
He looked as an ogre from orgies beneath.
"Great Allah!" he cried, "this tale seems un-
couth—
Ho, ho! to th' ramparts!—I 'll soon know the
truth!"

### PART SIXTH.

"HALT!" and they halt in the land of their
foes,
In th' land of th' hated, who wrought all their woes;
In sight of the palace o'ershadowed with trees,
Where the Sultan reposed in the soft lap of ease.
When the night veiled in shadows the land and the
waves,
Into squadrons Bravello divided his braves,
And posted them round the high castle walls,
Ready to charge when their brave leader calls—
To fight in the cause of Circassia's dark woes,
The ruin brought on her by villainous foes—
Deeds dire and damning, which caused many tears :
Th' theft of maidens, death of kindred and seers.

Hark ! " Charge on the ramparts !" falls fiercely,
    yet low ;
They charge ! through the gates the battering-rams
    go.
The Turks first repel, then flinch and fall back ;
Then like fierce tigers leap to the attack—
To fight and to falter before the onslaught
Of foes who alone for their loved ones fought.
The battle is fierce, for many do war ;
Bold warriors fall low in death by the score.
In front of the battle throughout the whole strife,
The blade of Bravello drank oftentimes life.
His warriors fought bravely and well their ground
    stood,
Their foes fell around them like leaves of the wood,
While th' eyes of th' death-god glow'd ominous
    light,
And th' ebon war-eagle scream'd dread through the
    night !
Feeling they fought for a cause that was just,
In the god of battle all placing their trust,
The invaders conquered in the short wagéd war,
Though by foes they 're outnumbered by many a
    score—
O'er the red field of Mars triumphant they bear,
Ere fair Morn had loosened her bright golden hair.

   \*     \*     \*     \*     \*     \*

No longer the sounds of dread battle roll ;
From stark, stiffen'd corses, each storm-toss'd soul
Hath winged its swift flight 'mid battle's loud roar
To the dim land of shadows—the echoless shore.

In the zenith above are myriads of stars,
And sadly they glow o'er the red field of Mars.
The war-horse lies dead, and dead the dragoon,
And infantry warriors by score and platoon :
All ghastly and grim 'neath the soft mellow moon.
Each spirit afar from the drear, dreadful sight,
On ethereal wings took its swift wayward flight ;
But, when all and each shall be called to their
    doom,
When the blast of the trumpet shall peal through
    the gloom,
These, with the many, whose sins are concealed,
Will stand all unveiled, all secrets reveal'd,
By the great recording angel, the scribe of the
    Light !
Who knows every deed of the day and the night.
With those that now fell Turkey's monarch was
    slain,
And 't was brave Prince Bravello's good sword
    bore th' stain ;
The vow was fulfill'd, which th' dead heard him
    tell—
Prince Agra avenged, fully, speedy, and well.
From out of the harem Bravello released
Many beauties ; the fairest, " The Star of the East."
When the bugle-call told each warrior to mount,
Soon lost on their ears was the musical fount,
Where the Sultan 'neath turban, from eyes of clear
    jet,
Oft gazed at the tall, towering mosque minaret—
At beautiful houris, that gracefully move,

Through the sweet minuet, a dance that they love,
When the low, dulcet tones of the soft, sweet guitar,
By fair captives played, oft wafted afar.
The prince leads his clan, which Zalumna endears,
And the laugh of their friends rippled sweet on her
    ears.
And now from Circassia, no more shall they roam,
Nor warriors nor maid—all are happy at home.
And ne'er braver knight fairer captive released,
Than the Knight of Circassia—the Star of the East.

# THE RHYME OF THE BORDER WAR.

## AN HISTORICAL EPIC POEM OF THE KANSAS-MISSOURI GUERRILLA WAR BEFORE AND DURING THE GREAT REBELLION.

### THE PRINCIPAL CHARACTER BEING

## THE FAMOUS GUERRILLA, WILLIAM CLARK QUANTRELL.

## MY WIFE.

God secretes in places lone and still
The rarest products of His will,
For contact with the world disarms
His fairest flowers of half their charms.

# CONTENTS.

# THE RHYME OF THE BORDER WAR.[1]

## CANTO I.

### INTRODUCTORY.

FULL many builders in our time—
  Some riches build, in doubtful ways :
I build the fair and lofty rhyme,
  Of deeds heroic sing the praise.

[1] " The more unpoetic a century appears, the more pressing
are its needs for poetry drawn from fresh, contemporary, and
immediate sources. . . . An age like our own, thronged
with such varied activities, throbbing with such manifold en-
ergies, struggling so fiercely towards the light, can never be
regarded as hopelessly prosaic. Poetry is not dead because it
sleeps ; it is ' immortal as the heart of man,' if poets depend
on themselves, and not on external circumstances. In variety
and depth of meaning, the nineteenth century will not, surely,
disappoint those who have the discernment to extricate, and
the ability to exhibit, the treasures it supplies. The eagle eye
will yet detect the ideal beneath and within the actual world ;
the seer will always read the permanent truths enshrined in
common incidents ; at the touch of the magician the apparent
confusion ceases ; like sun-gleams that turn the dew-drops into
diamonds, master-minds will never cease to reveal beauties
that lie at our very feet—but lie there unobserved. He whose
mind is. burnished by contact with the world most fully col-
lects into a single focus all the interacting rays of the light
around him ; he who bends his ear most patiently to the
' loud-roaring loom of time ' will best extract a harmony from
its seeming discords."—*Edinburgh Review.*

Though now I touch the breathing lyre,
　To sing past war, if of those days
Should other harps than mine aspire,
　It boots not who best wears the bays—
So that the poem hath expressed
The music of the poet's breast
With feeling that to time imparts
A light of pathos melting hearts—
That mystic power of poesy,
Defineless as the Deity.
I sing as now my whim suits best,
And leave to time and man the rest.
I sing of war—red cruel war,
　The desp'rate deeds of desp'rate men—
Of war, whose echoes yet afar
　Low thunder over hill and glen.

\*　　\*　　\*　　\*　　\*　　\*

Behold ! excited cities stir !
　See the deserted shop and field !
What in man's history doth occur?
　To what doth fruitful toil now yield ?
His iron front grim-visaged War
　Doth bold display with wrath unmeet !—
Lo ! yonder !　Mars' fierce, lurid star,
　And Battle stamps his bloody feet !
Oh ! to what ominous shadows dark
　Time's finger points prophetically !
I hear the widow's wail and, hark !
　The nursing babe's cry comes to me !

\*　　\*　　\*　　\*　　\*　　\*

Kansas ! land of many a change !
　Land of wealth ! of fairest things !

Where war and carnage oft did range,
  Now Peace and Beauty spread their wings.
Thy verdant plains, thy waving turf,
  All teeming with unnumbered men,
Were trackless as the ocean surf,
  And monarch was the Red Man then.
But Pike, the pilgrim, came at last,
  Soon followed by explorers bold,
Dissatisfied with all the past,
  Who sought for happiness and gold.
Then the bowie and revolver ruled,
And men alone in these were schooled.
Here the Border Ruffian came—
  Here the early pioneer
Found the Missourians would defame
  With slavery the whole frontier.
And Atchison [1] here came as they,
The President for but one day.
At old Lecompton, which now lies
In mouldering ruins 'neath the skies,
'T was Judge Lecompte who first essayed
  To hold a court upon thy soil ;
And though he coaxed, and swore, and prayed,
  Thy land was shamed by many a broil.
'T was here John Brown, the fanatic, made
  A name which many yet admire ;

[1] David R. Atchison was made President *pro tem.* of the
United States Senate on the death of Vice-President King.
On Saturday, March 3, 1849, President Polk's term expired.
President Taylor was not inaugurated until Monday, March
5, 1849. So that David R. Atchison was President of the
United States for just one day, Sunday, March 4, 1849.

He looked for sunshine—all was shade,
  His faith in fools his funeral pyre.
And there was "method in his madness,"
  And madness in his method wild ;
He sowed—the Negro reaped in gladness,
  The harvest of this frenzied child.
Here brilliant Lane his powers displayed
  In oratory capped with fire ;
Triumphant in his might he swayed
  The crowds that listen and admire.
Here bold Montgomery led his men
Like Roderick Dhu through Scotia's glen.
Brave Leonhardt,[1] a waif of time,
A good man in the days of crime,
Under Kossuth a hero fought
Ere he our western borders sought ;
In Kansas used to hardships rare,
Three ears of corn his daily fare,
Shared with his horse ; this scanty store
Supporting life and nothing more.
Pilgrim and genius, Ingalls[2] came
Among the first—here built his fame.
And sons afar [2] the war notes hear,

[1] Gen. C. F. W. Leonhardt.

[2] The distinguished statesman, John J. Ingalls, President of the U. S. Senate.

[3] Gov. Robinson, Gov. Shannon, Gov. Reeder, G. W. Brown, Editor of the *Herald of Freedom ;* Richard Realf, the poet ; Gov. G. W. Glick, U. S. Senator P. B. Plumb, Col. W. A. Phillips, Gen. Geo. W. Deitzler, Hon. Lyman Allen, Col. S. N. Wood, Major F. G. Adams, Secretary of the Kansas Historical Society ; Gov. Thomas A.

And like the Spartan braves appear—
From their dark guns swift vengeance hies,
While wider spreads dear freedom's skies.

Osborn, Hon. James Redpath, Hon. John Speer, Col. Sam-
uel Walker, Hon. James M. Winchell, President of the Wy-
andotte Convention, 1859; Hon. Samuel A. Stinson, Hon.
Eli Thayer, Hon. Thaddeus Hyatt, Gov. John A. Martin,
Edwin Coppoc and John E. Cook (these two men were exe-
cuted at Harper's Ferry, December, 1859, as accomplices of
John Brown in his attempt to liberate the Southern slaves),
Major H. H. Williams, Col. C. K. Holliday, Major H. J.
Adams, Hon. Archibald L. Williams, Gov. Geo. W. Smith,
Gaius Jenkins, Judge Samuel A. Kingman, Judge L. D.
Bailey, Gen. Thomas Ewing, Judge Wm. C. McDowell,
Judge Jacob Safford, Judge Nelson Cobb, Hon. E. G. Ross,
Governor of New Mexico; Judge O. E. Learnard, Judge
Robert Crozier, Hon. M. F. Conway, Col. R. J. Hinton, Gen.
A. L. Lee, Hons. T. D. and S. O. Thacher, Gov. T. Carney,
J. H. Kagi, Major James B. Abbott, Hon. B. F. Simpson,
Gen. James G. Blunt, Hon. M. J. Parrott, Hon. Isaac Sharp,
E. P. Harris, Hon. F. W. Giles, Gov. John W. Geary, Gov.
Robert J. Walker, Gov. Samuel J. Crawford, Hon. Sidney
Clarke, Col. Geo. W. Veale, Col. John Ritchie, D. W. Wilder,
Ross Burns, Dr. A. J. Huntoon, Hon. Jacob Smith, Hon.
W. P. Douthitt, Hon. A. H. Case, Hon. David Brockway,
Hon. P. I. Bonebrake, Col. D. R. Anthony, Enoch Chase,
W. W. Climenson, Gen. Thomas Moonlight, Hon. J. C.
Hebbard, Major J. K. Hudson, Editor *Daily Capital;*
and others who figured more or less in the history of Kansas.
Many self-sacrificing wives and mothers, youths and little
children, came to suffer, and, in some instances, to perish
from hardships—true martyrs to the march of civilization
westward.

Here journalism [1] first betrayed
The hope the law would be obeyed.
Then thy first bard, Realf [2] did essay
The Muse—his poems seem like day
Amid that one dark night of time,
When all was vengeance, hate, and crime.
Though distant, Whittier with his song,
Helped Freedom's mighty march along.
All through thy Border-Ruffian days
I find more to condemn than praise—
When Territory and when State
First dawned—a happy thing of fate—
When lucky Reeder saw death near,
When Shannon ruled the hour in fear—
One for his life compelled to fly,
One to resign compelled, or die ;
While Robinson and other men
That Kansas served as rulers then,
Got little to repay the trust
Save hope, which oft deludes, and must.
Thank God ! 't is passed—the wagon wheel
Gives place to iron trail and steel.
Here Rogers,[3] and like soldiers, brave,
Find rest without and in the grave—
Now through with war and carnage all—
Hang their tried swords upon the wall.
And here as elsewhere, as a rule,
The wise man jostles with the fool.

[1] *Free State, Speer's Tribune, Squatter Sovereign, Leavenworth Herald, Herald of Freedom, Kickapoo Pioneer.*

[2] Richard Realf.

[3] Gen. Geo. Clarke Rogers.

Thy poesy soars on sublime—
Here grovels the pretender's rhyme.
O Kansas ! thou hast wonders seen,
   While Territory and a State !
Thou art, like mortal man, I ween,
   A creature led by tyrant fate !
Here white man drove the red man back,
To be supplanted by the black ;
Though now and then a moment seen,
   The strange wild Indian of the plain,
His star is setting low between
   The Rocky Mountains and the main.
His fate and the buffalo's are one—
They gather to the setting sun.

\*     \*     \*     \*     \*     \*

The maiden Morn walks with the Hours ;
Their tread has wakened all the flowers
That now are smiling sweet and fair,
And whispering unto God in prayer—
Bright birds of beauty welkin wing,
And matin-hymns to Heaven sing ;
The east with omnipotent power,
Burns with the breath of God this hour !
That mystery of life—O strange bequeath !—
That hems man in from birth till death,
And aught he knows e'en further still,
Broods in the vale and on the hill !
A cottage sweetly veiled in vine
Of ivy, myrtle, and woodbine,
Stands fair with portal open wide,
Where two stand talking, side by side—

A lovely woman, sweet and young,
A man who looks from greatness sprung,—
Stand with a something in their eyes,
Which tells that gloomy darkness lies
Deep in their hearts : "O husband dear,
I tremble with my aching fear !"
Her pure frank eyes were bent on his—
   Sweet sunbeams in a sea of dawn—
When by his side all hours were bliss,
   When parted, life 'mid clouds dragg'd on—
"Oh ! have no fear !—hope, hope !" he said ;
"Hope that we meet ere moon hath fled !"
"The spring-flower blooming sweet and dear,
Is hope without one sorrow near,
But when 't is smote by chilling frost,
'T is blasted hope forever lost !"
She quickly, earnestly replies,
With anxious looks and plaintive sighs.
"The Union I must help restore !—
'T is hard to leave thee for the war !
My country calls and go I must !
The duty 's hard, but it is just !
And Kansas, our own home and State,
Is threatened with Guerrilla hate !"
He said, and kissed her rose lips dewed with wine—
   The wine of love and beauty sweet—
She looked so fair she seem'd divine—
   An angel strayed from near God's feet.
He long caressed her with a sigh,
Said : "God bless you, darling wife, good-bye !"
Then vaulting on his steed, once more

He scaled the tufted prairies o'er.
A solitude of flowers rare,
Blushed sweetly in the valley fair ;
But not so sweet as Ida Vane,
The bride whose brightest hopes did wane.
As innocent she seemed to be,
 There blushing 'mid the woodland bowers,
As fair young children playfully
 Strewing early spring-time flowers.
Too fair, too young, this one-week bride,
To tread alone life's path untried.
As rests the dawn upon the lake,
 She rested on the arm of God—
She knew He ne'er would her forsake
 Nor him who 'midst war's dangers trod—
Far off in war's dread battles wild,
 Where Death exulted in his power ;
She had a woman's love, a child
 In years—but fourteen times spring's flower
Had bloom'd since first she breathed the air
Of earth's sad sorrow and despair.
" Dear God ! from thy high home above
 Bend low and hear me, Father, please !
Dear God," she cried, " preserve my Love,
 In war where death lives in the breeze !
Father, I pray thee, guard mine own
 Dear Willie while away from me—
Please bring him back ere flowers now blown ·
 Have faded to Eternity !
Dear God, protect my Life, my Love,
 I ask of thee, whose mercy sees ;

Dear God, from thy high home above,
  Bend low and hear me, Father, please ! "
Thus prayed this fair wife, innocent
  And young—too young for such great cares ;
And yet, 'midst all the worst, low bent,
  God hears and heeds such earnest prayers.
A bay-flower glowed in beauty fair
From out the midnight of her hair ;
The wine of beauty in her face,
  Within her eye the wine of love—
The wine of all we love to trace
  In woman—virtues from above—
Was hers, the lovely Ida Vane's,
  One week ago fair Ida Bell,
But William Vane her heart obtains—
  The fairest girl in all the dell :
Her bosom glowed with love as bright
As light of stars a cloudless night ;
And like those sweet immortal flowers,
  True woman's love grows on sublime—
Like them it soars o'er mortal hours—
  It lives beyond the bounds of time !
Unto the young wife, through her fear
So heavy, sorrowing, sickening near,
All nature lost enchantment here.
Lo ! see yon placid lake so clear !
  Where lilies with their satin stars
Wave sweetly in the breezes here,
  With snowy beauty, nothing mars .
Near by the gold-eyed kingcup glows,
With purple clover and red rose,

Where flower-cradled, golden bees,
Sway to and fro unto the breeze ;
With arrowy sweep a river glides
   'Twixt hills, then flows on dreamily.
Where beauteous fish flash sparkling sides,
While sporting in the waters free.
The vales where doth God's grace appear,
The sylvan wilds—hills, forests here,
Invite the wanderer to draw near ;
Sounds of mysterious beauty breathe
   Adown the lonely, lovely vale !
'T would seem that unseen angels wreathe
   A crown of glory in the dale,
For some good being of this world,
And whisper of the boon impearled !
Here countless fragrant flame-like flowers
In beauty bloom 'round wildwood bowers ;
Here birds of beauty breast the breeze,
And hide amid the leafy trees,
And sing a lovely madrigal,
While each dear little heart is full.
The music of sweet, hidden hours,
The poesy of fairest flowers,
Were here—sweet breathing through the bowers ;
Too, the Silences their Sabbath keep,
Far, far within the forest deep.
As blushing to her bridal bed,
   The young bride walks in beauty fair,
With modest fears that she is wed,
   Yet joyous, for her heart is there—
Glides day's lingering sweet twilight
Into the chamber of the night.

## CANTO II.

### QUANTRELL'S [1] EARLY HOME.

THE mansion of the Hildebrand
    The fairest of Ohio's land,
Is glowing freely in the night—
Pendent a thousand brilliants bright !
Out moon and stars—in peerless light
To help make glad the festive night—
Bright banners float upon the walls,
And happy faces throng the halls,
And sparkling wines flow free as water ;
And every neighboring son and daughter
Adds to the mirth that ripples here,
Where silence reigned for many a year.
The tables in the banquet-hall
Are spread, and dancers to the call
Are lightly tripping to the notes
Of music as it onward floats—
All is wild wassail and good cheer ;
They quaff the wine and foaming beer.

[1] The correct name of the great guerrilla, known on the
border as William Clark Quantrell, was William Clark
Quantrill,—the last syllable of his name being spelt with an
*i* instead of an *e*.

Long years agone Hugh Hildebrand
Had left his home and natal land,
To spend the wealth at his command :
Foul envy whispered, young and old,
Abroad he 'd been an outlaw bold,
In foreign lands, in years since fled
And vanished with the other dead.
But where he 'd been, what done, how well,
It boots not to this rhyme to tell ;
Suffice he 'd kept his promise given
Unto a sister saint in Heaven :
That he 'd return from foreign joys
To watch and guard her orphan boys[1] ;
Suffice he homeward joyous came
His lovely cousin's hand to claim—
The beauteous, radiant Rosalie,
Sweet as the scent of summer sea,
As gentle as the rays of love
That light alcoves of Heaven above ;
In all so sweet, so good, so fair,
She seems of neither earth nor air,
But something far too good to be,
Aught save those stainless saints we 'd see
Could we but roam that world so high,
Beyond the borders of the sky.
She, this earth-sprite, 's happy now,
With rosy cheek and snowy brow ;
Oh, she enjoys her hours of glee,
For happy, blithe, and joyed is she,

[1] One of these boys was William Clark Quantrill, who in
manhood became the famous guerrilla chief.

As poet singing unto those
Living in a world of prose—
Beholds the magic of his powers
In weeds transformed to fairest flowers !
'T is the fair maiden's wedding night,
And each and every winsome wight
Is blithe and gay, and full of cheer—
Feels that both life and love are dear.
Each agéd servant shares the bliss,
The master's joys are hers and his ;
With ardor as in Eastern land,
Both Rosalie and Hildebrand
Loved with love's mysterious power—
As odors of the fragrant flower
Attract us till their petals blow
In close communion with us : know
Ye that the flower's perfume is love
Lost from the heart's o'erfilled alcove !
The past seemed living as of yore,
When Hildebrand, the elder, bore
The name of being free from care,
Supremely happy, debonair—
He masked his heart from them, I 'd swear.
With all the wealth that mortals crave,
And generous to a fault, he gave
And squandered like a prince of old—
His heart too warm to e'er grow cold.
Night in and out his halls he 'd fill
With friends from every vale and hill,
Till every garnished hall would be
Resounding to the revelry.

Thus lived he his wild life away,
In dissipation mad and gay,
Till death low laid him in his tomb,
And silence did his mansion gloom,
And bats and spiders lined the walls,
And phantoms walked his silent halls.
Night waxed and waned, and Morning fair,
A maid of beauty, loosed her hair
Ere all the guests had left the scene,
Where dance and song and wine, I ween,
Were plenty.   Thus and thus again,
Like his mad sire, the son insane,
Pursued this wild, destructive course,
Which had its end in time perforce.
His Rosalie, a flower too frail
For earth, now bloomed in Heaven's sweet vale.
He hung a wreath of love and flowers
Over her grave so sad and lone—
For her he wept ; the happy hours
Beyond the silent stars had flown.

## CANTO III.

### LULU EARL.

LO ! yonder is the sylph of morn—
　　A maiden young, and wondrous fair ;
'T is Lulu Earl, whose charms adorn
　　And breathe a glory everywhere—
An unkissed maiden, at the mere,
　　Whose knowledge of earth's sin confessed
Is nothing—for her soul is clear
　　As infant on its mother's breast.
The radiant angels breathe her name,
In Heaven they feel her spirit's flame ;
Her lily rounded arms so fair,
Her form of tempting beauty rare,
And face might bring this fair one harm—
For many are less good than warm.
Far, far within the hidden vale,
　　Where dwells the peasant poor and good,
There is on earth no nobler tale
Than her life and those in that wild wood.
Here Lulu's presence inly gave
A peace as when calm waters lave—
A happiness we know in dreams,
The poet's ideal maid she seems,
Who makes  bright even dark despair—

O God ! thou knowest she was fair !
In her sweet home—a forest bower—
She blushed, the wildwood's loveliest flower.
God secretes in places lone and still
The rarest products of His will ;
For contact with the world disarms
His fairest flowers of half their charms.

&ast; &ast; &ast; &ast; &ast; &ast;

A storm howls like a fiend in pain ;
In swaying fury falls the rain ;
Around spreads out the forest black ;
Above extends the roaring wrack—
And oft deep voices muttering call,
As through Plutonian darkness fall
The voices of the damn'd and lost,
Whose crimes the love of God hath cost !
Who wander boundless depths of Hell,
Plunged in vast wastes of darkness fell.
The hills unloosed their shadows vast,
Which wander down the angry blast.
A sound—as when God's voice doth sweep
Through space's vast and awful deep
In mighty peal, whose great voice awes
The powers He bids obey His laws ;
Now thunders bellow, loud and far—
By Peri heard on outmost star ;
All objects by the storm are hurled
As though an earthquake shakes the world.
Through swaying trees, o'er sweet-crushed thyme,
Upon a steed as black as crime,

A horseman lone pursues his way,
All hoping that some shelter may
Be found—and lo ! the lightning's glare
Shows him a cottage closed with care.
" Thank God ! " he said, " Heaven must be near,
Though Hell 's abroad, it would appear,
For demons of most fearful fright
Seem'd galloping around this night,
Until this cottage, fair and bright,
Seems to have banished ghouls of night."
" Had I a shelter for my head,
Methinks I would not ask a bed."
The lightning danced before his eyes,
And seemed to picture Paradise !
As, drunken with a heavenly wine,
He fancied things that seemed divine !
A form of flame,—a spirit form,—
Goes flashing through the rolling storm,
Calls to him from a cloud of fire,
Then fades in the empyrean higher !
" Methinks a fever racks my brain ;
Perchance I 'm mad or half insane !
For on this stormy night abroad,
I 've seen an angel sent by God ! "
Lo ! yonder comes the gray-eyed Dawn,
    And shadows dark float to the woods—
The genii of the storm have gone,
    And sought the deepest solitudes.
A-weary, hungry, wet all o'er,
    The storm-benighted traveller drew

His reins before the cottage door,
  And loudly cried : " Halloo ! halloo ! "
He hears door-bolts fly back, and now
Sees a fine face and massive brow
Protrude.  " Good sir, I shelter seek ;
The storm last night has left me weak,
And hungry too."  " Dismount ; we 'll share
The best we have of rustic fare."
The stranger to a couch now drew,
And Sleep her mantle o'er him threw.
His steed was resting 'neath a shed,
And by the children loved and fed.
The day-god, in his golden car,
Had driven down the skies full far,
When he, the stranger-guest, arose,
Donned his late wet, now fire-dried, clothes,
And, looking from his window, starts
At sight of one who deftly parts
The vines of honeysuckles sweet,
As on she glides on fairy feet.
A fair enchantress sweet she seemed,
So those that saw when waked still dreamed—
For where she stepped, unto the view,
Sprang flowers early, sweet, and new !
And bloomed more beautiful and fair
Than rarest flowers on earth elsewhere.
The blooming blush of her ripe mouth,
  Whereon the grace of beauty dewed,
Like scarlet rose blown from the south,
  Seemed to the eye of him that viewed.

Oh, quaff the nectar of her lips !
  Oh, drink the glory of her eyes !
Oh, young, fresh, beautiful, she sips
  The beauty out of Paradise.
How fair !—she 's vanished from his sight,
The day so sweet fades into night.
The stranger-guest scarce fast had broke
When her soft voice the welkin woke !
The music of her step he hears !
  The silken sound of her approach !
Ecstatic to his ravished ears,
  His coming words can never broach ;
Though, could he tell as many times
  As there are flaming stars in Heaven,
His thoughts of her in poet's rhymes,
  Not half of all his love were given.
She comes ! that gushing glory glides
Toward him, and near him now abides.
The wanton wind has opened rude
Her dress, and laid her bosom nude,
Unknown to her, for she was pure.
And could not such a thing endure.
" Good-morning !   My name, stranger fair,
Is Quantrell !—for yours could I dare ? "
Said he, the guest.   She blushed ; her hair
Veiled much of her sweet, shining face,
Tossed by the breeze that still kept pace
Full well.   " My name is Earl,' t is plain
Lulu Earl.   I trust you will regain
Your strength lost in the storm and rain,

Our home is small, but you are free
To all; I pray, at home you 'll be."
How fair ! how sweet ! how strangely dear !
   With love's blush mantling on her cheek,
Is she, the gold-haired maid, that here
   Stands trembling with a joy unspeak.
That mystery of the soul glow'd bright ;
'T was instant love—'t was love at sight.
She loved the stranger, on her part,
With all the passion of her heart.
He loved her more than he had dreamed
That he could love—so fair she seemed
To him—her heavenly hazel eyes
Broke on him such a sweet surprise,
He felt as though some Unknown Power
Had placed him in a Heavenly bower.
When they did part to them 't was known
That each the other's heart did own.
And with embraces warm and sweet,
As when o'er clouds two angels greet,
They parted with love's deepest vows,
To meet to marry 'neath the boughs
Of her sire's whispering forest trees,
Where chirps the wild bird in the breeze.

## CANTO IV.

### QUANTRELL'S SOLILOQUY.

L O ! yonder is the king of day
    Peeping o'er the forest gray !
Through camp the echoing noises gay
Sound the notes of a gala day.
Fitful the songs the soldiers sing—
Wild as winter and soft as spring,
As hate or love their spirits start
With passions deep that touch the heart.
It is the camp of Jennison,
And all his men are full of fun
And liquor—for the leader thought
They that drank most the better fought.
Lo ! who those men with soldier grace,
Conversing there, with face to face ?
'T is Jennison, and him we 've seen
Out in the storm and in the green
And lovely vale.   " Now, while away,
I found a spot more fair than day :
And made such friends I ask your aid
That no one harms them in the raid.
Since I have e'er been to you true,
This one request I make of you—
Avoid this valley ; change your route,

And I will be your faithful scout,
As I have been your trusted spy."
"Impossible, e'en though I try !
For my wild clan will me defy.
My wounds will keep me here for days ;
My clan have money sworn to raise ;
They know the land where you have been,
The richest all the country in.
Since I am wounded, sick, and sore,
Then either you must lead, or Moore.
Since you decline my place to touch,
Because my men have drank too much,
As leader, Moore must act as such.
Although I 'd like your wish to grant,
I 'm very much afraid I can't ! "
Though Quantrell showed not one alarm,
He needs to warn his friends of harm—
On the first steed which meets his eyes,
Far from the camp he swiftly flies !

&ast; &ast; &ast; &ast; &ast; &ast;

"They come ! they come !" said Quantrell, low,
To her he loved—while neared the foe.
With doors and windows bolted, barred,
In Earl's house the defenders warred.
Here Hildebrand displays a might
In marksmanship that proves his right
As tutor of his nephews—they
Ever as true an aim display.
Their foes still pour from out the woods,
Fierce demons from the solitudes !
Now back, that wild and hellish horde

Seeks shelter which the woods afford,
To wait a while, for night is near,
When they 'll attack with less of fear.
Lo ! yonder in her pale career,
The moon wheels by each tarrying sphere ;
And yonder from the umbrage shade,
Which spreading oak majestic made,
A form unseen save by that Eye
That sweeps all space below, on high,
Creeps through the high and thick-grown grass,
As sly, a serpent oft will pass,
And lo ! a flame leaps toward the sky !
The door opes and the inmates fly !
The rifle's crack the vale awoke,
Amid the battle's fire and smoke.

\*        \*        \*        \*        \*        \*

The morning breaks—an awful morn,
    Within the vale of Avadore,
Where Lulu Earl was happy born,
    And lived where all was peace before
The hour that brought the murd'rous band
To rob and slay on every hand.
That band had vanish'd with the night,
Like evil ghosts afraid of light ;
Their wounded warriors and their dead
    They took, and with them swiftly fled.
Hard by Earl's cottage four are dead,
    And here two others freely bled—
And one was young and very fair,
And one stood o'er her in despair.
'T was Lulu Earl who lay so weak,

'T was Quantrell stood, too full to speak.
For that dear one he loved so well
Was dying from her wound so fell.
" Dear Lulu !   Darling of my life,
My heart is broken in the strife,
And with thy pain, my soul, mine own ! "
" Dear Will, I 'll leave you soon alone !
I soon shall go, but have no fear—
Now opened is my spirit ear !
List !   I hear the silent-footed Hours
   In endless music onward go,
And close beside the sylvan bowers,
   I hear the lovely flowers grow ;
I hear the ' music of the spheres ' ;
   I hear the angels singing now,
Above the sky where Christ appears
   With pity written on his brow ! "
Low Quantrell sank upon his knee,
   All heedless of his own wounds sore,
And kiss'd the lips he could not see
   For tears that from his sad eyes pour.
" Kiss me, dear Will ! a farewell kiss ! "
She smiles as slowly to the bliss
Of Heaven she goes—she does not groan—
She smiles in death, and makes no moan ;
Like soft decline of summer day
She sweetly passed to God away.
As morning mist floats from the sod
Her spirit passed the stars to God.
All that in life 's most wondrous fair,
In death none with her could compare !

" This deep, dread silence ! is it death ? "
Thought Quantrell, with a painful breath.
" O wake ! and feel the breathing morn—
　　O wake, my loved one, wake, dear heart !
Didst thou not tell me, angel-born,
　　That nevermore again we 'd part ?
She wakes not ! God ! can this be death ? "
　　Close to her heart he placed his head,
And listened, holding fast his breath—
　　Long listened—cried : " My soul is dead !
O Christ, where art thou now ! " he cried ;
　　" Why didst thou take her, God, from me ?
Why hast thou me time's joy denied ?
　　She 's thine through all eternity !
All gone ! My Lulu gone ! Great God !
Do thus I feel thy chast'ning rod ?
Father, uncle—my Lulu's mother !
And my beloved and only brother !
He with whom 1 oft have roved,
Whom I loved—aye ! more than loved—
Lies stark ! his generous spirit fled,
Alas ! alas ! is dead, is dead !
Oh, was he not myself almost,
　　When born with me the self-same day !
Methinks I hear his pensive ghost,
　　That doth to me for vengeance pray ;
As there he lies, he so like me
Doth look in every feature free,
Did I not know I live through pain
I 'd swear my very self were slain !
All, all are gone save me forlorn—

Why was I left ?  Was it to mourn ? "
" No!  No ! "  " What voice is that I hear ? "
 " To avenge the dead you are left—
The dead that to you are so dear,
 So ruthlessly were you bereft ! "
When that voice died upon his ear,
 As " one crying in the wilderness,"
Cried Quantrell : " It is well !  I hear !
 I shall avenge ! ease your distress !
Hear me, high Heaven !  O God, me hear !
And ye ! my friends in spirit near,
I shall avenge each, all of you,
And make your murderers bitter rue
The hour they wrought this fearful woe,
In streams that through their vitals flow !
This tribute to your memory—
The golden past so sweet to me—
From this time forth I well shall pay,
From morn till night, from night till morn I 'll
 slay !
Five thousand men brought on my woes,
Five thousand men make up my foes.
I know them all—each, every one,—
And none shall my just vengeance shun !
Five thousand men shall feel my power,
Shall 'neath my hand of vengeance cower ! "

## CANTO V.

### QUANTRELL AND JENNISON.

'TIS eighteen hundred and sixty-two—
    The north winds pierce the deep hills
    through ;
September, and the leaves are browned
That fly the breeze, that cover ground,
And droop upon the trees around.
Missouri river waters flow,
All swollen in their channel go.
A hundred mounted men or more,
Armed to the teeth, are on the shore.
A moving arsenal each seeming,
From the many weapons gleaming
From belts and boot-legs—every side,—
All bristling as they onward ride.
All sudden south their way they take—
All sudden swifter progress make !
To land of Harris they have come
To take the products of his home ;
To get by right of might a share
Of the rich farmer's bounteous fare.
In front of that bold company
The leader rides, and marked is he
Above the vulgar herd of men—

Above the herd pent in the pen
Of common thoughts and things and ways,
Where one day shows the life of days—
Repeats the past, tells what''s to come,
As footsteps sound continual hum.
Though small of build, one understands
From looks, that he alone commands.
His air and aspect this confess
In language words cannot express.
His eyes are blue, the deepest blue,
And almost black they sometimes grew—
'T was when of wrongs their owner thought,
Of which the bitter past was fraught.
He was not handsome, yet his face
Express'd a strong, strange, winning grace ;
His form was sinewy, strong though spare—
Wronged, he was a lion from his lair.
The flag borne by a war-scarr'd son,
Tells unto each and every one
The chieftain's name—with black background,
The name of "Quantrell," dreaded 'round.
His hat—each bold, wild follower's too—
Toss'd high a plume of raven hue.
His fierce men no allegiance knew
Save to him who had ta'en them through
All kinds of dangers, wild and dread,
And yet did save them from the dead.
All quailed beneath his eagle eye,
All him obeyed and asked not why.
They looked upon him as a sage,
The mighty Nestor of his age.

They looked to him as to a God
Who held o'er earth a magic rod—
A potent wizard power, that wrought
Great wonders—with a mystery fraught.
In th' mysterious wise he 'd grown—
    Of the bright stars he 'd learned man's fate—
Beyond earth's confines the unknown
    He knew, but dared not to relate.
Napoleon cross'd the Lodi o'er,
    With followers that feared at first ;
So Quantrell led the way—before
    He went—his men against the worst—
It booted not the odds how great,
They trusted all to him and fate.
He seemed as cool in battle's roar
As though he walked the calm sea-shore,
And though war's missiles fell like rain,
He ever passed above the slain.
Hence many thought some Unseen Power
Protected him each woful hour.
Be as it may, it seems that fear
Had never whispered in his ear.
He lived aloof, what vengeance made,
A daring Northern renegade.
He cared not for the Southern Cause,
He cared not for man's puny laws,
He fought for vengeance and his foes
Fought 'neath the Federal flag.  His woes
Were great, for all he loved were gone
To that strange bourne where phantoms wan
Hold mystic rites—life's secrets learn,

For which all truly great souls yearn.
Aye, those he loved with all his heart,
  With all his soul, in their blood fell
By Jennison and clan ; the smart
  In his breast rankles like a hell.
Once, in bold Jennison's command,
  He rose above the ranks, soon earned,
Because the leader of the band
  Found he knew more than he had learned
Of war's black art—yet did betray
The greatest trust that cheers life's day.
Those promised to protect he [1] slew ;
  Would number Quantrell with the dead.
But fate decreed his foes should rue
  Through him, that sacred blood was shed.
Yet Quantrell, with a conscience keen,
Felt if he could he 'd rather been
A soldier on the Northern side ;
But fate and vengeance this denied.
All through the war his thoughts upbraid
That he lived on a renegade—
As when, by God from home and Heaven
Ambitious Satan, distant driven,
Far onward solitary went,
And far through space his journey bent,
With thoughts full bitter with defeat,
And a remorse pride could not cheat,
That he had with his Father warred,
And with his brother, Christ, our Lord,—
Though swift through dread immensity

[1] Jennison.

He flies the boundless, bottomless sea—
O'er frozen, over fiery worlds,
Past burning meteor as it hurls,
Expecting to some realm obtain,
Where he might e'er unrivalled reign ;—
Though Quantrell thus unhappy, he
Kept hidden all his misery ;
Provoked to vengeance, his loved slain,
A Nemesis he roamed the plain.
Thus hatred overpowers well
All other passions ; thus he fell.
He thought with feelings dread, aghast,
Death ravished all the golden past,
Which was so bright—too bright to last !
Alone, one panacea he found,
In war's dread thunders echoing round !
" Poole, post a guard on yonder hill ;
And then we 'll try and get our fill
From this old farmer's well-stocked farm ! "
The guard is placed to watch for harm ;
They hasten—enter through the gate,
Where earth seems not so desolate
As most spots where the iron feet
Of war had trampled down unmeet.
The farmer came unto his door
And hailed them as a friend of yore ;
This a surprise and too a foil
The foe each thought he would despoil.
When Quantrell scanned his features free,
Awoke a sleeping memory,
For there before his flashing eye

Stood one he knew in days gone by.
" Dismount ! " the mighty chieftain said ;
And at the word his men obeyed.
Beneath the farmer's broad, wide roof,
Which knew the mingled warp and woof
Of happier days, the guerrillas came,
Ate of the store the farmer's dame,
Assisted by her daughter fair,
Set forth,—a maid of beauty rare.
Oh ! she was wondrous, passing fair !
And she was happy—debonair—
A spirit she of fancy wild—
A dreamer was this lovely child.
But summers seventeen had flown
Since she had come, one of God's own.
She 'd heard the golden laugh of Flowers ;
Heard step of silver-footed Hours
As they walked on the mystic heights
Of all the mornings, noons, and nights.
Beneath the moon's and stars' soft light
She 'd heard the voices of the night
Go sweetly laughing back to God,
As she, the child of nature, trod
The forest path o'er sand and sod.
The past to her was like a dream—
The present hers—the future's beam
She knew not ; it is well, I trow—
That future 's hard and full of woe.
Alas ! how short the sight of man !
Beyond the future's veil none scan ;
The present is a flower we see—

The past lives o'er, a memory.
The future points with hope afar,
Like child that longs to grasp a star.
The outlaws all enjoy the hours
Well spent 'midst wines and vines and flowers.
Behold the ruby wine they pass,
It flames and dances in the glass !
Hark to the song that John McKeene
   Sings to guitar the young girl plays ;
By nature song is his, I ween
   In song a talent he displays :

"Give Heaven the good and Hell the bad ;
   Yield me the lovely and the fair,
For though my heart be sick and sad,
   A girl's sweet face dispels my care.
Drink ! drink the rosy, sparkling wine,
To woman, lovely and divine !

"Oh ! what 's the poet's lofty wreaths,
   To sweeter wreaths of woman's arms,
Encircling you, when beauty breathes,
   Her true love gemm'd by all her charms !
Then drink the rosy, sparkling wine,
To woman, lovely and divine !

" Then drain the foaming, sparkling glass,
   To her who brings such peace and bliss ;
Whose tender eye we cannot pass
   Without we long to woo and kiss !
Drink ! drink the rosy, sparkling wine,
To woman, lovely and divine ! "

When he had closed, fair Annie's eyes
Gleamed with a sudden, sweet surprise.
The singer was a handsome man ;
The maiden did his features scan
Until she found his eyes on her,
And then she blushed to find they were.
Her heart was not a frozen lake
  On whose cold brink fond Cupid stands,
But it was warm, like winds that wake
  In June, blown from the Southern lands ;
This love we sometimes see, apart,
  Forever glowing fresh and new—
A flower that grows from near God's heart—
  Immortal, radiant, sweet, and true.

\*       \*       \*       \*       \*       \*

Low sinks along the purple hills,
Which shadow vale of flower and rills,
And gives the forest, black and dun,
The aspect of a thing to shun—
That its dense wilds do deep afford
The stronghold of a robber horde—
The setting sun, and softly glances,
Farewell to earth as night advances.
When Quantrell and his men-at-arms
Left their kind friends.   Said he : " If harms
Thy foes one single hair, good sir,
Of yours or your good folks, I swear
To make them rue the hour they came
To do thee wrong—so sure my name
Is Quantrell.   Though I 'm deemed a ghoul,
God knows I am not near so foul—

Deemed wretch on earth, astray from Heaven,
Who lost the route that God had given,
I have one virtue 'midst my crimes—
I bear a grateful heart all times.
Who my dark hours tries to make less
Will ever find me in distress
A friend ; and never be it said
When needed most I ever fled,
Though foes unnumbered trod him down
And all the world gave him a frown.
Men struck my heart a bitter blow,
They pose as patriots, but my foe ;
I 've naught against stars, stripes, or states,
A victim I of all the fates !
Ohio [1] is my boyhood's home—
Fate forced me from that land to roam !
A twin—my brother slain, and all
I dearly loved.   Their ghosts now call
For vengeance from the hills and vales.
Hark ! now I hear their mournful wails !
The South outlaws me—doth ignore—
    Because I will not spare a foe
Of those who brought forevermore
    A bitter and eternal woe.
For Southern rights I do not call,
Th' Confederacy must surely fall !
I stand alone !—I 'm not afraid !—
An outlaw and a renegade !
Farewell !" he said.   Each man's good-bye
Is spoken in a hand toss'd high.

[1] Canal Dover, Tuscarawas County, Ohio.

O'er each guerrilla's head defined
His black plume nodded to the wind.
They hasten on ; their friend's kind eyes
Fain follow them along the skies.
Lo ! Luna rises soft and bright
Above the battlements of night !
O'er outlaw'd loveliness of wilds
Where fairest forest flower smiles.
Lo ! see upon yon great hill's height,
Beneath the floating moon's pale light,
The tall guerrillas' shades appear
Those warlike phantoms mortals fear,
Seen but a moment in the mist,
Then pass like shades the sun hath kiss'd !

\*        \*        \*        \*        \*        \*

The soft, round moon did yet blush red,
Like beauteous rose above the dead ;
And like the lamps the saints hang out
For sin-freed spirits on their route
To Heaven, burned bright across th' skies
And lit far space to mortal's eyes ;
When, like ten thousand demons driven,
That have no hope to be forgiven,
There rose a mad and mocking yell
That sounded like a direful knell !
Piercing the deep wolds through and  through,
And sweeping the wide prairies too.
Jayhawkers came, and came Redlegs,[1]
Because good Harris oped his kegs

[1] An independent clan, fighting under the Federal flag, and peculiarly uniformed with red stockings and knee-breeches.

Of wine, his cupboard, larder, all,
To Quantrell's men, for carnival.
This outrage to the Jennison cause,
Brings punishment by outlaws' laws.
A dark form neared the Harris home,
And call'd : " Halloo ! awake and come !
I 'd speak to you and ask advice ! "
The farmer answered in a trice.
But scarcely had he loosed the door,
When he fell dying on the floor,
And loud report of carbine shot
Rang on the night air round the spot !
They fire the house—see it consume,
And crumble to a Jennison tomb ! [1]
The horsemen, led by Jennison,
Sped Quantrell's men with knife and gun,
And when they overtook that clan
There was a battle every man
Of them will ne'er, will ne'er forget,
Though dews of fivescore years may wet
His brow ; for it was fierce and hot,
And angry poured the whistling shot !
And savage foes from hand to hand,
Stained with their blood the shifting sand.
Of those who fought in furious rage,
Many were young on life's strange stage ;
Some felt the winter of their age ;
All mingled in the battle cloud,
While surged the voice of conflict loud !

[1] The term applied to the remains of the houses burned by Jennison.

As fierce the fight as Wilson Creek,[1]
Where the brave dead fell fast and thick.
With ensign " Quantrell," a black flag high,
Proudly flaunted the smoky sky ;
While high the patriots' flag streamed out,
O'er Redleg and Jayhawker rout.
The serried ranks of friend and foe,
Fought hand to hand and toe to toe,
The war-horse rears and strikes as fierce
As rider, whose sharp bowies pierce
The quivering flesh and harder bone—
When fall the mighty with a groan.
It was a fierce and awful fight !
    The men that died in conflict great,
They fought as demons in Hell's light,
    For some poor fickle boon of fate—
That light so dreadful in its glare
It makes e'en darkness welcome there.
Yells rose to anxious, listening stars !
    Near kindred to the Great Unknown—
They sank until earth's centre jars,
    And Neptune startles on his throne !
As oft here Quantrell plainly showed
    Why his feared name was dreaded so ;
Why his foul fame e'er redder glowed
    'Long border, wheresoe'er men go.
While foes his death forever sought,
    To lay him bleeding on the sods ;

---

[1] The battle of Wilson Creek, which was a great victory
for the Union forces, 5,000 of them whipping 20,000 Rebels.

He handled weapons quick as thought
   And sent them howling to their gods !
As down the midnight depths of Hell
   A fiend is hurled by unseen hands ;
A fiend that dared to mock God, fell
   From high, where Heaven's great rampart stands.
" 'T is useless that the just assail !
It seems the fiends these days prevail ! "
Cried Jennison, when Quantrell fell
Upon his troops and scattered well ;
Till, vanquished, he afflicted grieves
O'er troops now scattered like the leaves !
For few that lived, with him had fled,
Leaving their own unburied dead
With Quantrell and the men he led.

     *     *     *     *     *     *

When John McKeene knew all the truth,
His heart was touched with tender ruth
For her, the black-eyed girl he loved,
From whom he, war compelling, roved.
With a short leave of absence, he
Returned to her he longed to see.
He found her, and he vowed to take
Swift vengeance on their foes, and make
The murderers of fair Annie's sire
Deep rue the deed.    'T was her desire
To part no more from her fond lover,
Though yet he lived an outlaw rover.
Whether the cause is right or wrong,
Whether the man is weak or strong,

Woman goes where her heart dictates ;
The rest she leaves unto the fates.
As McKeene's wife, she vowed she 'd go
In Quantrell's ranks, for weal or woe.
Her toilet quick she donned—attired,
Her waiting steed she vaults, and fired
With love's desires, they scoured the lea—
All lily pale, yet dauntless she.
On through the solitudes they rode,
Till found a holy man's abode ;
No time to lose, since wait their band,
Since dangers lurk on every hand.
They on their fiery steeds await
The marriage vow that them would mate.
The man of God pronounced them one,
Then like two phantoms they were gone.
In man's attire now changed the life
Of Annie, the guerrilla's wife.
Her and her husband's honeymoon
Was passed 'mid scenes of blood ; no boon
Of peace or rest was theirs ; they saw
The awful import of life's law ;
They realized in battles red
The beauty of that peace far fled,
That war's black art was Hell's dark plan
To feed on God's best gift to man.

\* \* \* \* \* \*

It is the song-told month of June,
The air re-echoes many a tune,
The angels sing to God on high,

While basking 'neath His tender eye.
When seem great Presences to dwell
On hills, in woods, and flowery dell.
Great beauties may all radiant be
On Earth, which man 's too blind to see ;
A thousand poems unexpressed
May be within the poet's breast,
Which angels read that wander by,
Sweet pilgrims from beyond the sky.
'T is morn ! and near Lee's Summit town
McKeene and wife are riding down
The prairies green, with friends but few.
The Seventh Missouri comes in view !
But eight unto a thousand strong,
A fight begins, but lasts not long.
As Spartans fought in days of old,
So fought the few guerrillas bold,
Till seven were slain ; among the seven
Brave John McKeene his life had given ;
And she, his wife, in soldier garb,
Lay wounded by her dying barb.
And when a soldier sought to slay,
She quickly doth her sex betray ;
For ere he 'd time her death to track
She 'd pulled her long hair down her back,
And looked at him with woman's eyes,
Which woke in him a soft surprise.
Her beauty held him like a dream—
He could not move, so fair the béam !
Like summer moon through clouds of night,

She broke upon his ravished sight !
Oh ! strangely sweet her voice did seem—
Like Heaven-sent whispers in a dream !
Spoke as she lay, sad, weak, and wan :
" My loved are dead ; the morning's dawn
Shall never break for me with light.
God ! am I dreaming ? all is night !
And am I left to tread life's way
Alone, alone ! O gently lay
That form so dear low to his rest ;
Press light the soil above his breast ! "
The fountain of her soul in tears
Flows 'long the shore of bitter years.
Beneath a giant oak's dense shade
The corse of John McKeene was laid.
The fair one found in convent's halls,
A home where Mercy sweetly calls.
Deep in recesses of each heart
   Some sacred cherished secret lies,
Which tenderly is laid apart
   From the rude world's inquiring eyes.
Sister Celeste[1] (Annie McKeene)
Sleeps with the just and blest I ween.
God ne'er forgets the sore-tried soul,
Unknown to fame or at fame's goal,
But high in dark mysterious realm

---

[1] The devout Sister of Mercy who died a few years ago of yellow fever, at New Orleans, while in the faithful discharge of her duty in attending to the wants of those afflicted with yellow fever.

The Mighty One directs the helm
Of all that 's been, is, e'er will be,
Through time and through eternity.

## CANTO VI.

### WILD BILL.

L O ! Phœbus climbs the hills of morn !
 And white-robed Day is newly born.
Far o'er the prairies, fair to see,
Wild yellow sun-flowers flourish free
For miles and miles, a golden sea !
One mile, and scarce a mile, apart,
 Are now encamped two warlike clans—
But soon from their still rest they 'll start,
 Prepared for battle's dread demands !
Soon shall arise the voice of war,
And death will lead the wild uproar !
As black as crime out one flag flows,
With "Quantrell" writ in red it rose ;
While o'er the other, fair as light,
The stars and stripes wave proudly bright !
Th' brave o'er whom the Union banner
Floats in such a winsome manner,
Approach their foes, whom Younger leads
To battle where the warrior bleeds.
Why is not the great guerrilla here
Whom all his foes so well do fear ?
Low lying nigh a river scaur,
Where ten to one his foemen are,

Bold Quantrell waits a desperate fight.
His officer, with force bedight,
He had despatched upon a scout
To forage through the land about,
Bushwhack, and any foeman rout.
All suddenly Cole Younger heard
A voice, all others he preferred—
A voice, in tones so deep and loud
It seemed to pierce the trembling cloud.
From Younger's lips this warning fell :
" My boys ! we 're on the brink of Hell !
That sound is Wild Bill's[1] border yell !"
Bold Younger to himself now thought,
" I have a foe I have not sought !
Though in my day's best fighting hour,
This foe will try my greatest power—
Try power of each and every man ;
He leads a fierce and desperate clan !
I do confess beneath my breath
I dread to fight this son of death.
If Quantrell was but here, how proud
I 'd rush into the battle cloud.
Though I 'm a Hector in the fight,
Wild Bill 's Achilles in his might ;
But, pshaw ! I 'll trust all to the fates—
We 'll war like devils at Hell's gates !
Buffalo Bill and Texas Jack,
I see, help lead the yelling pack !
And Wild Bill wisely still retains,

[1] William Hicock, famous as " Wild Bill."

' The Evil Spirit of the Plains,' [1]
That thunderbolt of might and war,
Leaves awful carnage near and far.
These men seem demons fierce and fell,
Whom Satan seems to shield too well.
From what I learn they 're on a scout
To spy fierce Quantrell's secrets out.
They search in vain, for Quantrell 's deep,
And e'er doth his own secrets keep ;
And ever sleeps where none can say,
Safe hid, that gold may not betray.
Boys ! ere we enter in this row,
I want to tell you here and now,
That your best fighting must be done,
Or when goes down yon wandering sun
He 'll look upon us dead and stark.
Gird up your loins—each weapon mark—
See that each cartridge is at hand,
And each good weapon to command !
We fight Wild Bill—he comes this way—
That means he comes to murderous slay ;
Though drunk or sober, Bill's intent
Is to lay low a regiment
With crew he from the wilds obtains,
His Indian-fighters of the plains—
Hark ! once more Wild Bill's border yell !
Our foes are nearing—lie low well !
Down with the steeds !—in ambush, so
We 'll have advantage of the foe,

[1] W. F. Cody, *i. e.,* '' Buffalo Bill,'' known among the Indians by this title.

And get the ' drop ' on them I know !"
Down sink the steeds, well trained to war,
And all is still as at death's door
When death alone is there, no more.
The desperate crew that Bill doth lead
Now dashes by at headlong speed ;
Cole Younger's clan arise and fire,
And battle shrieks with mad desire.
Now Younger cried with hurried speech :
"To horse ! and for your foemen reach !"
They mount, they charge, fire oft and well,
While Bill and boys on their ranks tell ;
Where Wild Bill fought the dead do swell
To thrice the number elsewhere slain.
He flies, he flashes o'er the plain—
He kills before, behind the same—
Shoots on all sides, true is his aim ;
He fires with such rapidity
One stream of fire forever free
Flames from the mouth of his fire-arms,
For each hand a revolver warms.
His thundering yells incessant rise,
Which tell his foes he them defies ;
His long hair snaps and cracks behind,
And lashes the complaining wind ;
He bristles like a porcupine
With weapons growling in a line—
An arsenal that spins and flies
Before the watcher's wondering eyes.
Savage the conflict, dread and hot ;
Swift, sure, and oft the fighters shot ;

Oft saddles empty as men die,
Riderless steeds the prairies fly.
The doubtful combat they maintain
Till night's deep shades involve the plain ;
When Younger sent one of his men
For Quantrell, lying in the glen
Hard by Blue River, waiting then
For Jennison's and Ewing's men.
Came Quantrell quick at Cole's desire,
But found none on whom to wreak his ire ;
Wild Bill had learned of Younger's aid,
And vanished in night's friendly shade.

## CANTO VII.

### YOUNGER AND HIS MEN.

EARTH clothed with grass—with each fair
    thing
Of flowers—of all the gems of spring,
In beauty dreams ; thus kissed by Heaven
'T would seem that man had man forgiven.
Day blushes on the summit height ;
   There dwells a calm and holy still ;
The warring winds that howled all night,
   Soft whispers breathe upon the hill !
As bridal bark with silken sails
   First leaves its moorings on Time's shore,
And happy speeds before soft gales
   Adown Life's river, each explore.
The blithe bird winds his dulcet horn,
Whose tones float through the depths of morn,
For silver springs of beauty flow
From his fond spirit, rich I trow.
And morning broke upon a sight
Of carnage of a fearful fight !
Upon Cole Younger and his men
Hiding their lost in the shady glen.
'T is done ; each warrior turns him round
To seek his rest upon the ground.

Quoth Younger : " Boys, our fate is well,
Though many of our comrades fell ;
We warred with Titans, not with men,
Be proud of the battle in th' glen,
For many of Bill's warriors slain
Lie silent on this sombre plain.
Such, such is war—no use to weep
O'er those that woo eternal sleep ;
They 're gone beyond our power to keep.
To-morrow may see us as they ;
God pity every one, I say !
Boys ! while we rest I 'll tell a story,
Here on the field of battle gory :
In Texas, Wild Bill, with a score
  Of Indian fighters of the plain,
Was driven to a bloody war,
  And many of their foes were slain.
'T was on a time when Bill, the devil,
Went south, ' to hold the Texans level.'
His followers were fifty odd,
And they were rough and ready shod
For any conflict great or small.
In Shelby County—it was fall—
Two hundred thieving ' Regulators '
  Came down upon them like a flash ;
But soon they rued, these Texan traitors,
  That they had made their reckless dash ;
As most of them in battle fell
So few were left the tale to tell.
Their bloody hurt yet rankles sore,
And since that day they 're less for war.

They wakened Wild Bill and his crew,
They wakened Bill who fifty slew.
Each time he fires a foeman dies,
Thus hundreds fall before his eyes.
'T was this that made his bristling name,
'T was thus he got his ' drop ' on fame.
Had I not worn a steel breastplate,
Death now would triumph o'er my fate.
Full fifty times balls struck my breast,
To flatten on my armor vest.
This steel-made cap upon my head
A hundred times has stopped his lead."
He could acknowledge, and he would,
The prowess of a foe withstood.
" Well, boys ! up now, let us away ;
Dawn crimsons at approach of day !
And ere goes down yon rising sun
Quantrell meets Ewing and Jennison.
Down near the Blue he ordered me
To fail not at the battle be."
He leaps upon his war-horse, light,
And spurs him toward the coming fight,
His followers close upon his flight.

## CANTO VIII.

### THE SNI HILLS.

FROM out the deep, on golden wings,
    The blushing angel Morning springs !
And her fond smiles of beauty dwell
On hill and plain with magic spell—
Dwell on the mist-clothed hills of Sni,
Which, tower-like, seem to touch the sky,
Deep in whose fastness Quantrell lay,
To fever's slow torments the prey.
Reflects he on his years of life,
On childhood, boyhood, manhood's strife,
And all his life's acts pass him by
Like sheeted ghosts we oft descry
When night engulfs the world with shade,
And angels breathe " Be not afraid ! "
Among his many deeds of war
There 's one he deeply doth deplore.
Olathe, Lone Jack, other places
Gave him no pain—but one disgraces
All others—and he cursed the day
When his spy did his trust betray,
And thus made Lawrence all his prey.
He cursed his weakness at that hour
To check his men's fierce brutal power,

Who slaughtered with a mad desire,
Inflamed with liquor's fatal fire—
Like maddened bloodhounds in their ire.
He cursed his base and treacherous spy,
Who told to him a cruel lie—
Led him to think that those were there
Who brought him all his mad despair ;
Who tore asunder each loved tie,
And waked his sleeping battle-cry—
Revenge ! revenge ! he shrieked in vain,
Nor trampled he the guilty slain.
Alas ! too late ! in frenzied ire
He learned the truth ! lo ! bursts forth fire !
Not he who once held magic power
Can check his madmen in this hour.
Yet there was one deed which sublime
Should glow 'mid his dark deeds of crime,
One deed that 's hallowed with the light,
One star of beauty through the night.
When his wild crew their thirst for blood
Glutted on hundreds of the good,
From out the Eldridge House he led
Two score or more with stealthy tread,
Them to the city's south conveyed,
There to protect them he essayed ;
He placed them in a barrack, then
With his fire-arms defied his men.

\*     \*     \*     \*     \*     \*

Hark ! what sound of hurrying feet
  Awakes the silence of the hills ?

And yells that caverns all repeat,
   To wind that wanders where it wills !
The fierce and cruel ghouls of war,
The open-mouthed cannons loudly roar.
Forgetting all his sickness now,
   The great guerrilla chieftain rose,
And mounting his black steed—his brow
   Is scowled—he spurs to friends and foes !
His men retreat !   His loud war-cry :
   " Halt ! right about ! beat back the foe ! "
They halt—they charge—on him rely
   Who e'er hath brought them out of woe.
" Yield not ! though all the foemen host
Are led by Hector's mighty ghost ! "
Though Quantrell's genius was in war,
   He gave his quick commands as short
As words express—to army lore,
   Not speech, he ever had resort.
" 'T is strange ! " he thought, " that Anderson,
   The reckless Bill, should thus retreat !
That Frank or Jesse James should run,
   Todd, Poole, or even Younger beat
A back track when 't is wise they should,
With odds too great to be withstood—
Not strange, for they have wisdom good.
But Anderson ! now goes he back,
Upon his red and bloody track ? "
This all through Quantrell's mind quick flashes,
As on his crime-hued steed now dashes
The chief—Anderson he 'd sent out
Upon a far and dangerous scout.

The guerrillas well the fight maintain,
Since Quantrell is with them again ;
His deep defiant thundering yell
All their wild fears doth quickly quell ;
His well-known and assuring voice
Made their once fearing hearts rejoice,
Although outnumbered ten to one.
But where is he, Bill Anderson ?
" Dead ! " a guerrilla said ; 't is true—
" Died 'mid a score of foes he slew."
On his proud battle-footed steed
Quantrell again his force doth lead.
It is an awful, fearful fight,
For neither foe will take to flight ;
The dead are falling left and right.
The awful clang of conflict roars,
Shakes hills and distant shelly shores ;
Like loud terrific thunder's roll,
Flashing bright light from pole to pole ;
The sounds of battle echo far
    Throughout the misty hills of Sni,
Loud thunders dread the voice of war,
    And seems to shake the distant sky.
The stern Avenger—Renegade—
    The fearless chieftain, Quantrell, fought
Coolly, which his men's fears allayed,
    Who well his lion spirit caught.
Day wanes, night nears, the carnage still
    Goes on—red Murder walks his rounds,
Oft blanches pale—disturbed the hill
    Trembles at war's terrific sounds.

The Redlegs and Jayhawkers fought
  With frenzy, fury, fierce and wild,
'Neath Jennison, but all for naught,
  For Quantrell, the avenger, smiled
Upon his men, a potent smile—
  A smile though grim and like the war ;
His men from it took hope the while,
  And cyclone-like, their foes before
Them, their red hands of vengeance hurled,
As leaves by storm swept o'er the world.

## CANTO IX.

### GENERAL EWING'S CAMP.—THE POET.

THE breath of spring, soft, fresh, and rare,
  With fragrance sweet of unknown flowers,
Comes wafting through the yielding air,
  And bathes with love the hazel bowers.
And one who wore the scallop shoon,
Who lingered yet in life's fair noon,
Was pacing as a sentinel,
Before a tent, white, wide, and tall ;
Where gallant Thomas Ewing slept—
Above, the stars their vigils kept.
Tom Ewing loved this child of song,
Who could tell adventures strange and long
In the richest, happiest, flowing rhyme ;
Romances of a bygone time,
He sang as well of deeds sublime.
E'en things uncanny, dark, and dull,
From his refining crucible
Reflected fair and beautiful !
And every thing, crude though it be,
Came from his soul in beauty free ;
In liquid music's numbers given,
As though Christ handed joys from Heaven.
The poet's heart was full of woe :

She, whom he loved, who loved him so ;
The daughter of his country's foe,
Was distant, in the wilds afar,
And her near kin his foes all are.
But deep within his heart he swore,
Her hand he 'd claim, although the roar
Of thousands of war missiles dire,
Poured forth their deadly heated fire.
"She 's mine !" he said, "the danger 's great—
   But love the greatest odds defies.
Who would not dare both death and fate,
   To win so sweet, so fair a prize ?"
With his swift courser and fire-arms,
He ventured to defy all harms,
And bear the lovely girl away,
Who pined in secret for the day
When he, the child of song, would come
And bear her from her sylvan home.
He wooed her with the poet's power
Of love, that blooms a heavenly flower.
He told her that, perchance, her name—
Her love for him one beauteous flame,
With his—would live in song and fame ;
Greater than kings with kingdoms strong,
Are the mighty kings of song.
For kings and kingdoms pass away
As snow beneath the sun's hot ray,
The true bard's verse will live alway,
Like one eternal summer day.
She listened to his songs of love,
   And hence was lost to all save him ;

His poems burned like stars above,
  Like magic worked on woman's whim.
His song could win Amazon's heart.
Who can resist the poet's art,
His that fine frenzy of the brain,
Which the true poet doth retain ?
There was no sin that Ethel gave
Heart, soul, and all, unto the brave
And noble son of silken song
Against friends' wishes !—wherefore wrong ?
An angel in its flight afar—
  God's messenger—may pause, nor wrong,
To list a moment to some star
  Which hath immortal power of song ;
Nor would God chide that angel sweet,
Though learned to love that star so meet.

*        *        *        *        *        *

Night on the plain ! the moon divine,
  Through Heaven's boundless depths sails on,
Nor mist nor cloud now stains the fine,
  Fair glories in the night's sweet dawn.
O beautiful ! O angel night !
  Fair night of June from God above,
'T would seem that in thy holy light
  E'en iron hearts would melt to love.
The poet's dreams of conquest tell—
'Neath window of the peerless belle,
His daring vow he now fulfills ;
With song he wakes the vales and hills,
And her whom long his soul did mourn ;
And well his singing robes adorn,

While touching soft his harp of love,
To her who longed with him to rove—
To fly to distant happier lands,
Beyond the wild and troubled strands :

" Dear Ethel ! fair, sweet child of God,
    From love's own fountain we do drink—
From love's own fountain, o'er which nod
    The passion-flowers, upon the brink.

"Snow-bosom'd love ! Oh, I love thee ;
    Thy kisses are more rich and rare
Than all the other mouths that be,
    Of all the many rose-lipped fair.

" I see thy face in every star
    That blossoms on the field of night ;
O love ! thou knowest I 've come far
    To gaze upon thy beauty bright !

" Thy voice sweet murmurs in mine ears,
    In dreams—in dreams you smile on me—
Like music of the happy spheres,
    I breathe this melody of thee.

" From clouds that float at eventide,
    Soft, purple-tinted, gold, and blue,
I see one fair as God's own bride :
    She smiles ! lo ! darling, it is you !

" The thought-flowers of thy mind so high,
    So beauteous blush far o'er earth's sod,

That angels wing 'twixt earth and sky,
 And carry all those flowers to God.

" A golden bell of Heaven rings now
 The matin-hour of thy sweet prime ;
The flower-time of thy life, I trow,
 Is breathing odors rich as rhyme

" Of Byron—sweet as Shelley's tone—
 In their grand lays of life and love.
Dear girl ! fair girl ! thou 'rt all mine own ;
 A gift God sent me from above !

" Oh ! sweet is summer's twilight hour—
 The hour when day sinks to his rest ;
And like a weary child each flower
 Sleeps on its Mother Earth's broad breast.

" Sweet is the star of eve, that pale
 Far glows beyond the shores of night,
When are heard the robes of angels trail
 Adown their Heaven-lit halls of light.

" But Ethel ! thou art lovelier far
 Than twilight hour with dreams so fair—
Than star of eve—than angels are,
 E'en though their radiant beauty 's rare.

" Dear one ! so like a rose you seem,
 Sweet blushing lone in woods afar,
Accept this rose I plucked in dream,
 From sweet land nestled by a star.
[*Here a rose is thrown into the maiden's window.*]

" Oh, rose-lipped, rich-lipped one !
 Kissed with the dewy wine of love,
I long to clasp thee as the sun
 Burns for the loveliest star above !

" In dreams I 'm kiss'd by thee, who smiles ;
 Though thou art far, sweet memories wreathe;
Though we be parted by long miles,
 Sweet odors of thy soul I breathe.

" The music and the poetry,
 O love ! of thee, sweet being, near,
Is sweeter than all else to me,
 More lovely and more dearly dear.

" Alone with thee and God, oft I,
 Deep love-drowned by thy charms so rare,
Do pluck the star-flowers from the sky,
 And place them in thy silken hair.

" Oft gaze down in thy star-lit eyes ;
 See thy sweet, gentle spirit smile,
And linger there, in Paradise,
 Afar from every thing that 's vile.

" The rose that thy cheek blushes fair,
 A poem blooms all poets greet—
Which kindred angels of the air
 Read with delight, for it is sweet.

" Were I a dream in thy fond breast,
 What dearer Heaven could there be ?

I then would be forever blest,
　　From every secret sorrow free.

" Ope ! ope thy milk-white arms to me ;
　　Caress me with thy kisses warm ;
Swoon on my kiss alone for thee,
　　While I clasp thy fair blushing form.

" Come ! let me sink and dream and rest,
　　O Queen of angels ! sweet and fair :
Upon the heaven of thy breast,
　　And fondly love thee ever there.

" Ethel ! my beautiful ! mine own !
　　To look upon thy face inspires
Sweet dreams I ne'er before have known,
　　And kindles all love's sacred fires.

" Oh, every moment kept from thee
　　Is bliss that 's lost forevermore—
A gulf of sorrow unto me,
　　Where waves in fury lash the shore

" You look so fair I deem it true
　　You bathe in dew of Heaven-grown flowers
Which God did plant himself for you
　　About his angel-builded bowers.

" On purple pinions wing the Hours—
　　Happy since thou seest them fly—
And lovely are the beauteous flowers
　　Whene'er they know that thou art nigh.

" The perfume of thy love for me
   Is sweeter than rose scent so bright,
Though Queen of all the flowers that be,
   Has not the sweets thy charms unite.

" In the deep clear Heaven of thine eyes,
   O lovely music-footed maid !
I see the joys of Paradise
   And feel to highest Heaven I 've strayed.

" I never lived till I knew thee,
   For never have I loved before ;
I used to walk the earth, but free
   I now along the skies do soar.

" O Morning Star of all my love !
   A sea of glory dreams afar,
When I behold thee, my sweet dove,
   With beauty fairer than the star.

" And when I feel thy loving kiss,
   A golden glow of happiness
Steals through my soul—it is a bliss
   That language, dear, fails to express.

" With sweetest words that love can frame
   In poetry I 'll sing thy praise ;
Aye ! I shall garland thy dear name
   With beauteous, melting, lovely lays.

" Oh ! it shall e'er be my delight
   To guard thee waked and in thy dreams ;

I 'll kiss thee to thy rest at night,
And watch thee till the morning beams.


" The hours I pass with thee, dear one,
Are silken hours of peace to me,
When flowing streams of sweetness run
Through all my soul with melody !


" The fair blush of thy blooming years
Doth fill my days with golden gleams ;
And wrapped in sleep, your love endears
And fills my night with beauteous dreams.


" O Ethel ! in thy sweet young years
You bloom, 'midst all, the fairest rose ;
Thy heart of hearts you hide with fears
You would not to the world disclose.


" When I thy circling zone embrace,
And kiss thy lips for me alone ;
My heart, my soul, my being trace
Thy goodness which but Heaven can own.


" When sad o'er buried hopes I grieve
Beside a lone, neglected tomb,
As summer sweet, serene as eve,
Thy smile makes all my being bloom.


" Thy eyes light up my soul of gloom
As Earth lights 'neath the kiss of Heaven ;
And life flowers toward a perfect bloom—
Flowers fair like soul by Christ forgiven.

"When Morn her eyelids opens wide,
  And glances on the world below,
I long to have thee by my side—
  The fairest of the flowers that grow.

"When day walks o'er the gulf of Time,
  As Christ walked o'er the troubled sea,
E'en midway in the hours sublime
  My yearning soul goes out to thee.

"When comes the hour King Sol doth pray
  To God—far in the west, ere fled—
Ere sinking down in ocean gray
  To sleep among the mighty dead,

" I long for thee, sweet star of night !
  And hearken to the roving hours,
That whisper of thy beauty bright
  And lovely hope's delightful bowers.

"Dear Ethel ! strangely dear to me,
  You float my day and nightly dreams
Like some fair star we ever see,
  That on us down from Heaven beams.

"O Ethel ! dearest, darling love !
  I 'll love thee while the years increase ;
Thy beauty comes where'er I rove,
  And brings me pleasure, hope, and peace.

"Oh, when I sip of thy sweet lips
  The purple wine of love I quaff ;

I heed not time, though by it slips,
    For through me sweetest pleasures laugh.

" O noble, lovely, loving girl,
    Rest, rest secure that I am thine,
Throughout life's wild and stormy whirl
    I 'll love thee with a love divine '

" Of all fair ones that I have chanced
    To meet, I 've thought, 't is she I 've sought !
But when I in each soul advanced
    I 've found a waste where there was naught.

" No flower of fragrance blossomed there—
    Each soul was like a fair sad tomb,
Which stands in snowy, blank despair,
    With no sweet rose and no perfume.

" But when I found thee, then I cried
    In joy, for well I knew thy soul
Was blushing with the sweets denied
    To others—I had reached the goal.

" Hope breathes in beauty sweet and fair,
    Of when thou 'lt nestle by my side,
When thou art—t' whom none can compare—
    Mine own, my loved, my beauteous bride !

" In dreams upon thy beauteous breast
    Then let my feverish being sleep,
For I am weary and would rest
    Where cares are not. nor shadows keep."

When closed his song, the loved and fair
   Young girl doth in hope's castle dwell,
She longed to fly with him who dare
   For her war's dangers brave so well.
Down from her window by a rope
   She swung his eager eyes to charm ;
Swift as winged Love keeps pace with Hope,
   She in her lover's arms fell warm.
"Thy song was sweet ! Oh, sweet indeed,
And wakens those that must not heed
Thy sweet, thy pure, thy lovely lay !
O Claude ! O dearest Claude, away !
Around us all, where'er we turn,
They come ! I see their torchlights burn !
Their stern, fierce faces now deride—
They 've sworn I shall not be thy bride ! "
Her eyes burn through her silken veil,
Where love and passion sweet prevail !
Her vermil lips, ripe, rich, and sweet,
Melt on each other when they meet.
Those luscious lips in sweet repose
Bloom on her face a breathing rose.
Her breath like that fair flower as sweet,
It charms each zephyr it doth meet.
Her swelling bosom panted high ;
Her soul's warm passion through her eye
Came melting as her bonny head
Lay on his breast with whom she fled.
Lovely as moonlit Venice dreams
The ages by, so beautiful she seems !
The poet sees they 're hemmed in quite,

And sees no way to pass in flight,
How, with his lovely burden, fight !
Thrice now his raven charger neighed ;
Thrice now his hands on weapons laid.
A new thought thrills him : he would try,
And pass high o'er his foemen nigh ;
His steed which doth pursuit defy,
Could leap proportionately high.
He told his plan to her who lay
Upon his breast, like Hope at day.
Defiance shot from his dark eyes ;
Swift as a flash away he flies
With her, the lovely and the fair ;
Swift as a flash they cleave the air ;
They pass the heads of those below,
They leave behind the following foe.
His steed, one 'midst a million horse,
Had mighty lungs of iron force.
As sometimes powerful mind in man
Accomplishes what none else can—
Does that which others dare not try,
He wins—they gaze with wondering eye !
While other steeds fagged in the chase,
He onward hastened in his pace ;
While foes grew weary, weak, and hot,
Far o'er the ground he swiftly shot.
A wizard's gift he seemed, a boon
To him who wore the scallop shoon.
The thunder-footed courser fled
Like some great phantom from the dead.
Did all men well his swift steed know

Who would pursue the flying foe ?
The radiant Ethel Golder sleeps ;
She knows she 's safe with him who keeps
Her in his arms, and she feels blessed ;
Wearied in flight, she sinks to rest.
As there she lies, so sweet and white,
Kiss'd by her lover, God, and night,
A fair bark she by tempest tossed
In dangerous waters lone and lost.
On, on they dash ; the tall pine trees
Pass by them like a long blue breeze ;
His raven courser, black as night,
Swift rushes on like storm in flight ;
Thunders along like some vast train—
He knows the way, and has the rein.
On, on through night—o'er plain and hill,
Past mountains, where the wolf his fill
Of howling pours to ear of night,
Which oft the great-eyed owl doth fright,
Who wings his sullen flight anigh,
The flying triune passing by.
Trees, rocks, and mountains whirling seem
By them as if it were a dream.
Like voice of sad and troubled deep,
    The moaning night-wind strikes the ear,
As if some mournful ghost doth weep,
    Remorsefully its earth career.
Dim in the clouds the hills above,
Strange phantoms weirdly seem to move,
And shadow lake, long, wide, and deep,
Whose waters lie in glassy sleep.

Orion and the Bears give light,
From the dim cloudy shores of night.
"Star-whispering night ! canst thou not tell
    Life's secrets to my yearning soul ?
Canst thou not tell me where doth dwell
    The Great God at the highest goal ?
A sentence from the golden lips
    Of yonder star so fair and bright,
Might wisdom shed to man, who dips
    The blackened waters of earth's night ;
Yet like a melody far fled
God 's silent on the mountain-head.
Oh, this will be till He appears
Far gazing o'er the countless years !
Wake ! maiden in thy loveliness—
That thy sweet gaze my spirit bless—
And with me listen to the sea,
Which speaks a tender memory ! "
She wakes ! love's blush is on her cheek,
    Red as the rich and rosy wine,
And sweetly from her eyes do speak
    A beauty that is all divine—
A beauteous love that lives sublime—
That lives beyond the reach of time,
Like flowers immortal, fair and sweet,
That bloom in Heaven at Jesus' feet.
On, on they dash ; the landscapes are
By them traversed, then left afar ;
Now through a moonlit valley sleeping
    Beneath a robe of fairest flowers,
While far above star-souls are peeping
    On twilight earth and mortal hours.

The Hours have chased the stars away,
There blushing comes the stepping Day,
As Night's skirts trail far down the skies,
Before the watchers' wondering eyes
Dew-spangled scenes the earth adorn,
'Neath lifted eyelids of the Morn.
The opal-colored morning calls
Blithe birds and happy madrigals.
Now Claude Lorraine, the poet, thought
On life, on man—on what man wrought—
His aims, ambitions, and desires.
Again his Ethel sleeps—she tires
With the long ride—'t is well ! when fine
She was so flowery—feminine—
For she was saved the rude fierce shocks
Of nature, where the forest mocks.
The bard hears Nature's sweet refrain,
This poet strange—strange Claude Lorraine.
O man ! thou stranger on the earth—
Forever restless from thy birth.
Thy love, O wretch ! for what is not
Makes life's foiled hopes a hapless lot,
Each great man marks where'er he trod
In his lone pathway up to God.
Who tells a truth that 's real and clever,
Tells it to the world forever !
Each breeze that blows across the brow
   Bears something of God's wealth of love—
Oh, garner what He yields you now,
   And profit wheresoe'er you rove !
The sky so soft above the earth,
   Is veil of blue God spreads between

Man's world and where the saints have birth—
  They that see man, by man unseen.
Is this the noon of earth?—its prime?
  Is this man's hour, elate and wise?
Or do we live in that sad time,
  'Midst wreck of earth's fair paradise?
Greater than conqueror or king,
  The thinker of his throne of Thought
A sceptre wields—puissant thing—
  By which mutations great are wrought.
The true bard's poems ne'er will die,
For God inspires them from on high.
When earth, time, man, have passed away,
Heaven's angels will his songs essay.
As glorious Shakespeare's mighty name
Far stars the skyey heights of fame.
Christ's life 's a poem more sublime
Than any given unto rhyme.
There are dark times when naught can bless
The poet's sense of loneliness,
E'en 'midst the press of outward life—
When doth awake the inner strife
Of soul with unseen powers that be,
To learn life's strange, strange mystery;
There e'er seem hues of tender grief,
Like yellow on the autumn leaf,
When thoughts of poet seem to burn
To read the secrets of etern.
A greater mystery th' life on earth
Than that we live beyond as now,
From life grows life—another birth—

From whence came man, and how ?
Hark ! songsters waked, sing merrily. .
And other notes of melody,
We hear—we, of the keener sense,
Who list with hearts and souls intense ;
O'er earth the distant melody
That 's sung in Heaven eternally,
Above earth's battlements and portals
The song that 's sung by the Immortals ;
A song—a poem—grand, sublime—
'T is little dreamed this side of time.
'T is this for which on earth forevermore we
    yearn,
To comprehend God's poem, th' Epic of Etern.

    \*       \*       \*       \*       \*       \*

Like mighty rush of torrent goes
   The jet black courser on his way ;
Far from the presence of the foes,
   Earth drinks the full-blown blush of day.
And she, the silken soul of love,
Looks in her lover's eyes above ;
While he sees all of Paradise
In the sweet beauty of her eyes ;
As o'er the golden twilight sea
A voice steals like a memory
Of happy love, the bard is blessed,
By Ethel's lovely arms caressed.
" Too fair, too pure for time's vile touch
Art thou, dear one, I love so much !
Oh, night comes not when by my side
Thou art ; O Darling, there abide ! "

Her love was like impassioned light—   •
  A yearning, burning, steady fire ;
She threw her soul, a star so bright,
  Impulsive to her heart's desire.
He kissed her rich vermilion lips,
  The burning beauty of her eye
He drank, and from her being sips
  The glory of her spirit nigh.
Once more she sleeps—for she 's at peace
  And happy in her lover's arms ;
And now his reveries increase,
  For whom the mystical hath charms.
The stars are tears that God once wept,
  Far back, when e'en Etern was young ;
When all of life save He yet slept
  In womb of Chaos yet unsprung.
His tears fell through the endless waste
  Till angels sprang to life and light,
When, with their beauty charmed, they placed
  Them on the garland brow of night.
The soul e'er lives—to Him goes back
  From whence it came to earth and time ;
Aye it will live when stars grow black
  And fade—live on fore'er sublime !
Though Wrong may riot for a time,
  And Evil veil in robes of Good,
As o'er prose soars sweet song sublime,
So Right shall rise o'er Wrong's black flood.
As, fashioned by the hand of God,
  Yon mountain, clothed in mist and snow,

Looms o'er the clouds where none have trod
  Save angels that guard man  below,
So, fair in loneliness doth sleep
Yon lake's wide waters bright and deep.
God's open, piercing eyes see all !
  His mighty hand of awful force
Compels the dreaded storm to fall,
  And guides the wandering planet's course.
Far through the clouds and storms of life
  The pole-star of unburied truth
Shines bright, e'en though the selfish strife
  Of some may blind their eyes, forsooth.
We fret because of limitation,
And ever yearn for far progression ;
Perchance when God the gates of Truth
  Opes with the key of eternity,
'T will prove to all his tender ruth
  In veiling earth with mystery !
The Universe, though great and grand,
Is in the hollow of God's hand.
Two souls are in the poet's breast,
They e'er produce a wild unrest ;
One yet would cling to earth and time,
One o'er the stars would soar sublime.
" Midnight," the poet's glossy steed,
Still onward passed in wondrous speed,
While lovely Ethel slept away,
Under the rosy depths of day.
Mountains rise as the courser scours,
Higher than Ilion's haughty towers.

The flower of life, though long or brief,
Opens its petals leaf by leaf.
Through yon wild forest dark and wide
Perchance lone spectres ever glide ;
Perchance these woods of ebon night
Conceal some fearful ghoul from sight,
Where fiends oft curse the straying light
That violates eternal night !
As ghastly as the Gorgon's head .
The evil things these forests tread.
Here the weird witches of the midnight air
Howl round the hills and shake their hissing hair.
I love to rove at early morn,
    And breathe the scent of daisies rare,
When Summer, Spring's fair child, is born,
    To walk the vales a virgin fair.
. I love to hear the march of God
    As He dread thunders through the deep !
It tells me here on earth's low sod
    He doth o'er all a vigil keep.
The morning star of life is still
For me soft glancing on the hill ;
Yet gloom oft settles on my soul
And waters dark, unceasing roll,
As Raphael found the gates of hell
Strong barricaded by a spell,
When he was sent from Heaven to see,
How wrought the sons of sorcery.
Oh for an atmosphere more clear
    Than that of common men and things,
To soar high o'er the welkin here,
    On purple azure, golden wings !

Here on a hill of golden hours,
I reach the summit's fragrant flowers.
'Midst pensive hours that boon is sweet,
  Unknown unto the vulgar wise,
The poet in his soul's retreat,
  Above all other things doth prize !

     *     *     *     *     *     *

O God ! shall open-throated war
O'er this fair land forever roar ?
From this too long afflicted land,
Hurl crime with Thy almighty hand.
Through endless days, Truth, in her sway,
O'er Falsehood sails, high on her way,
As the immortal starry spheres,
Sail o'er the battlements of years.
Some mortals' reason proves to be
Of vision short—but sophistry—
As woman's suffrage wrongs her rights,
It yields her thorns, her roses blights,
It hurts the home, the marriage tie,
It wakes the little children's cry,
It steals the soul's sweet poesy,
Its trend is immorality.
Woman's course is high, toward Heaven's light,
Why drag her down to paths of night ?
The rights of children suffer wrong
Through time the mother gives the throng.
Her social life leads from her door,
Her life political the more.
Her child to guide, good thoughts instill,
The mother's place none else can fill.
Her child in charge of heedless ones,

Embraces things the parent shuns.
Should its bark ride the waves of time,
Its life perchance is vice or crime.
She who the little child well trains,
Till it the path of God attains,
Exerts an influence bright alway,
When thrones, empires, and worlds decay.
Through love, man's sweetest heritage,
She rules the great, the mightiest sage.
To keen insight this suffrage beams
The theorist's Utopian dreams.
Blind leaders !   I predict it here :
Woman betray from her high sphere,
And ruin will the home assail,
And discord on the earth prevail.
Idolaters of theory, stay !
No Nestor's counsels guide your way.
You 'd add to woman's duties, more—
Man's burdens, till life's work is o'er.
You 'd change the laws of nature, you ?
Attempt what God refused to do ?
Unchecked, man's actions are *too* free,
So limits law his liberty.
When ignorant millions [1] menace us,
Why multiply our perils thus ?
History repeats—what was will be—

[1] Anarchists, Communists, Nihilists, Socialists, foreigners, and the very ignorant native-born Americans. When the male vote of these classes already threatens our Government, is it wise to double the power of these dangerous elements by giving their wives and daughters the ballot ?

Beware !   Rome's fall was anarchy ! [1]

\*     \*     \*     \*     \*     \*

Up from the azure hills of God
A living presence seems to rise,
And soar above the heavy clod
Of earth unto fair Paradise.
The dewdrop on yon fragrant flower
May be the tear of some sweet star
That weeps for joy that God's great power
Shields all creation near and far.
Oh, could the music of my lyre
    Follow the high flight of my will,
To highest Heaven I would aspire,
    Beyond the poet's holy hill !
Oh, life 's a strange mysterious dream,
    Commingling with the day and night ;
I long have tried to find that beam
    Which will make all things clear and bright.
Aye, vast as night, as endless morn
    I 've sought life's great, mysterious truth
In vain—with me this feeling born,
    Hence melancholy 's mine forsooth.

---

[1] The exhaustive and logical treatises by the historian, Francis Parkman, in "The North American Review," October, 1879, and January, 1880 ; the concessions of the suffragist author, T. W. Higginson, in "The Forum," January, 1887 ; the Sixteenth Amendment dissertation by U. S. Senator John J. Ingalls, in "The Forum," September, 1887 ; the conclusions of Gail Hamilton, in "Woman's Wrongs" ; the experiences and confessions of Mrs. Kate Gannett Wells, whose earnest work for the advancement of her sex is widely known ; the experience of Rev. Brooke Herford, and others, with limited

The nameless tumuli on th' shore
   Of lone seas with unhappy skies,
May hold a germ forevermore,
   Of knowledge hid from wisest eyes.
Eternal whispers breathing 'round,
   Breathe the warm soul of other days.
I feel the import deep, profound :
   God is not far from him who prays—

woman suffrage in England ; the opinions of such famous and
conscientious thinkers as Ralph Waldo Emerson, Rev. T.
DeWitt Talmage, Mrs. Anna Jameson, Miss Mulock, John
Boyle O'Reilly, Richard H. Dana, Prof. W. W. Goodwin, of
Harvard University ; Rev. O. B. Frothingham, etc., prove to
an unprejudiced mind that fanaticism instead of wisdom dictates the extreme views of those who would lead as advocates
of woman suffrage. And T. W. Higginson, the eminent
author and prominent woman-suffragist, concedes some of
the evils of woman suffrage in " The Forum " of January,
1887, in the following language :

   " It is logically possible, and we must frankly recognize the
fact, that the enfranchisement of women in a number of the
States will give a majority of the votes to the women, and the
men of these States will be numerically as powerless as the women are now.   It will be equivalent to a transfer to a wholly
inexperienced constituency, not merely the balance of power,
but its very substance.   Not often in the history of the world
has a body of voters deliberately opened its ranks to admit a
reinforcement larger than itself.   Yet in almost every one
of the older States of the Union this will literally happen on
the day when women are enfranchised. . . .   Whatever
may have been the corruptions of our political life, they have
thus far had the limitation of being entirely masculine ; the
familiar intercourse of the sexes, in legislative halls and com-
mittee rooms, is a thing of the future.   The actual conduct of
legislation, and still more of political parties, involves an im-

When his cause is both wise and just,
And earnest prays because he must.
I hear the bells of heaven—they ring
   The ending of epoch old :
O Wisdom, brood and spread thy wing
   More freely o'er the new unrolled.
Great minds most honor worth and brain,
Small minds to honor wealth are fain.

mense deal of the most private and confidential conference by
day and evening. Who that remembers the Woodhull and Claflin
period of our social history, or the Beecher-Tilton controversy,
can look without some anxiety to the utterly unrestricted
mingling of men and women, in periods of great excitement, and under the strongest inducements to use whatever
means of influence may prove most potent in dealing with one
another?   There will be no point so vulnerable, no mode of
attack so promising, as those growing out of the question of
personal chastity, in these untried relations.   To all the present opportunities for scandal there will be added a new one ;
and this in the hands of an unscrupulous antagonist will be
worth all the rest put together.   This consideration is strength-
ened by the fact that the promoters of such scandals will not
be the vicious, but the virtuous portion of the community, and
especially women themselves.   Once create the impression, no
matter by what device—the handkerchief of Desdemona, the
diamond necklace of Cagliostro—that a man and woman prominent in public life have become entangled in wrong-doing, and
nothing can save them.   It is a curious but well-known fact
that the very purity of women makes them most suspicious
where they are purest ; and when another woman excites this
distrust, it takes with fatal frequency this particular direction.
The intestine feuds which rent twenty years ago, the Woman
Suffrage movement, gave striking illustration of the tendency
of this form of suspicion, as could easily be shown by instances, were it well to rekindle those slumbering embers."

Who never doubted, never thought—
　In conscientious doubt is power,
From this the greatest things are wrought ;
　'T is to th' soul as perfume to the flower.
Great men are numbered by no year—
　The life of each immortal name
Is in the thought-prints which appear
　Along the skyey heights of fame.
That I might tread the Milky-Way ;
　Forever wander 'mid the stars,
I then perchance might find some day,
　A key to ope the gate that bars
The way to highest, pure, clear light,
Above earth's long and sombre night.
Like moonlight on the breast of night,
Sweet dreaming of God's Heaven-lived light,
So lovely slept sweet Ethel fair,
On bosom of her lover there.
Like twilight o'er a sinless world
Her silken hair o'er bosom curled ;
But when they passed a holy grail,
With water filled from Heaven's sweet vale,
'T would seem some sprinkled Ethel's face ;
She woke to feel her love's embrace,
Hear th' tolling of the vesper bells
Which from cathedral sweetly swells.
" Thou hast awoke to give me bliss,
　Dear Ethel ! Oh, thy charms inspire !
I feel immortal when thy kiss
　Sinks deep into my soul of fire !

What cannot love, forsooth, effect?
  It drew Diana from the spheres ;
Mount Ida's youth it did elect ;
  It holds the rein o'er endless years."
Low, soft, yet audible and sweet,
  To him and Heaven she breathed his name—
Her velvet voice his ears do greet
  As if from Aidenn's heights it came.
' Dear Claude !  " she whispered, " thou art fair ! "
  And heaved a plaintive, ardent sigh—
" I love to breathe the virgin air
And hear the happy birds sing nigh.
These hours are sweet—these hours are given,
Love-flowers God hands to me from Heaven."
Lo ! there in beauty 'neath the skies,
Broad Kansas prairies meet their eyes !
The lovely home of Claude Lorraine
Is shadowed on the endless plain.

## CANTO X.

### BATTLE OF WESTPORT.

ALL summer Price had forced his way,
    With his fierce army of the Gray
Toward North and distant setting sun,
While Curtis, Blunt, and Pleasonton
Disputed every foot he stepped,
With Kansas men who never slept
So sound but they remembered well
The foes that came so fierce and fell.
Many a man of Kansas soil
Had shouldered arms the foe to foil ;
They swarmed on prairie, hill, and glen,
To full three times ten thousand men—
Men who were fighting for their all ;
And the invaders to the wall
They swore to drive—fierce hurl them back—
As swift as cyclones forests rack.
Price fiercely fought to Westport—there
Looked longingly to Kansas, where
He saw afar more spoils and fame,
And thought to win a brighter name.
But this he found a task full sore—
That fame was his, ah ! nevermore !
    *     *     *     *     *     *
October claims of time a share—

'T is Sabbath morn ! Day's dawn is fair ;
'T is eighteen hundred and sixty-four,
And into Kansas cross, Price swore
He would that day, the twenty-third.
Hark ! voice of coming battle 's heard !
The bugle now awakes the air,
Breathing sad tones of beauty there.
The sullen tread of hosts is heard,
And neigh of war-horse fierce ; the word
Of stern command. All now is still,
The wind is lull'd from hill to hill.
All suddenly red flames burst out
    From cannon on a breastwork high,
Behind which lay the Rebel rout :
    And iron balls scream down the sky,
And bombshells burst before, behind,
While Death and Ruin ride the wind ;
Swift carbine bullets shrilly sing ;
Dread notes of death, earth, heaven, ring !
Th' Federals pour their swift replies,
War's thunder mounting to the skies.
Many a strong and mighty man
Falls dead, falls dying, spent and wan.
The breastworks topple, tremble, fall,
Before shot, shell, and cannon-ball ;
Down on each other rush fierce foes,
And dark in deadly combat close !
They close in sable clouds of smoke :
A yell bursts out which Sol awoke ;
For instantly his heavy head
Uprises from his Orient bed.

And 'midst the roar and thunder dread
  The battle-shaken hills do groan ;
A thousand ghosts of fallen dead
  Shriek madly to their God Unknown !
The battle thickens in the van,
  The awful revelry of death
Would melt the hardest heart of man ;
  Would make him catch his faltering breath.
The fight goes on—more fearful grows ;
  Dun clouds of battle black the air ;
The shrieks, the groans, 'midst dying woes
  Are mingled in war's dread despair.
The battle roars like to the blast
  That drives the forest from the shore ;
And thunders like the storm that vast
  Sweeps Hell's great dreary regions o'er.

  \*    \*    \*    \*    \*    \*

Day wanes, the battle 's o'er, and Price,
  Defeated, leaves the foughten field.
The dead are heaped and cold as ice,
  And they increase as the dying yield.
The warriors comfort as they can,
And cheer each dire afflicted man
By some kind act or promise given,
Which smooths his way, we trust, to Heaven.
I sympathize with those who fall
Down stricken by the deadly ball,
For I have felt the cruel thing
Tear through my flesh with angry sting.
War is the worst curse of all time,
Against both God and man a crime.

Here lay the bleeding trooper dying,
   And there the cause—a broken shell ;
And, powder-burnt, his steed is flying
   Swift from the sight of Death's foul spell.
Each bird has flown, from awe is still ;
The wolf, in fear, howls from the hill.
The prairie-dog barks fierce and wild
Before his earth-house door defiled ;
While his household of snakes and owls
Beneath are listening to his howls.
Night thickens ! wolf and dog are still,
And silence broods o'er plain and hill !
Still ! All is still since battle-blast,
Save when some new-born phantom passed ;
Lost ! shrieking for some beacon light
To guide it through the starless night.
Men died so dreadful on that day,
Some of the souls that fled away,
Not said in vain, of flesh bereft,
Were stained with blood of corses left !

   *    *    *    *    *    *

O Muse ! we now must here recite
   The valor in each army there,
The brows of those who led the fight
   Deserve the crown of laurels fair ;
So does each private soldier too,
Whether he wore the gray or blue.
We should not men in haste condemn,
   For they and we may each be right—
As life's environment doth hem,
   We see the truth by different light.

Grant fought the Union to restore,
   For State rights Cockrell fought his part—
Each saw the star of truth before,
   Which shed a radiance o'er the heart.
The Rebels thirty thousand strong,
Their foes wellnigh as numerous throng.
McNeil, the dauntless, showed his skill
In war, and showed it with a will.
Here Jennison and Ford restore
The scenes that marked their paths of yore.
With his brigade, Moonlight,[1] the brave,
To Price defeat his prowess gave,
Two days before that Rebel crew
He fought upon the Little Blue.
And Hinton[2] proved a patriot here,
A soldier without fault or fear.
The militia under Blair's[3] command
Sad havoc wrought on every hand.
Here Simpson[4] and his cavalry tell
In prowess where the foemen fell.
Here Walker[5] his front ranks did lead,
Astride of his uncertain steed.

[1] Gen. Thomas Moonlight, present Governor of Wyoming.

[2] R. J. Hinton, author of the "History of the Army of the Border."

[3] Gen. Charles W. Blair, of Leavenworth.

[4] B. F. Simpson, late U. S. Marshal.

[5] Col. Sam. Walker, of Lawrence, whose steed had the disagreeable habit of going over to the enemy's lines during battle, a habit which had caused the death of several of its owners.

Here fought one Boone, the grandson bold
Of Kentucky's mighty hunter old.
The Shawnee County Regiment
Fought like veterans of the tent.
Of men of war, whom war called there, ·
Topeka [1] proudly claims a share.
The valiant Bonebrake, Case, and Burns,
   Veale, Brockway, Williams, Huntoon there,
Smith, Douthitt, each his laurel earns—
   Which e'er should shine in poesy fair.
Here Major Ross [2] and his true men
In marshalled ranks crossed hill and glen.
'Mid thickest of the fearful fight
The Major spurred his steed of night ;
Nor cringed he 'neath the battle cloud,
His arm too good, his heart too proud.
Here Hoyt, the hero of the Blue, [3]
Fought brave and well the battle through.
Joe Shelby and his cavalcade,
Of Death proved they were not afraid ;
They 'd seldom heard a milder note
Than came from out war's dreaded throat.

[1] P. I. Bonebrake, Ross Burns, A. H. Case, Judge David Brockway, Arch. Williams, Dr. A. J. Huntoon, Jacob Smith, W. P. Douthitt, and Col. Geo. W. Veale, all citizens of Topeka.

[2] Ex-Senator E. G. Ross, Governor of New Mexico.

[3] In the fight at the Blue, Col. Hoyt, with a portion of the Fifteenth Kansas regiment, made " one of the most gallant sabre charges recorded in the history of the war."—O. H. Gregg's " History of Johnson County, Kansas."

Here Colonel Moore[1] and valiant band
Fought under Shelby's fierce command.
Here Edwards[2] did both armies show
He was the Federals' bitter foe.
Though now he wields the mighty pen,
The bickering blade he wielded then ;
His men were brave as brave could be,
They fought and they died recklessly.
"T was here Todd, the guerrilla, fell,
A reckless, daring child of Hell,
To whom peace seemed a waste of time,
Who gloried in the hour of crime.
Here Marmaduke his forces led
With pomp of war, amid the dead.
Here Fagan, Cabel, Gordon, too,
And Jackman, Thompson—leaders true
Unto the Southern cause—command
For Price troops fighting on each hand.
And more were they that battled well,
Whose names no mortal tongue can tell—
Hurled from the earth by war's great crime,
Oblivion long hath veiled from time.
The deeds of valor on the day
Of Westport's battle, Westport famed—
As Bunker Hill is famed for aye,
As Lexington 's immortal named.

＊　　＊　　＊　　＊　　＊　　＊

Ah, Price ! thou wrought thine own defeat,

[1] Col. John C. Moore, the well-known journalist and lecturer.

[2] Major John N. Edwards, the able writer, now editor of the *Kansas City Times.*

When thou offended thy great power,
Who best knew war's black art—'t was meet
Quantrell had been with thee this hour.

\*    \*    \*    \*    \*    \*

The storm of war has blown afar,
The star of peace shines o'er the field,
Transmuted swords to ploughshares are—
To break the sod and bread to yield.

# EXTRACTS FROM COMMENTS OF THE PRESS ON " POEMS OF THE PLAINS."

### FROM THE " LONDON (ENG.) LITERARY WORLD."

We next come to three American bards ; and first, of Thomas Brower Peacock, the poet of the Wild West. " Buffalo Bill " had not yet appeared at Earl's-court when Mr. Peacock's modern epic, " The Rhyme of the Border War," appeared, and won praise from critics so hard to please as Matthew Arnold. With all its defects of form, it is the work of a poet, and " Wild Bill," " Buffalo Bill," and their companions find in him a *vates sacer* whom more distinguished warriors might envy them. " The Rhyme " is reprinted in the present volume, but the main bulk of it consists of miscellaneous poems, some new and some not, which are grouped together under the title of " Poems of the Plains." Though at times unconventional, Mr. Peacock is always worth reading, and much of his verse is full of fresh and vigorous feeling.

### FROM THE " CHRISTIAN UNION," NEW YORK.

In Mr. Thomas Brower Peacock's " Poems of the Plains," we meet with most decided poetic talent." " The Rhyme of the Border War " gave Mr. Peacock the right to be called a poet. There is a strength, a vigor, a sweep of mental vision in these poems which incontestably show an insight into the realities, a faculty which is never absent from true poetry.

### FROM JOHN BURROUGHS.

Of the trans-Mississippi poets Thomas Brower Peacock easily leads them all.

### From Edgar Fawcett.

Mr. Peacock displays earnestness and a national spirit in his work, " Poems of the Plains and Songs of the Solitudes." His longer poems have evidently been labors of love.

### From Gertrude Garrison, in the (N. Y.) " Journalist."

" Poems of the Plains and Songs of the Solitudes " is the title of a handsome volume of poems by Thomas Brower Peacock, of Topeka, Kansas, who is known as the Kansas poet. . . . The author has acquired some fame by his " Rhyme of the Border War," " The Vendetta," and other poems previously published. His themes are stirring Western ones. Red men, wild riders, brave men, and fair beauties of the pioneer days are thrown together with much poetic fire and fine imagery. Mr. Peacock lacks nothing in poetic feeling and refinement of thought.

### From Francis Parkman.

His poems show feeling, spirit, and a good deal of force.

### From the " St. Johns Globe," New Brunswick.

The poems contained in this volume are of an original order of genius, and are marked by a strong, fiery, vigorous treatment—a breath from the plains they so vividly and in such a picturesque manner portray. Mr. Peacock fulfills the conditions necessary to a correct carrying out of the ideas popularly entertained as to what a poet is, inasmuch as he is preëminently imaginative, a dreamer of dreams, a creator of pictures. With the exception of Bret Harte and Joaquin Miller, there are no other poets who bring out, as does Mr. Peacock, the strange beauty, the richness, and the pathos of Western life.

### From the " People and Patriot," Concord, New Hampshire.

The " Songs of the Solitudes " are esteemed by many to be fully as meritorious as the " Songs of the Sierras." The new poems cover a large variety of subjects, secular and religious, love and war, real and idealistic, and evince the true poetic spirit.

### FROM " THE LITERARY WORLD," BOSTON, MASS.

It is impossible to read " The Rhyme of the Border War," and not to recognize that the author has got hold of his theme in a very resolute manner. If some of Mr. Peacock's contemporaries could acquire a little of his exuberance, the field of current verse, while possibly more than ever like an unweeded garden, surely would not be so stale, flat, and unprofitable as it is now.

### FROM THE " NEW YORK NATION."

The late Matthew Arnold is mentioned in the Appendix as one who thought well of the work, and found in it, apparently, those qualities of distinction and interest which he declined to recognize in Emerson and others.

### FROM OSCAR WILDE.

Mr. Peacock certainly writes with great vigor, freedom and enthusiasm, and these are admirable things.

### FROM THE " ST. LOUIS REPUBLIC."

Mr. Peacock has quite a reputation as a poet in the Far West. He is a Kansan—in fact the poet-leaureate of that new and progressive State.

### FROM THE " WORCESTER (MASS.) SPY."

Mr. Peacock is a young man, resident of Topeka, Kansas, and has won already high reputation as possessing poetic power and a gift for melody and versification. Several of the poems in this volume are narratives of considerable length, and one of them, " The Rhyme of the Border War," will be found of historic, as well as poetic value. Scott's poems are evidently his guide, in some measure, in form and style of treatment.

### From the "Boston Times."

Mr. Peacock is a Western poet, and displays high claim to distinction. His poems are full of imagination, picturesqueness, and freedom of strength that make them often exhilarating. This volume contains numerous beautiful thoughts expressed with striking force, and will afford rare pleasure to many. The true merit of the poet has won golden opinions from the most eminent critics, and this inherent worth will create still further appreciation from future readers.

### From the "Chicago Inter Ocean."

Messrs. G. P. Putnam's Sons have issued a new and revised edition of the poems of Thomas Brower Peacock, the Kansas poet. The longest and best poem of the volume is "The Rhyme of the Border War," in ten cantos. It is a poem of great strength, and one of the best war poems ever written. The historian of that wonderful period has at no time gathered so many facts in the same space, or caught more certainly the spirit of its actors, than has Mr. Peacock.

### From the "Christian Advocate," Pittsburgh, Pa.

Mr. Peacock seems to be, in his poetry, just what the really great poet of America should be, *i. e.*, truly and exclusively American. Our glory lies in our individuality. Mr. Peacock is American to the core, and he is one, possibly the best, of the few American poets treading paths which he himself must pioneer.

### From the "Leader," Cleveland, Ohio.

The scope of his imagination is surprising, and his lofty spirit appears to have been born amid the scenes of nature's grandeur, and upheld by a desire to sing their greatness. . . . The narrative poems will no doubt be read with pleasure for their exciting interest.

### From the "Cincinnati Christian Advocate."

We occasionally pick up a volume of genuine poetry, or

one in which the true spirit of poesy is interfused through all. Such a volume is " Poems of the Plains and Songs of the Solitudes," together with " The Rhyme of the Border War," by Thomas Brower Peacock.

### FROM THE " TOLEDO BLADE."

From G. P. Putnam's Sons comes " Poems of the Plains and Songs of the Solitudes," by Thomas Brower Peacock, appearing now as a new and revised edition, showing that it has already obtained popularity. Some idea of his especial gifts of expression may be seen from the following lines culled from different poems :

> " The dew-drop on yon fragrant flower
> May be the tear of some sweet star,
> That weeps for joy that God's great power
> Shields all creation near and far."

> " Battle stamps his bloody feet ! "

> " God secretes in places lone and still
> The rarest products of His will ;
> For contact with the world disarms
> His fairest flowers of half their charms."

### FROM THE " JOURNAL," INDIANAPOLIS, IND.

The poems vary in length from a few stanzas to many pages, and cover a wide range of thought and feeling. Some of the themes are essentially American and Western, and are handled in strong, original style. The book contains some striking passages.

### FROM THE " CHICAGO STANDARD."

His lines have great vigor, while evidences are abundant of a fertile imagination and a power of poetic expression which go far to justify much that has been said in his praise.

### From "Zion's Herald," Boston.

The West has been too much absorbed in the spread of civilization, and in the accumulation of money, to inspire and foster the poetic muse. Even genius must be properly housed, else it will not thrive. The muse of poetry has not, therefore, been awakened to best work in our great West. Joaquin Miller and Bret Harte have possessed this limitless field. In this volume a new aspirant appears to us. He comes, however, with golden opinions for fugitive poems from Matthew Arnold, Victor Hugo, Bayard Taylor, Ray Palmer, and many others.

### From the "Baltimore American."

Mr. Peacock has already acquired quite a reputation as a writer of verse, and this "Poems of the Plains and Songs of the Solitudes" will in no wise lessen it. Many of the descriptions of scenery are finely conceived and delicately portrayed, and there is a vein of romantic pathos permeating the entire collection, which makes it doubly charming.

### From the "Baltimore Sun."

His imagination is as exuberant and boundless as his native prairies.

### From the "American Magazine."

Mr. Peacock has the not very general quality of having something to say in his poetry, and of saying it.

### From the "Boston Post."

His style is formed on Byron. It seems marvellous to find here, out on the Western plains, two long tales of Oriental adventure. . . . The really singular poem, however, is American in subject, and is nothing less than an historical epic of which the hero is the guerrilla, Quantrell, and in which Buffalo Bill is a leading subaltern. Local history is put under contribution for it so directly that one might call it a journalistic epic. These three hundred pages are not without fire and a certain rendering of the tumult and spirit of battles on horseback with the pistol and rifle.

### FROM THE "PITTSBURGH (PA.) POST."

He had the good fortune to win the notice of Victor Hugo and Matthew Arnold. So much for the poet. Mr. Peacock has unquestionably the poetic gift. He is unconventional ; has the freedom of the Wild West, and his poems are exuberantly American.

### FROM THE "TRANSCRIPT," PORTLAND, ME.

The poem that has attracted the most attention and won the highest praise is " The Rhyme of the Border War," which contains many fine passages of descriptive scenery and portrays the characters that figured in the troublous times of the early settlement of Kansas, and the days of Quantrell.

### FROM THE "NEW ORLEANS STATES."

Peacock's reputation has been established for a number of years as the laureate of the Western States, his " Rhyme of the Border War," first published nine or ten years ago, having beyond a peradventure secured his claim to that appellation. That splendid epic, which celebrates the doughty deeds of the famous guerrilla warrior, William Clark Quantrell, and which in many of its dashing passages falls no whit behind the elan of Scott's " Marmion," is included in the present volume, with many others of the author's select poems, written —some very early, some later in his lifetime. The characteristic charm of Peacock's poetry is its absolute immunity from any taint of staginess ; his freedom from the trammels of regulation laid down by this or that school of poetry is the freedom of the deer in the forest, of the lark in the empyrean.

### FROM THE "PHILADELPHIA PRESS."

Mr. Thomas Brower Peacock publishes a fresh edition of his collected " Poems of the Plains and Songs of the Soli-

tudes " (New York : G. P. Putnam's Sons). The remarkable
" Rhyme of the Border War," an epic of the Kansas-Missouri
guerrilla war, in which Quantrell is compared with Satan, is
also included in the volume. Mr. Peacock is the talented
Kansas gentleman of whom Oscar Wilde wrote : " Topeka
has a poet which seems to me a feather, perhaps I may call it
a Peacock's feather, in the city's cap."

FROM THE " PRESBYTERIAN BANNER," PITTSBURGH, PA.

There can be but one opinion as to the author's themes of
romance and song being almost exclusively American. No
other country could produce such originals as Kit Carson,
Buffalo Bill, or such a hero for an epic poem as Quantrell,
the Guerrilla.

FROM THE " CHICAGO JOURNAL OF INDUSTRIAL EDUCATION."

Many of the poems are illustrations of border life and history, and breathe the genuine spirit of the West. Strong,
free, untrammelled, with many an outburst of poetic warmth
and vigor.

FROM " THE POST," WASHINGTON, D. C.

Mr. Peacock has a healthy, virile imagination, good descriptive powers, and a happy command of language. Some
of his poems will live

FROM THE " LEWISTON (MAINE) JOURNAL."

His poems show a true appreciation of nature, and his
thoughts find expression in words evidencing poetic power.

FROM THE " POST-EXPRESS," ROCHESTER, N. Y.

The author has both imagination and strong poetic feeling.

FROM THE " BURLINGTON HAWK-EYE."

A splendid volume of virile verse comes from the pen of
the poet of sunny Kansas. Breathing the bracing air of the
plain, this poetry seems instinct with its myriad voices. . . .

The most noted poems in this book are "The Vendetta" and "The Rhyme of the Border War." The latter is a stirring historical epic, which has already brought its gifted author much fame.

### FROM THE "SALT LAKE TRIBUNE."

The author of this book is still a young man, but he has received most flattering encouragement and praise from some of the foremost men and journals of the age. There is much of the nature of the poet in the author of this book. Much within the book is most commendable.

### FROM THE "ALBANY (N. Y.) ARGUS."

That he is a writer of merit cannot be denied, for he has won golden opinions from many of the most eminent critics. . . . . While the author's latest poems are unquestionably his best, his earlier ones deserve the commendation they have received.

### FROM THE "BOSTON GLOBE."

It may be said that no one can dispute Mr. Peacock's claim to be a poet. There are passages and ideas which go far to sustain his claim.

### FROM THE "PHILADELPHIA TELEGRAPH."

"The Kansas Indian's Lament" and "The Doomed Ship Atlantic" are good examples of Mr. Peacock's gifts. He is best in descriptive and narrative pieces.

### FROM THE NEW YORK "CHRISTIAN INTELLIGENCER."

The author is richly endowed with poetic talent, and is making good use of it.

### FROM THE NEW ORLEANS "TIMES-DEMOCRAT."

He has been fortunate in attracting the attention of and winning golden opinions from some of the most eminent literary judges of Europe and America.

### From the "Chicago Advance."

In a volume entitled " Poems of the Plains," Mr. Thomas Brower Peacock has gathered a large number of poems, the most important of which is " The Rhyme of the Border War," in which the historic struggles connected with the early settlement of Kansas are portrayed with much spirit and vividness. . . . He seems to be always real and sincere, and does not affect impossible emotions, or attempt to " woo the muses " or revive the dead paganism of old Greece. He is honestly American and himself.

### From the "Grand Rapids Eagle."

In describing the scene of the battle, Canto V, "The Rhyme of the Border War," the poet reaches one of the grandest passages written by American poets.

### From the " Nashville Democrat."

The book, " Poems of the Plains," contains some real gems in both melody and verse.

### From the Pittsburgh (Pa.) "Chronicle and Tele-graph."

" The Kansas poet " brings out in a new edition his " Poems of the Plains," and joins with it in a handsome volume his two previous works. These poems have attracted a good deal of attention, aroused some criticism of an un-friendly nature, and received a considerable amount of praise. The portrait of the author is handsomely engraved upon the first page of the book, and a critical preface by Thomas Danleigh Suplée follows. Then come the poems. There are a great many of them and they are of unequal merit—but all of them can be read with interest, and many of them with satisfaction.

### From the " Milwaukee (Wisconsin) Sentinel."

It is sufficient to say of the poems in this book, that they bear out the author's reputation as a writer of imaginative and romantic verse.

FROM THE "CINCINNATI ENQUIRER."

The book possesses many merits, and there are flights of fancy in it which bespeak genius of an unusual order.

FROM THE " KANSAS CITY TIMES."

Mr. Peacock's poems are full of fire and imagination, free from the trimming-down process which gives smoothly rounded sentences, and sickly sentiment, from which all naturalness has been unsparingly culled.  As a true poet-son of Kansas, Mr. Peacock stands in the lead, and if all his other work was as naught, and he should never again touch his pen to paper to inscribe poetic measures, his name would live in his three great poems : " The Doomed Ship Atlantic," " The Vendetta," and his " Rhyme of the Border War."

FROM THE " TOPEKA CAPITAL."

Mr. Peacock, as is well known, is the most noted poet in Kansas, and his works have attracted the attention of foreign as well as home critics.  The thought expressed in Mr. Peacock's later poems is more vigorous, more mature, and decidedly better expressed, and at the same time displays quite as much poetic feeling as his earlier ones.

FROM THE " WICHITA (KANSAS) EAGLE."

That Mr. Peacock is a poet, and a superior one, cannot be doubted.  The poems are pregnant with truly poetic inspiration, rich with noble thought, and worthy the most flattering commendation.

FROM THE " UNION," JUNCTION CITY, KANSAS.

We are gratified to know that Mr. Peacock's literary reputation is expanding and attracting world-wide fame.

# EXTRACTS FROM COMMENTS OF EMINENT CRITICS, REVIEWS, AND CLIPPINGS FROM THE PRESS ON "THE RHYME OF THE BORDER WAR."

PUBLISHED 1880.  G. W. CARLETON & CO., NEW YORK.

---

### FROM MATTHEW ARNOLD.

He takes a subject which interests him and he treats it with liveliness and vigor.

### FROM M. VICTOR HUGO.

I am very much pleased with Thomas Brower Peacock's poem, "The Rhyme of the Border War."

### FROM BAYARD TAYLOR.—Manuscript sheets—"The Rhyme of the Border War."

The thoughts, for the most part, are grandly conceived, and there are passages of the highest type of poetical composition, mingled with some which are not so good,—thoughts that are sublime in their conception and expression. The poem does not lack true poetical spontaneity, philosophy, or prophecy.

### FROM HUGH HASTINGS.

"The Rhyme of the Border War" is throughout a tale of love and strife, of consuming passion, and rapid action. The battle scenes are stirringly described. The work altogether shows the poetic power of one possessed of fertile imagination and true poetic fire.

318

### From Louise Chandler Moulton.

There is in Thomas Brower Peacock's poems the breadth and freedom and vigor of the West. They are picturesque and heroic. I find them most interesting, full of vigorous life.

### From George Ripley.

While the rhythm of Thomas Brower Peacock's poems could be better in places, the thoughts show a high order of poetical genius.

### From Ray Palmer.

His poems clearly show that he has naturally a liberal measure of poetic sensibility, imagination, and fancy, and other gifts essential to the poet.

### From Samuel S. Cox, A. M., M. C.

The poems of Thomas Brower Peacock are always pleasing and sparkling, and show the true lyric style.

### From "Potter's American Monthly."

Thomas Brower Peacock, known as "The Kansas Poet," through his many previous poetical effusions, has well earned the reputation. We find many gems of poetic thought expressed in words both chaste and select. In fine word-painting especially does he show a most gratifying skill ; some of his poetic imagery possessing much original and striking beauty. His peroration to Kansas is exceedingly graphic and fine. His descriptions of the battles fought by the bushwhackers are equally well and forcibly expressed.

### From the "Literary World," Boston, Massachusetts.

It is a poem of love and battle. There is no lack of spirit and fire.

### From the "Philadelphia Times."

Thomas Brower Peacock is regarded by the *London Saturday Review* as the great American poet.

FROM GEORGE H. PICARD, AUTHOR OF "A MATTER OF TASTE," "A MISSION FLOWER," "OLD BONIFACE," ETC.

I give his " Rhyme of the Border War" the loftiest place in Western minstrelsy.   It is heroic in treatment, melodious in expression, and highly original in its conception.   His poetry is far above the puerile warblings of the average poet of the day.   In many instances it is sublime.   It was a masterly conception to found a long epic poem upon a theme so devoid of all that has been regarded as picturesque, as the Kansas troubles. To me there is something absolutely thrilling in his descriptions of guerrilla warfare.   I like especially his spirited lines on Quantrell.

FROM THE "NEW YORK COMMERCIAL ADVERTISER."

Border wars have ever been a fascinating theme with poets of heroic bent.   The freedom of life, the loneliness and loveliness of nature, the daring and danger of human passion, all tend to inspire the breast of one imbued with poetic sentiment and vivid fancy.   Its author, a young man, has the spirit of poetry within him, and in many passages sings with ease and wealth of imagery.

FROM THE "CHICAGO INTER-OCEAN."

This is a poem of real merit, and, true to history, it marks a wonderful era in our time, and one yet vivid in the minds of thousands of living men and women.

FROM THE "DETROIT FREE PRESS."

The poet has shown taste in the choice of his subject, and considerable skill in telling his romantic story.

FROM THE "ST. LOUIS REPUBLICAN."

The narrative generally runs smoothly in rhyme, and there are some good strong lines, sinewy with thought, and flashes of poetic fancy.   He does not waste many words in metre and rhyme-hunting, and scales the rough places with a bound instead of going a long way round.

FROM THE "ST. LOUIS HORNET."

"The Rhyme of the Border War." This late poem of "the Kansas poet" is an epic of ten cantos, historical and clear-cut, and is very like the "Vendetta" of the same author, save that there is more power, greater girth of poetic beauty, more vivid pictures, in the last effort. Indeed, a marked superiority must be conceded to the new poem. The book is brimful of grand thoughts, exquisite imagery, pathos unsurpassed, passion that stretches into the realm of the blest, and depths of grief, a broad theology, a boundless humanity—all in the garniture of true and superb poetic rhetoric. The picture of Ethel is one of rare beauty : the genius of the author seemingly revelling in the bright dream of the loveliest type of God's handiwork.

> "Lovely as moonlit Venice dreams
> Th' ages by, so beautiful she seems."

And she is not all etherial, for

> "Her heart was not a frozen lake
> On whose cold brink fond Cupid stands."

And more than once :

> "Beneath the moon's and stars' soft light
> She 'd heard the voices of the night,
> Go sweetly laughing back to God."

These are but fragments descriptive of Ethel, and we unhesitatingly assert that there are dozens of stanzas in this portion of the book that are gems of ideal poesy, and that lose nothing by comparison with the ancient and modern poets in this special field. The following from the battle-field is a bit figurative :

> "And 'midst the roar and thunder dread,
> The battle-shaken hills do groan,
> A thousand ghosts of fallen dead
> Shriek madly to their God unknown."

Here is a potent and sublime truth :

> " God secretes in places lone and still
> The rarest products of His will ;
> For contact with the world disarms
> His fairest flowers of half their charms."

At times the poet plumes his wings for flight into the illimitable :

> " We hear—we of the keener sense,
> Who list with hearts and souls intense,
> The song that 's sung by the Immortals,"
> Above earth's battlements and portals.

It is impossible to do justice, in this brief critique, to the book. Indeed, we have selected at random, almost, the few lines above recited, but we do not care to say that they are the best. They are not the best. The volume is strewn thick with pretty thoughts and rounded into rich rare music, by the subtle brain and pen of this young and gifted poetic dreamer of the Far West.

### From Enrique Parmer, author of " Maple Hall Mystery," etc., etc.

" The Rhyme of the Border War." The poem, from first to last, binds us as with a spell, and we read with rapt attention to the end of the last canto. The subject is one of vast interest, for it embraces a period in the history of American politics that will ever be fresh and vivid in the memory of men. It is a fine effusion, masterly in itself. It is not only the earnest of nobler creations—it is a living, palpable creation itself.

We cannot, with our brief space, speak of the plot, the history, or lay open the characters that figure in the poem ; we must content ourselves with what we have written—not forgetting to say that the author of " The Rhyme " must, some day, attain a legitimate place among the brilliant stars that deck the poetic sky in the Western Hemisphere.

Thomas Brower Peacock has won golden opinions from critics of high standing. A year ago he published a volume of poems, but since that time has attended more strictly to business of a more prosaic nature, but no doubt the while revelling in a poet's world, his fancies and thoughts unconsciously weaving themselves daily into beautiful verse. Every young aspirant in the field of poetry thinks he must be either sad, sour, or wicked, like Byron, Shelley, and Poe ; but Mr. Peacock has not seen fit, because he has poetic inspiration, to affect what he is not. His poetry is of a healthy, elevated character, and no taint of the fleshy school, no sensualism. He, like many of us, ponders on the question of life, as these lines prove :

" O what is life to man ? and what is man ?
    Immortal ? or the mere shadow of an hour ?
Is earth all ? or has life a broader span,
    Beyond time reaching with eternal power ?
The star far hanging in heaven's high tower
    May once have been a drop oozed from a rose !
Then if a star is but the essence of a flower,
    Will not man, far the greatest life earth grows,
Live on beyond the grave and find naught to oppose ? "

Again :

" Then what 's all beauty but a tempter's bait ?
    It lures us on, it leaves us all alone,
To muse upon the unforeseen of fate—
    We live for what we know not."

In contradiction of what has been said of Mr. Peacock, we may say he does not essay as much as he is capable of doing. Therefore those critics who have unjustly spoken of self-consciousness and vanity in this author little know the man or poet.

There is neither self-assertion nor over-estimation. He, like most poets, talks of his poetry, is ambitious for a place

among the laurel-crowned, but by no means wishes to claim
it ; he would rather earn it, and at all times courts honest
criticism, and not fulsome, indiscriminate praise.  This is
merely a word or two about the Kansas poet, and in no sense
of the word a review of his book.

FROM THE " KANSAS CITY REVIEW OF SCIENCE AND IN-
DUSTRY."

This is a handsomely printed volume by a gentleman of
Topeka, who has already acquired a fair reputation as a
writer of poetry.  This reputation will be in no wise lessened
by his latest effort, which contains many genuinely poetic
fancies and lofty passages.  The introductory lines are especially good, and many of the descriptions of scenery and
character are finely conceived and delicately portrayed.
Among these we can only take time to mention the poet and
song which abounds in such gems.

FROM THE " ST. LOUIS SPIRIT."

This work is from the author of the " Vendetta," and in
many respects surpasses that effusion.  There are verses, and
plenty of them, in the description of Ethel, that are not sur-
passed anywhere.  They are superb.  There are dozens of
verses that would do no discredit to any of the ancient or
modern poets.

Occasionally the poet drops into commonplace descriptions, but the same may be said of Byron, Longfellow, and
others.

We can pick out scores of gems, real inspirations, that
stamp the author as no ordinary verse-maker.  They are
skirmishers in the van and types of the great army in the rear.

FROM C. G. COUTANT, IN THE " TOPEKA MAIL."—EDITORIAL
OBSERVATIONS, MAY 17, 1883.

Thomas Brower Peacock, the Kansas poet, has suddenly
come to the front by having his poem of the " Border War "
lauded in the *London Saturday Review.*

This poem is reviewed at length by this high English authority, and it is pronounced worthy of more than a passing notice.

Such treatment can hardly fail to make the volume sell, and cause Kansas to feel proud of this much-lauded Poet of the Plains.

There are some writers in the State who have been slow to recognize the true worth of this poet, who will now be ready to sing his praises. These, of course, Mr. Peacock will forgive on account of their ignorance. They will have a chance to learn something by carefully reading the volume anew. They will have a chance to find out that the value of poetry does not consist in sing-song verse, but in originality of thought and depth of sentiment. The poet who dares not go out of the beaten path of every-day couplets will never rise to make a name in the world.

If Mr. Peacock will now revise his poems they will become popular the world over ; and if the advice of the *Mail* is taken, our Peacock, who is now in high feather, will set about the work at once. Shakespeare says : " There is a tide in the affairs of men, which, taken at the flood, leads on to fortune." That tide is now rising for the Kansas poet, and if he is true to himself he can safely anchor in the harbor of fame.

### FROM THE " ST. JOSEPH HERALD."

" The Rhyme of the Border War." Mr. Peacock's progress has been very great since his last volume appeared. The handsome and modest young man has given much time to reading, and has grown much in thought and power of expression.

### FROM THE " LEAVENWORTH TIMES."

This work, the fruit of the brain of the Kansas poet, Thomas Brower Peacock, is one which deals with Kansas entirely, with the exception of the period when the guerrilla warfare was carried into the neighboring State of Missouri.

There are many fine passages on the book, and it should meet with a hearty reception.

### "From the Pittsburgh (Pa.) Telegraph."

Mr. Peacock is a gentleman of the finest poetic taste and genius in the Far West, and already has published a volume that has commanded the praise of Eastern journals and literary periodicals.

### From Oscar Wilde's Letter to a Topeka Gentleman, Published in the "Capital."

Topeka has a poet, which seems to me a feather, perhaps I may call it a Peacock's feather, in the city's cap.

### From the "Topeka Times."

"The Rhyme of the Border War." It possesses the stamp of true poetic genius. There are many passages of much beauty. In the battle scene the poet becomes sublime:

> " The fight goes on—more fearful grows ;
>     Dun clouds of battle black the air ;
>   The shrieks, the groans, 'midst dying woes,
>     Are mingled in war's dread despair.
>   The battle roars like to the blast
>     That drives the forest from the shore,
>   And thunders like the storm that vast
>     Sweeps Hell's great dreary regions o'er."

### From the "Topeka Daily Capital."

Few American poets have met the recognition accorded our poet, Thomas Brower Peacock, by the great English authority, the *London Saturday Review.*

# CRITICAL COMMENTS ON THE VENDETTA AND OTHER POEMS.

First Edition, 1872 ; Second Edition, 1876.

FROM THE "CHICAGO INLAND MAGAZINE."

The Vendetta is a tragic romance, and the scenes and characters are Corsican. The survivor of a family becomes outlawed, becomes a sea-rover, accomplishes his vendetta vow, slays all the opposing Corsicans, and then voluntarily sinks beneath the waves of the sea.

There are many beautiful passages in this poem ; it is eminently rich in description and metaphor, while here and there the inner life of the actors crops out with unusual force.

It would be impossible to do justice to this poem by citing any extracts we could find space for, in this brief article.

The poetry of Mr. Peacock, though grave is not morbid ; nor it it misanthropic. There is, it is true, now and then a quaint bit of mystery, that drifts beyond the evolution theory, as when in " Reverie " he hints :

" That maiden fair, we see, with many a charm,
May once have been a pearl beneath the sea."

But he never makes the head giddy with paradox, nor swings the heart upon a wild and chaotic tempest of doubt and selfishness. He deals not in spectres and unsocial horrors. He is true to what he feels, and right or wrong he speaks it as it is. He is not bombastic nor grovelling, and he steers clear of intellectual cant and literary quackery. There is an odor of freshness and originality in the book. The tone is highly moral, and there is not a line in these pages

327

that the gravest, purest, and noblest need blush to read.
There is no gall nor wormwood concealed along the lines, nor
is our author always gay, light, and laughing.    He writes with
an enlarged humanity ; he writes with much insight into the
inner workings of the human mind.    He seldom draggles his
pen in the slough of casuistry.    His intellect goes whither it
will ; he climbs the hills, races on the plains, rides upon the
waters of the great deep, and gathers from every element the
secret in them.    And now he sends these creations of his
brain out to be recognized and appreciated.    They deserve
from the wise and the brave, from the old man and the maiden,
the warmest welcome.    Gonzails is the outlaw in "Vendetta."

> " But where is he, Gonzails ? had he no one
>   'Midst all the fair whom he could call his own ?
>   Ah, yes ! he loved and was beloved by one,
>   A peerless beauty of the tropical sun,
>   Whose love was pure as heaven's transparent streams—
>   She loved him as the poet loves his dreams."

And then again :

> " Ah ! here 's what allures, here 's what entices,
>   Leads man to virtue or deep into vices ;
>   Nor sylph nor nymph more graceful than is she—
>   Fair Inez, the beautiful ' Pearl of the sea.' "

In " Reverie " the poet lets fly another arrow :

> " Then what 's all beauty but a tempter's bait ?
>   It lures us on, it leaves us all alone."

And this from " A Secret of the Sea " :

> " Great bolts of thunder loudly crashed,
>   And living lightning ran the sky,
>   And here and there it angry flash'd
>   Like some fierce demon's vengeful eye.

> " Time wings his constant flight—now wan ;
>  The blast strays homeward o'er the deep ;
>  The weary clouds move slowly on ;
>  In his far cave the storm doth sleep."

The " Atlantic Doom " contains some passages of rare beauty and power, which we cannot reproduce in our limited space, without marring their fair proportions.   The vessel already doomed, rides on into darkness :

> " Descending Night, with visage dark,
>  Drops her black mantle o'er the bark ;
>  And o'er time's pathway journeys on."

Part first of " Star of the East " opens with a scene in the Turkish capital.   This poem is perhaps one of the most elaborate in finish in this volume.   There are in it many descriptive passages of a very high order of merit.   Except the Vendetta it is the very best poem the author has yet published, and one of great beauty and power.   What more did Thomas Brower Peacock need than his hill-slopes, dells, seas, and living beings ? In the one he finds the fulness of nature ; in the other the essentials of humanity.   What if a young poet's reviewers outnumber his readers ?   What if some critics are scoffers ? There are others who bring him admiration unqualified.   Let him stand unshaken before his detractors, and let him not be exultant in the homage of his friends.   There was a time when Wordsworth had little else besides critics, and how long has it been since the genius of Poe has put his detractors to silence ?   We close with one more extract from the " Vendetta," and would remark that we like the poem better with each successive reading.   It is certainly not the production of a mere verse-maker ; any one can see that.   It is no mean order of genius that conceived this poetic romance :

> " Well may they fear—for means the flash and roar
>  The mightiest elements are at fiercest war,
>  The angry storms fling huge destructive shafts,

> In deepest scorn each warrior hoarsely laughs,
> And marshall'd far around in densest crowds,
> Live thunders swiftly leap from clouds to clouds,
> Hurling their deadly massive bolts afar,
> Hitting the very vault of distant Heaven !
> Which jars each high hanging planet star,
> And shakes the earth to its foundations even ! "

We are not sure that we have been wise in our selections from this author. We have indeed not picked out the pearls, and have not endeavored to put the poet's best foot foremost. We have but dipped in here and there among the mass with almost closed eyes, believing, as we did, that we could not easily produce anything without some merit. And now that we have drifted through to the end, we confess that we found more to admire than we expected ; and that while there are faults, still the good in them outweighs the errors ; and we are conscious, too, that the young poet whose inspiration was gathered upon the dead levels of the Far West, has by this work of his brain won a place of no common significance in the galaxy of poetic genius.

### FROM ENRIQUE PARMER, IN A CRITIQUE WRITTEN IN 1877.

This man whose lips have touched the rim of nature's poesy, who drifted without bluster into the wind-swept forests of song, is young in years, and his genius is now stretching its wings for its first flight. Thomas Brower Peacock is gifted with poetic genius. The author of " Vendetta " develops in that effort alone evidences of all the elements of the poet, while in the minor poems, many gems of purest ray flash out, which foreshadow the dawn of brighter imagery for the grand thoughts that lie here and there in the pages of the book. His poetry is thoroughly human—a poetry which reproduces, as we read it, all the feelings of our wayward nature—which shows how man was made to mourn, to be merry, to doubt.

The descriptive and the picturesque have a large place in his writings. A picture with him is more than the mere drapery of a passion. The chivalric past has as yet received but little of his veneration. The conflicts of the ancient rival factions have somewhat greater enchantment than the gorgeous falsehoods of departed ages, to warm his fancy or to rule his pen. He has little to do with rank or reverence except when he enters the pale of the supernatural.

His imagery is true, it is also original. He meditated by himself, and he studied the outward phenomena of nature with strange enthusiasm ; hence it is not surprising that this youthful poet should have enriched his mind 'with truth, freshness, and originality, and that these should appear in imagery and description.

The reader will find many beauties, many curious fancies, many strange pictures wrought out with marvellous power. He will find wild romances, painted with a master pen, long rolling verse, almost as good as that of "Childe Harold," occasional bursts of inspiration vivid as that of Poe or Shelley, description as dignified and orthodox as that of Wordsworth, while many stanzas are as musical and enrapturing as Tennyson's "Locksley Hall."

FROM DR. R. SHELTON MACKENZIE, IN THE "PHILADELPHIA PRESS," MAY 9, 1873.

We judge from the poems themselves that Mr. Peacock is a young man, enthusiastic yet practical. "The Star of the East," a Circassian story, is the best sustained poem in the volume, and breathes of the distant Orient. "The Vendetta," with its scene in Corsica, is more diffuse. Several of the minor effusions possess considerable merit. Having formerly noticed Mr. Peacock's poems, we shall only say that to open with "The Vendetta, A Tragic-Romantic Poem, in Five Cantos," was a bold step for a young author. However, "nothing venture, nothing have" is a time-honored adage, and Mr. Peacock evidently possesses a spirit which, in the words of Othello, "makes ambition virtue."

The new miscellaneous poems show improvement in construction and a deeper and more searching course of thought than before. He is evidently mastering his art. His rhymes are generally very correct, a great point in these days of prevailing carelessness. The only piece in Mr. Peacock's volume which we decidedly condemn is the last, entitled "Metaphysical," and its demerit is, the more we read the less we understand it. Such is the character of metaphysics in verse, even of Wordsworth's.

#### FROM THE "PITTSBURGH POST," OCT. 14, 1876.

"The Vendetta, and Other Poems," by Thomas Brower Peacock. We have before us this work from the pen of one of the most brilliant young writers of the West. It is singularly free from the crudities that so often mar the productions of young beginners, especially in the line of versification. Mr. Peacock's book is emphatically something more than verse—it contains a great deal of real poetry, with occasional bursts that equal Keats and Poe in their peculiar lines of poetical fancy. Here is a little fancy in "Egeria" that is full of vivid imagery :

> "The stars forevermore enshrined
>    In their high homes far o'er the sea,
>  In their dear beauty me remind,
>    Egeria ! darling one, of thee."

"The Vendetta," which gives the title to the volume, possesses a great deal of poetic beauty and unusual force and depth and warmth of expression. The present volume is an earnest of the splendid contributions to American literature that Thomas Brower Peacock will yet make.

#### FROM THE "DETROIT FREE PRESS."

The author has paid less regard than he might with propriety have paid to the recognized laws of versification ; but there are traces here and there of real power and poetical insight. "The Vendetta," the poem which gives title to the work, is the largest and most pretentious in the collection.

### FROM THE "CHICAGO INTER-OCEAN."

This volume takes its title from a somewhat ambitious effort founded upon the Corsican vendetta. While it is marred by defects, it contains many fine passages. "The Star of the East," a metrical romance, is better, and the minor efforts are best. Mr. Peacock seems to possess a vivid imagination and an easy command of language.

### FROM THE "UTICA (N. Y.) HERALD," JUNE 9, 1876.

The opening poem, "The Vendetta," is a "tragic-romantic poem," in five cantos; and while it presents verses of much beauty, its prevailing tone is one of such exuberantly sombre woe that it falls somewhat short of being in complete accord with the best songs of the day. Some of these poems denote skill and true poetic refinement.

### FROM THE "WAVERLEY MAGAZINE," BOSTON, JUNE 24, 1876.

We have read some of the poems, and we are pleased with the absence of affectation or imitation in his diction, and his thoughts seem to flow from a soul which is full of poetic fervor.

### FROM THE "NEW YORK NATION."

Mr. Peacock's poems are of a high order of merit. Here is an apostrophe to chastity, from his poem entitled "The Vendetta":

> " Thou Chastity ! that long hath held
>    The world in virtue's modest check,
> Man owes to thee, in heart, joy knell'd,
>    For the little pure saved from vice's wreck—
> Warm thanks to surface ever gurgling up,
> As o'erflows nature's sparkling chaldron cup."

Here is a much warmer passage, taken from the same poem, descriptive of the person of the Countess Inez Galvo, afterward mistress of the sea-rover, Gonzails:

" Ah ! here 's what allures, here 's what entices.
Leads man to virtue or deep into vices ;
Nor sylph nor nymph more graceful than is she—
Fair Inez, the beautiful ' Pearl of the Sea.' "

FROM CAPTAIN HENRY. KING, IN THE " TOPEKA COMMON-
WEALTH."

The recent " Atlantic " disaster has inundated the news-
papers with poems relating to that terrible calamity—some
good, some so-so, and some execrable.  Among the best we
have seen is one written by the Kansas poet, Thomas Brower
Peacock.  It contains some fine word-painting, and some
poetic imagery of original and striking beauty.  Mr. Peacock
is the author of a small volume of poems, published a few
months since, which has received favorable mention in the
*New York Nation* and other first-class critical journals.

FROM MR. WILLIAM FINN, IN THE " BOSTON LITERARY
WORLD."

In one line—

" The vesper's chime and low of kine,"

the author has expressed what it took Gray two to do the
same :

" The curfew tolls the knell of parting day,
The lowing herd winds slowly o'er the lea."

The third verse brings to mind many passages in Moore, and
the fourth reminds us of Byron's Alpine descriptions, and in
the fifth we have something of the nature of Poe's " Raven."
There certainly is a multifarious power in these six verses.

FROM THE " LEAVENWORTH TIMES."

We have before us a volume of poems from the pen of
Thomas Brower Peacock.  There are some real poetical
thoughts in the book.  Perhaps the best thing in the volume

is the tragical poem entitled " The Vendetta." It is founded
on the peculiar custom of retaliation sanctioned by the religious superstitions of the Corsicans, and describes a bitter feud
that existed between two families, and the part taken by the
masculine representatives of each household. A love-scene,
of course, is introduced, because there can be no first-class
tragedy without a woman.

The poet thus pictures the flow of a stream:

> " Here lost the mountain streamlet strayed,
>     Through meadows green and forest glade,
>     Now winding east, now winding west—
>     As fearful where—which course the best—
>     Like agony of thought, which love so oft inspires ;
>     A soul still fluttering 'twixt two fond desires."

### From the "Kansas City Journal of Commerce."

" The Vendetta, and Other Poems." Advance sheets of
this volume, which is soon to appear, have been sent to us,
and, in comparison with the former publication by the same
author, show marked improvement and advancement. In
the higher aspects of the work he has given many evidences
of poetic power. His figures are well chosen and forcible,
the sentiments are all that could be desired in elevation and
purity, and his conceptions for the most part gratifying. The
parts of the book before us abound in fine thoughts.

### From the " Topeka Commonwealth."

We have been favored with advance sheets of " The
Vendetta, and Other Poems," by Thomas Brower Peacock, of
this city. " The Vendetta " is the most ambitious. Mr. Peacock, unlike many other literary men, while evidently an ad-
mirer of Byron's genius, does not suffer his moral sense to be
perverted by the brilliant wickedness of that great but mis-
guided personage ; hence the pure tone of all Mr. Peacock's
effusions. There is nothing in this volume that might not be
read aloud in any company. Next to " The Vendetta," and

quite equal to it in merit, we think, is "The Star of the East," the scenes of which are laid in the romantic country, Circassia, and based, as the author states in his argument, on well-authenticated events. The minor poems comprise "Egeria," "Reverie," "The Haunted Lake," "The Close of Day," "Vennova," and others. This hasty notice is made after a still more hasty perusal of the work, and hardly does it justice. We have, in fact, dwelt only on one of its merits—its moral tone.

FROM JOHN N. EDWARDS, IN THE "KANSAS CITY TIMES," JUNE 8, 1873.

"Poems by Thomas Brower Peacock" is a modest little volume containing some real gems, both in melody and versification. Upon the great prairies, drinking in such inspiration as came from the isolation and solitude of their illimitable horizon—from the stars that people the blue heavens with visions and dreams—from the longing and strivings the true poetic nature ever feels when alone with the night and with immensity—the poet has created for himself an ideal world filled with the darlings of his genius and his imagination. These he has sent forth on a mission of recognition and appreciation. They will be welcomed often and brought tenderly into many a pleasant place.

FROM RICHARD REALF, "PITTSBURGH COMMERCIAL."

I have examined "The Vendetta, and Other Poems." I find much to praise. The author, Thomas Brower Peacock, unquestionably possesses poetical genius of no common order.